Civil Disagreement

Civil Disagreement
Personal Integrity in a Pluralistic Society

Edward Langerak

Georgetown University Press
Washington, DC

Library of Congress Cataloging-in-Publication Data

Langerak, Edward.
  Civil disagreement : personal integrity in a pluralistic society / Edward Langerak.
    pages cm
  Includes bibliographical references and index.
  ISBN 978-1-62616-033-0 (pbk. : alk. paper)
  1. Courtesy. 2. Integrity. 3. Respect. 4. Pluralism. I. Title
  BJ1533.C9L36 2014
  172—dc23

                             2013204838

This book is printed on acid-free paper meeting the requirements of the American National Standard for Permanence in Paper for Printed Library Materials.

15 14   9 8 7 6 5 4 3 2 First printing

Printed in the United States of America

CONTENTS

PREFACE

A pluralistic society is one that includes individuals and groups with different and conflicting convictions about what constitutes a good life. These convictions are so important to the personal identities of its members that their integrity requires open disagreement with one another. But maintaining the social and political ties necessary to a peaceful society requires that they disagree in a civil way. Hence my title, which conveys the double point that in a pluralistic society there will be disagreement among persons of integrity, and that the disagreement can and should be civil.

I wrote this book after several decades of teaching ethics and political philosophy to liberal arts college students. These are the students of whom Allan Bloom, in the opening of *The Closing of the American Mind*, famously said, "There is one thing a professor can be absolutely certain of: almost every student entering the university believes, or says he believes, that truth is relative.[1] My experience is that Bloom is wrong. Rather, most students are trying to cope with the conflict of convictions, and trying to do so in a way that allows them to be true to themselves and still be appropriately open to the differences they experience all around them. Indeed, my experience in teaching ethics is that the most difficult problem for students is not arriving at their own reflective view about hot-button issues such as abortion or gay rights (though that can be hard enough); the most difficult problem is how to respond to the fact that others flatly disagree. If we could dismiss those who disagree as comparatively ignorant, corrupt, or unintelligent, the cognitive dissonance could readily be resolved. But the problem is that we often have to admit that those who disagree seem to be as informed, good-willed, and smart as we are, and sometimes, to our chagrin, even more so. As social scientists have noted, these days this problem arises well before the college years; thus many young people find themselves trying cope with it well before they have had an opportunity to explore thoughtfully the available options.[2] This book is written for those who want to explore those options; it assumes that the reader is motivated to ask, "How should I respond to the sort of intelligent diversity I encounter on issues that matter to me?"

So how should I respond? Well, one way to keep my bearings is to assert some variation of "I'm right and those who disagree are wrong." I will later argue that this attitude can be maintained in a humble and respectful manner, but to most thoughtful young people it comes off, initially at least, as arrogant, implausible, and sure to alienate friends. Hence the more common way to cope is to assert some variation of "Who's to say?" In chapter two I claim that a plausible version of this attitude is quite compatible with "I'm right and those who disagree are wrong," but one can see why it sounds to traditionalists such as Bloom like thoughtless relativism.

I discuss relativism in the final section of chapter two. I think that there is an objective truth about relativism, which, of course, tips you off to what I think it is. I do think that it can be developed and defended in sophisticated and intellectually respectable ways. I also think that it frequently is accepted too quickly and in ways that generate intellectual sloppiness and moral and spiritual malaise. But even if it is accepted by some or by many, it simply adds another minority view to the pluralism of our society, and therefore it also will have to confront the problems of how to cope with disagreement. For example, relativists cheerfully grant that fundamentalist dogmas are true for those who believe them, but this does not settle the important issues, since there is still the practical problem of how to respond when other views are not only different but also inspire actions that the relativists believe are harmful. An infamous example of this was the horror of terrorists flying passenger planes into the World Trade Center. I think it is foolish to blame relativists (or postmodernists) for 9/11 or even to charge them with paralysis in reacting to terrorism; they can in all consistency insist that we should fight terrorists. But the fact that so many commentators argue that relativists cannot take a firm stand against terrorism shows that relativists, like the rest of us, must have a coherent framework of ideas and attitudes about how to respond to disagreement and conflict.[3]

And this point brings me back to the students who Bloom says are relativists. Even if they are, they still need to ask questions about appropriate tolerance and intolerance, especially with respect to others who are intolerant. My experience is that when they say "Who's to say?" they usually do not mean to imply that there is no right or wrong on such issues as terrorism or even less dramatic issues such as gay rights or cheating. Nor do they mean to say that the truth is whatever people think it is. Rather, they are trying to articulate the point that informed and articulate people of goodwill are going to disagree on many important matters. Trying to reach consensus may be a good start, but there is certain to be continued disagreement. And with respect to that disagreement, "Who's to say?" is often a way of asking "Who's to judge?" and "Who's to enforce?" So it is really a question about how to get along with others when there is continued disagreement and do so in ways that respect everyone's personal integrity and simultaneously recognize the responsibility to take firm—sometimes even intolerant—stands on disputed issues. And that is what this book is about.

My intended audience is primarily citizens with questions about how to combine personal integrity with open-minded respect for differences. This audience includes college students taking ethics, religion, and political science courses, or any courses in which issues of pluralism are prominent. I have tried to keep the text itself clear and concise. But I hope my audience will also include scholars who are informed about the history and literature of the issues and debates I discuss. So I have put elaborations, references to current debates, conceptual clarifications, and bibliographical comments into notes. I believe the text can be understood without these notes, but I have tried to write the longer and more important notes in a way that they can be read as independent comments.

I have been working on the issues discussed in this book for many years and have been helped by many colleagues, students, and friends to clarify my thinking, sometimes through civil disagreement. Presenting these ideas at St. Olaf's Philosophy Department colloquia has been extremely useful, and I thank my colleagues for their criticisms and encouragement. People who have read more than their fair share of the manuscript and have given me very helpful comments include Doug Casson, Adam Copeland, Karen Gervais, Jeanine Grenberg, Anthony Rudd, Edmund Santurri, Doug Schuurman, the late Fred Stoutland, Charles Taliaferro, and Robert Van Howe, as well as two anonymous readers for the publisher. I have been blessed with many excellent teachers who have helped me understand the topics of this book; one whose teaching and writings have been especially important to me is Nicholas Wolterstorff, and I'm grateful for all that I have learned from him. I thank Tricia Little Streitz and Eric Erfanian for using their computer skills to help me with the manuscript. My wife, Lois, has been both civil and loving for these many years and I gratefully dedicate this book to her.

Notes

1. New York: Simon and Schuster, 1987, 25.
2. The pioneering work by Perry, *Forms of Intellectual and Ethical Development,* 1998 (first published in 1970), takes a developmental approach: Students often arrive at college with an unstable relativism, having discarded an earlier and naïve absolutism, but soon see the need for commitments that simplistic relativism cannot handle. My experience is that many children encounter issues of relativism soon after they begin watching television, including *Sesame Street.*
3. For discussions of postmodernism, relativism, and response to terrorism, see Fish's "Postmodern Warfare," 2002, and the symposium that includes Fish, Rorty, and some of their critics in *The Responsive Community* 12, no. 3 (2002): 27–49.

CHAPTER ONE

Conversations and Arguments

Is it possible for a group of human beings to live their lives together without sooner or later having serious disagreements and conflicts? This question raises an ancient debate. On the one hand, it seems that too many of us—maybe at some level all of us—are self-interested creatures who see ourselves in insecure competition with each other, a competition that applies to family members as well as to strangers. Conflict seems inevitable. On the other hand, maybe this tendency is caused by corrupting social influences that are not inherent in human nature. In other words, this sin, though common, is not original, in spite of the jest by some theologians that original sin is the one theological doctrine that is empirically verified.[1]

States of Nature

In the Western conversation, this debate is highlighted by the sharp difference between Thomas Hobbes and Jean-Jacques Rousseau on what they called "the state of nature." What would human life be like independent of civilization's influence—human nature in the raw? Hobbes thought it would be war; life would be nasty, brutish, and short.[2] Since humans would see that their desires for the same things bring them into conflict, and since they would see the advantage of doing unto others before they do it unto you, they would inevitably fight preemptive and preventive wars. However, Rousseau thought that Hobbes was projecting modern malaise onto primitive peoples. Rousseau claimed that, in the state of nature, people would cooperate in hunting and gathering bountiful amounts of healthy food. There would be plenty for everyone, and the inherent feelings of affection would cause people to get along just fine—until the agricultural revolution would start us down the slippery slope to property rights, envy, insecurity, greed, and all the other vices that civilization brings.[3]

Who is right? The early 1970s brought exciting news to cultural anthropologists: a Stone Age tribe was discovered in the Philippine rainforest that seemed to have been isolated from modern civilization for thousands of years. The gentle Tasaday, as they were called, were a tribe of twenty-six members who lived in caves and in an environment rich enough that several hours of hunting-gathering each day provided them with all their needs. And what amazed the *National Geographic* researchers was that they not only seemed to live in blissful harmony with one another, they also seemed not to have any words for fighting, quarreling, enemies, disagreement, or anything like that.[4] So do we have some empirical evidence that supports Rousseau against Hobbes? Alas, it turns out that there is much dispute about whether and how long the Tasaday were, in fact, separated from more modernized tribes. Indeed, it is quite likely that the "discovery" was something of a hoax.[5]

Nevertheless, the episode sparks the imagination. We can imagine that an isolated tribe of people with simple wants that are easily fulfilled by a generous environment could live in sustained, if unexciting, harmony. Moreover, if we assume cultural homogeneity, including agreed-on answers to life's basic questions—what it is all about and how we should live it—we can imagine that even hard times could be confronted without significant conflict. In 1994, prehistoric art that is at least 32,000 years old was discovered on the walls of the Chauvet Cave in southern France. These paintings of animals are 15,000 years older than the famous paintings at Lascaux, but are just as powerful and sophisticated.[6] The remarkable artists experienced the scarcities of an ice age, but the evidence suggests consensus on religious rites and even on artistic tastes. With Rousseau, we can imagine here, at the dawn of human history, peace and harmony—and no words for conflict or disagreement. Of course, Hobbes could use his imagination, too, and he would likely appeal to a proposed theory that the animal paintings were probably efforts in magic to assist artists in getting more meat than their neighbors, efforts only a few steps from fighting.

Ever since Plato there have been armchair designs for utopias that avoid conflict. Most people find Plato's *Republic* unattractive because of the manipulation, even repression, required to keep people in their places. Plato himself had doubts about how long it would last.[7] Thomas More's *Utopia*[8] seems more congenial, and may even have had an influence on Karl Marx's prediction that, with the advent of a classless society, the state would wither away and people would live forever in harmony. History has not been kind to this prediction, but there have been some efforts, with varying success, to establish small utopian communities of the sort More imagined. For example, until well into the last century, the Shaker communities had been impressive examples of largely harmonious group living. That they allowed no sexual activity may have contributed to both their short-term success and their longer-term demise, so a better example may be the Amish and Mennonite communities, which, in many ways, are flourishing. In addition, perhaps 3 percent of today's population consists of tribes of indigenous peoples, many of whom seem to have flourished without serious internal conflicts for hundreds and even thousands of years.[9] However, the implications of such communities for our world are questionable. Apart from the worry that these communities may involve more internal conflict and coercion than outsiders readily see (we know there are occasional divisions within the communities and there are occasional news stories about vulnerable members being victimized and then hushed up), their survival does seem to depend on a fairly strict separation from the rest of the world.[10] I conclude that it is worthwhile to raise the possibility of homogenous harmony; it stimulates our thinking about human nature, but it also underscores the limited conditions of such harmony. In short, the answer to whether individuals in a homogeneous society could avoid serious disagreement and conflict would, at best, shed only a little light on the issue of conflict in a pluralistic society. So we move to our world, one with many differences and, in fact, many different kinds of differences.

Encountering Difference

Already 35,000 years ago there likely were significant differences in beliefs and practices in the various parts of the lightly inhabited world. However, the relative isolation of the groups meant that any differences usually did not have to be confronted. The groups that interacted and intermarried probably tended to share similar tastes and beliefs; even the strangers were not very strange. There is some evidence that, for early humans, dislike of differences and avoidance of strangers actually enhanced reproductive success; those with an "us–them" attitude toward strange others passed on their genes to more children than did those who were more comfortable with otherness.[11] If so, we may be biologically hardwired with tendencies that, in today's world, have the opposite of survival value. Of course, humans are hardwired with a range of biological tendencies, and once we become conscious of them, we can, within limits, choose which ones to accentuate and which ones to play down, especially as we raise our children.

Experience suggests that children can be taught to be fairly broadminded about differences. A pluralistic society, therefore, can avoid a lot of grief if it raises its children to accept lots of human differences, such as diversity in color, cuisine, aesthetic tastes, political beliefs, and social practices. Such acceptance is the positive contribution of multicultural education and sensitivity. We learn thereby that some differences need not merely be tolerated; they can be celebrated, and found agreeable. For example, when I take college students on terms abroad, I encourage them to eat the local foods and attend the local festivals. Often they learn to appreciate differences they initially found strange, if not disagreeable. But there are limits. When encountering traditional attitudes and practices that they regard as oppressing women, for example, their question is not whether they should approve, but whether they should express their disapproval (and, if so, how). This issue, of course, is complicated by the fact that they are guests, and their goal as students is mainly to learn rather than teach. The point is that many differences can and should be celebrated, but others cannot and should not; indeed, they can be hard even to endure. Among the latter are some that merely turn the stomach, such as drinking snake blood in a crowded night bazaar. But others also contradict the conscience, such as brothels—located next to the snake stalls—filled with young girls for the entertainment of men who think their virility is fortified by drinking snake blood.

Convictions, Commitments, and Integrity

Some culinary practices can turn your stomach, and that is disagreeable. But it is not a matter of conflict; you can simply avoid eating what others find agreeable. Of course, how the animals are treated—such as those snakes—may be a deeper issue. And most of us will experience genuine conflict when we see cultural practices that we interpret as exploiting vulnerable human beings. This is because we have deep convictions, and not just tastes, preferences, and casual beliefs. Convictions are sometimes understood as unshakable beliefs that do not require proof or evidence.[12] This definition may be a bit strong; convictions can be firmly held and quite settled without being unshakable. And, rather than thinking they do not need proof or evidence, people may think that their convictions are proved by the authorities they trust or by positive evidence in the lives they lead. In any case, these convictions are deeply held and are often central to our identities. Convictions can be descriptive beliefs about how things are and the way the world works: For example, "every event has a cause" and "people are usually responsible for their choices" are such factual claims. But the convictions that shape our character are usually the ones that have an evaluative or prescriptive force or implication: "thou shalt not steal" and "honor your parents." These convictions associate with personal commitments, which involve attitudinal and behavioral dimensions, resolutions to live and act in particular ways. In the next chapter we will see the importance of distinguishing convictions and commitments, even as we associate them. Some commitments are so loose that associating them with "convictions" may be misleading.[13] About many matters of etiquette, for example, we can adopt a "When in Rome do as the Romans" attitude without compromising our integrity. This point is true even though there are some people who are inappropriately more rigid about manners than about morality. We can be loose about certain matters, but most of us also have some basic commitments that are central to our identity and self-respect.[14]

"Integrity," from a Latin root meaning "whole," sometimes connotes a reasonable level of *coherence among one's fundamental commitments*; in this sense, a life of integrity is one without serious fragmentation in the purposes we pursue. The next chapter will discuss how value pluralism can raise difficulties for this sense of integrity, at least for simple interpretations of it. Another, probably more common use of integrity also appeals to coherence but connotes *coherence between one's convictions and one's actions*.[15] Your convictions can tell you *what* to do but it is your commitment to them and to your own integrity that tells you to *do* it. And this is the sense of integrity that can be challenged by pressure to be broadminded about what you regard as questionable practices.

Most of us have some convictions and commitments that we cannot override without psychological pain or change of personal and moral identity.[16]

Postmodern Convictions

Are there intellectual and spiritual currents that encourage people to take nothing seriously, to drift without basic convictions, avoid strong commitments, and resist few temptations? Some social critics have accused postmodernism of cultivating the sort of relativism that undermines moral clarity and saps the willingness to take strong stands against evils, even evils as great as the terrorism of 9/11. *Postmodernism* refers to movements in literary criticism and philosophy that reject "modernism." Modernism is associated with the 18th-century Enlightenment confidence in human reason to discover scientific and moral truths that all intelligent persons of goodwill can learn to accept. Postmodernism, in contrast, is associated with contemporary pessimism about universal truths or "meta-narratives" that transcend cultural particularities and parochialisms. It asserts that we are all embedded in our own cultures, which is often thought to imply that appeals to universal principles or rights are illegitimate. Does this view imply pessimism about moral clarity or about our ability to oppose what in our culture we see as evil but which others might see as heroism? Not according to two of the most prominent American postmodernists.

For Stanley Fish, the pessimism is merely about reaching agreement: "the distinction . . . is not between affirming universals and denying them but between affirming them because you strongly believe them to be such and affirming them because you believe them to have been certified by an independent authority acknowledged by everyone."[17] We can take a stand for what we are sure is universally right, but we must realize that we cannot certify our view to ourselves or others with an argument from reason or some other source of authority that is or should be recognized by everyone. However, for Richard Rorty, the postmodern pessimism (which he prefers to characterize as "irony") is deeper. It is about our own epistemology—about what we think we know—and not merely about what we can convince others to accept through objective appeals: "insofar as [an ironist] philosophizes about her situation, she does not think that her vocabulary is closer to reality than others, that it is in touch with a power not herself."[18] For Rorty, we cannot even legitimately think that our beliefs are universally true, much less prove them to ourselves or others. One can see how some critics might think that such a view implies loss of moral clarity or inability to take a stand against evils that some others think are goods. Rorty, however, argues that an ironist can *commit* herself to her conviction, *believing* she is right—and even be willing to fight for it—without claiming to *know* it in the traditional sense of knowledge as justified true belief. What Rorty gives up is not forceful stances, but the need to think that such a stance requires a purportedly universal justification.

So some postmodernists are pessimistic about what we think we can prove, while others are pessimistic about what we think we can know, but most of them assert that such pessimism is simply realism about the human condition and that it in no way implies paralyzing skepticism about right and wrong or timidity about opposing those they think are wrong. Critics may claim that postmodernists misread the implications of their own views, but the relevant point for us is that most of them agree that strong convictions and commitments require persons of integrity sometimes to refuse to accept or even to tolerate certain actions or practices. In other words, they can believe that our integrity puts appropriate limits on our agreeableness.

Integrity and Balancing Commitments

Will a person of integrity hold certain commitments unconditionally and unchangeably? Perhaps, though we must remember that people undergo conversions and "born again" experiences resulting in deep and basic changes. Calling these difficult changes a loss of integrity would elicit resentment in those who see them as a rebirth. Still, given the deepest commitments you now have, are there some things you would never do?[19] If so, we will put such commitments at one end of a spectrum and, at the other, those "loose" commitments that you allow to be decided by social context, such as matters of refined etiquette and proper manners. Notice that you have many commitments between these ends of the spectrum, commitments that may be very strong, yet conditional; you take them to be significant obligations but you recognize that sometimes you have to choose among them, since you cannot satisfy all of them in a given situation.[20] These include commitments involving your various roles as student or teacher, child or parent, employee or employer, friend, colleague, or citizen. It is not difficult to find examples where your commitment to your work or to an important cause conflicts with, say, your commitment to your family or friends. In the 1980s, developmental psychologists Anne Colby and William Damon did an intensive study of twenty-three "moral exemplars" who were noted for their service to others and their moral commitments and motivation.[21] They found that these people often had to choose among conflicting commitments, ones that they simultaneously felt in a given situation but ones that they could not simultaneously satisfy, and that "the most frequent conflict . . . was their need to divide their efforts between their families and society at large. . . . The brutal fact is that moral heroes do not always make ideal parents."[22] Of course, most of our moral life does not involve dilemmas about which commitment overrides which. When I am in the grocery store, I do not have to deliberate about whether to steal some chocolates. Even whether to steal bread in order to feed my family is not something most of us have to decide. Generally our moral decisions can be made on the run, and we can rely on our experience to discern almost automatically the obvious thing to do. But circumstances can arise where the decision is not so obvious, as in the oft-cited case of Heinz, who must decide whether to steal a drug in order to save his wife's life.[23] Alas, it seems that one of the most interesting parts of our moral life consists in setting priorities among our conditional commitments, and that such decisions are made only with a sense of loss and regret. Even when we do the *best* thing, it is also the least *bad* thing and, as I will discuss further in the next chapter, the overridden commitments will leave their moral traces of regret, if not remorse.

To summarize, we can and should cultivate broadminded acceptance as a way of coping with some potential conflicts, but there are deeper conflicts where our moral identity and integrity require that we stand for what we believe by opposing what we see as wrong. Some of these stands may involve unconditional commitments, but even conditional commitments can be overridden only with some discomfort. Of course, one can avoid such discomfort by eliminating one side of the conflict, a tempting tactic when the conflict is between ourselves and others rather than an internal one between our own loyalties. Thus it is no wonder that for much of history the human race tended to cope with disagreements by fighting over them. Fortunately, enough humans eventually saw the advantage, instead of fighting, of reaching agreement on some things while agreeing to disagree on others. The question now is how to reach such agreements, and what to do when we cannot.

Uses of Conversation

Well, we can talk, as Aristotle long ago noted in his *Politics*, when he linked our capacity for speech with our being the distinctive type of social animals that we inherently are:

> But obviously man is a political animal in a sense in which a bee is not, or any other gregarious animal. Nature . . . has endowed man alone among the animals with the power of speech. Speech is something different from voice, which is possessed by other animals also and used by them to express pain or pleasure; for their nature does indeed enable them not only to feel pleasure and pain but to communicate these feelings to each other. Speech, on the other hand, serves to indicate what is useful and what is harmful, and so also what is just and what is unjust. For the real difference between man and other animals is that humans alone have perception of good and evil, just and unjust, etc. It is the sharing of a common view in these matters that makes a household and a state [polis].[24]

Aristotle here integrates three important features of human life: First, we go beyond using mere voice, which expresses only feelings; we use speech to communicate ideas. Second, chief among the ideas that we communicate are moral convictions; and, third, shared moral convictions are what unite us in families and city-states. Underlying these points is Aristotle's belief articulated throughout the "Politics" that humans are inherently social animals, that individuals are normally members of a larger body or group. Moreover, the group or groups we are part of, as well as the particular roles we have in the group, are what give us our moral identities. It is shared understanding of roles and values that unite the groups, according to Aristotle. Today he might not be so sure that no other animals use speech, and he would surely notice that many people live in pluralistic states, ones without a unified vision of good and evil. So today, even as we agree that humans use speech to talk about our moral convictions, the question is how can we use it to cope with the differences that divide us without fighting over them.

Some conversational optimists think that if we would only communicate respectfully and listen carefully to each other, we would find much common ground, at least enough that we could avoid serious ideological conflicts. Indeed, one of the patron saints of classical liberalism,[25] the 19th-century British philosopher John Stuart Mill, worried that freedom of public speech would eventually expose all errors, and that the resulting consensus might make society mentally lazy. He thought society may eventually have to hire skilled "devil's advocates" to give error its best run for the money so that the rest of us, by rebutting them, would have a more lively and firmer grasp of the truth.[26]

That free speech has not, in fact, brought such consensus does not imply that it never could, since the way our society actually exercises its freedom of speech is often deeply disappointing to those who have high hopes for careful conversation, especially careful conversation about differences. Of course, good conversations take many forms, and only some of them are intended to discuss differences of opinion. We do many different kinds of things with speech: We exchange greetings, give information, complain about the bugs, make promises, announce opinions, express feelings, propose marriage, pronounce two people husband and wife, ask questions, explain ourselves, lay blame, admit fault, apologize, exhort congregations, tell jokes, scold children, write poetry, deliver lectures, recommend restaurants, warn enemies, predict the weather, appeal decisions, thank our lucky stars, and chat about the news. One should not dismiss even our dangling conversations as little more than superficial sighs or idle talk, since they can be nurturing parts of our communal lives. Still, even if the purpose of most of our conversations is something other than making assertions, or discussing our differences, or trying to reach agreement, Aristotle makes an important point about the link between our speech and our discussing values; it is when we notice value-laden disagreements that we have an especially strong reason to think and talk things through. This point brings us to the question of what we mean by values.

Four Types of Claims

We can have all sorts of disagreements that do not involve values, and those that involve values need not involve distinctly moral values. A common way of sorting out types of claims (or statements, or assertions—I shall use the terms interchangeably[27]) is to distinguish among empirical, metaphysical, conceptual, and value claims.

Empirical

Empirical claims are descriptive claims about the way the world is (or was, or will be) that we decide are true or false—or probable or improbable—by using our physical senses. Often we can use our senses directly, as when we decide that the flowers outside the window are yellow and brown, but many of our empirical claims are verified or falsified only indirectly, as when we rely on scientific experiments. It is worth noting that many of the concepts used by natural and social scientists refer to things that are not directly sensed, and often they *cannot* be directly sensed, such as electrons and racism. Rather, scientists set up experiments or make observations that, combined with theory—often a substantial amount of it—yield inferences about things unseen. So marks on a photograph of reactions in a smoke chamber yield claims about elementary particles, and descriptions of crowd behavior yield claims about racism, in both cases only when combined with theories.[28] Notice that explanations referring to history, as well as predictions that certain policies will (likely) lead to particular effects, are generally empirical claims, and that these can be at least as controversial as value claims. There is much more debate about the causes of child abuse, for example, or about how to prevent it, or about whether "recovered memories" of it are reliable, than there is about whether child abuse is wrong. So we should avoid the surprisingly common error that empirical claims are what we agree on while value claims are what we argue about.[29]

Metaphysical

Are all descriptive claims empirical? Or are there some that we would not allow to be falsified by empirical evidence? It may be tempting to think that the only meaningful descriptive claims are those that we can arrive at by using our physical senses. But most people seem to have beliefs about how the world is and how it works that seem metaphysical rather than empirical.[30] That every event has a cause,[31] for example, is something that children perhaps first learn from empirical experience, but for many people it has become the sort of belief that they would not give up even if they could not find the cause of a given event. It has become one of the beliefs that they now use to organize their experience; they bring it to their experience rather than derive it from their experience. Beliefs about determinism or free will and some theological beliefs—perhaps elicited by religious experiences that transcend empirical experience—may be further examples of metaphysical beliefs. The classification has less to do with subject matter and more to do with how one arrives at or defends the belief. Those who treat answers or nonanswers to prayer as evidence for or against God's existence, for example, are doing their theology in an empirical mode: Their hypothesis is that if we act on certain independent variables (pray for rain), then there will be an empirically noticeable effect on certain dependent variables (rain will come), and the relevant theory attributes them to something unseen (God answered my prayer). Of course, if my prayer is not answered and

I count that as evidence against God's existence, I am still doing theology in an empirical mode. Some religious people think it is wrong to put God to the test this way, and they may take a more metaphysical approach to their theology, either relying on a type of experience that transcends the physical senses or on fundamental considerations that they use to make sense of their empirical experience, such as the belief that there must be a sufficient reason for the existence of the universe. Metaphysical claims, then, are believed by anyone who accepts descriptive claims that empirical experience by itself will not falsify or verify. We are *Homo credens*—the believing animal—according to a recent study of personhood and culture, and we all use fundamental beliefs to make sense of our world, something that Hollywood exploits in movies such as *The Truman Show* or *The Matrix* when it pulls the rug out from under our shared "plausibility structure."[32] Our fundamental beliefs are often part of a "stance"[33] that we take toward the world, an attitude that includes emotions and value-laden beliefs about which aspects of our experience can be trusted to provide knowledge and guidance. We will see that these beliefs may be justified to those who hold them, but not by empirical evidence, since they are the foundational beliefs we use to make sense of our sense experience.

Conceptual: True by Definition

In addition to empirical and metaphysical claims are conceptual ones, including those that are true by definition. You may have inferred from experience that all bachelors are unmarried, but once you know the meanings of the words you do not have to look to know that it is false that there is a married bachelor in the next room. So this first type of conceptual claim simply relies on the meaning of the words used. Notice that confusion can occur when one person treats as an empirical claim what another is using as a conceptual claim. You say that all crows are black and, as a counterexample, your birdwatcher friend shows you an albino crow. If you stick to your guns and insist that if it is not black it cannot be a crow, you are simply telling us something uninteresting about how you define "crow."

Sometimes this move is more subtle. Consider the following argument, used surprisingly often to defend psychological egoism: (1) Whenever you do something you do it because you want to; (2) doing something because you want to is in your (perceived) self-interest; (3) therefore, everything you do is in your (perceived) self-interest. Notice that the conclusion is not ethical egoism—that you *ought* to pursue only your (perceived) self-interest. Rather, it is the empirical claim that that is what you always in fact do. The first claim is meant to be true by definition of what it means to perform an action—you *choose* to do it, unlike an automatic reaction, such as a sneeze. The second claim might look like an empirical generalization: When you satisfy your wants you are acting in your own self-interest. Unfortunately, as an empirical claim, it begs the question; it merely states the conclusion and avoids the question whether you can ever want to do something independently of calculating your self-interest, perhaps out of altruism or duty. Now, if egoists say, "But having your wants fulfilled is part of what we mean by doing things in your own interest," they make it into a conceptual claim that is not only dubious but also one that they cannot simply combine with the first conceptual claim to yield an empirical (psychological) conclusion. In fact, a close look at the argument shows that "want" is probably being used in two different ways; in other words, the argument *equivocates* on an important concept, and such equivocation always turns a seemingly valid argument into an invalid one. In the first claim, a synonym for "want" is "choose": Whenever you perform an action, you choose to do so. But if one uses "choose" as a synonym for "want" in the second claim, it clearly begs the question of whether all your choices are self-interested. If, to avoid such circularity, egoists use in the second claim a more loaded notion of "want-fulfillment" (for example, interpreting it as "self-interested wants") they have used "want" in a different sense from the first claim; rather than beg the question they now equivocate, and they cannot link the first claim with the second one in a way that entails the conclusion.

The upshot is that this first kind of conceptual claim is very common because we often find it useful to notice that some claims are true or false by definition. However, we must be careful when using such claims in arguments that we avoid unnoticed equivocation.

Conceptual: Giving Definitions

That words can be ambiguous and vague brings up a second kind of conceptual claim that is often required for clear-headed thinking. In addition to claims that are true or false by virtue of the meaning of the words, conceptual claims can be clarifications of ambiguous and vague words and concepts. An ambiguous word has more than one meaning, though each meaning may be quite precise, as with "bat" or "iron." A vague word lacks precision, though it may be fairly unambiguous, such as "bald" or "bearded." Many words are both ambiguous and vague—hot, cool, hard, beautiful, true—though often the context makes them quite clear. Conversations in a pluralistic society will often include vague and ambiguous concepts that are not clear even in context, concepts like toleration, fairness, and respect. This is usually not a problem; since the real world does not appear to us in crisp categories, any language that maps reality (or, at least, is useful in coping with it) will be somewhat open-ended. But, as we saw in the previous paragraph, mischief can occur when someone equivocates on an unclear concept and uses it in different ways in the same argument. Hence sometimes we must do conceptual analysis and clarification by explicitly defining our terms. One way to do that is to look up the term in a dictionary. Notice that what today's dictionaries usually give are empirical reports of how the term is actually used. This means that for interesting words it will give more than one report, and one may have to choose among them. Another way to clarify is to provide your own definition of how you are using a term. Sometimes you can simply arbitrarily stipulate that you are using a new term in a particular way, as when a mathematician informs us that a particular symbol will be used to stand for a specific number. But usually when we try to clarify a debate we offer a definition that captures how we think clarity is best achieved and confusion best avoided in the use of that term. I will be doing that later for terms like "relativism" and "reasonable" and am doing it right now for "clarify."

Sometimes when we offer definitions, we can give what are called "essential properties" for what we are trying to define, as when we say that having three angles is a necessary condition for something to be a triangle. If we can find several necessary conditions that add up to a sufficient condition for what it is we are trying to define, we can give a precise and informative definition. The difference between a necessary and a sufficient condition is straightforward. If something lacks one necessary condition for what we are trying to define, it simply cannot be an example of that type of thing no matter what else it possesses. If the capacity for self-consciousness is a necessary condition for being a person, then no matter how much a robot can look and act like a person, it cannot be one. If the capacity for self-consciousness is a sufficient condition for being a person, then if a chimpanzee can say "I" to itself in a mirror, it is a candidate for personhood.

You might think that one would never mix up necessary and sufficient conditions, but people sometimes do that. Consider the following argument, which has been used by intelligent and knowledgeable people in the abortion debate: If we use the absence of brainwaves in human beings as our criterion for the death of a person, then consistency requires that we use the presence of brainwaves (which can be detected in fetuses in the first trimester of pregnancy) as a criterion for the presence of personhood. This argument confuses what the "brainwave" criterion for death uses as a *necessary* condition for personhood—brainwaves, the absence of which thereby indicates the absence of personhood—with a *sufficient* condition. In other words, it claims that if we use the absence of brainwaves as indicating the absence of a necessary condition for personhood, consistency requires that we must also use the presence of brainwaves as a criterion for the presence of personhood; and it thereby slips from a necessary to a sufficient condition. This mistake is analogous to saying that since the absence of oxygen—a necessary condition for fire—can be used as a criterion for the absence of fire, consistency requires that we also use its presence as sufficient for the presence of fire. (Notice that rebutting the above argument does not show that brainwaves in humans is *not* sufficient for personhood, since one might have a separate argument for that claim; the rebuttal only shows that one cannot move automatically from a necessary to a sufficient condition.)

The above examples show that one must be careful when one tries to define a term by suggesting necessary and sufficient conditions—essential properties— for its referent. Indeed, 20th-century philosopher Ludwig Wittgenstein is well known for claiming that we rarely, if ever, find essential properties for anything, even everyday things like chairs and games, much less complicated things like persons. He suggested instead that we use "family resemblances." Just as we can list a number of features that enable us to know that two people are siblings, without claiming that any one of the features or even a group of them are either necessary or sufficient for knowing that they are siblings, so we can give a list of family resemblances for what we are trying to define. For example, instead of making self-consciousness a necessary or sufficient property for personhood, we might suggest it as one of a list of "person-making" characteristics—being human, having speech, having certain types and levels of intelligence, making complicated tools, etc.—without insisting that any one or group of them is necessary or sufficient for personhood. This route will not have the precision that some people like, but when the concept we are trying to define is open-textured and thereby is difficult, even dangerous, to pin down, this route can at least give us some clarity, including clarity about why more precision cannot be found. We will have opportunity to notice this when we try later to define concepts such as "public reason" and "reasonable viewpoint." And it can certainly help us avoid equivocation; we simply make sure we do not slip from one set of family resemblances to another set in the same argument.

Normative, or Value, Claims

Finally we come to "normative" or "value" claims.[34] As Aristotle noted, this is the kind of claim we so often find ourselves talking about in public discussions. Normative claims consist of prescriptions and evaluations, only some of which are moral. There are various types of "shoulds" and "ought nots" in our prescriptions, and various kinds of "goods" and "bads" in our evaluations, all of which indicate distinct points of view (or realms of value) from which we make normative judgments.[35] The normative pie can be divided in various ways, but typical points of view from which we make judgments include the moral, the economic, the aesthetic, the religious, the intellectual, the political, the legal, as well as that of etiquette. When we evaluate something complex, like a college, for example, which participates in a number of realms of value, we can judge it from a variety of normative points of view. Its curriculum can be intellectually first rate while its campus is aesthetically displeasing and, as an economic investment, it can be better than some and worse than others. These different points of view come with distinctive types of norms, or value-laden criteria, and something can rank high on some norms and low on others of the same type, as when an automobile, say, aesthetically has clean lines but clashing colors. Something can also rank high from one point of view and low from another, as when an aesthetically undistinguished automobile turns out to be highly economical. So overall value judgments can be quite complex, involving different realms of value and different norms within each one. No wonder Aristotle noted that we talk about them a lot.

What distinguishes different realms of value has to do with what is relevant when making judgments from the different points of view, and that is an ongoing debate. Presumably the economic criteria that make a painting a good investment are not the same as the aesthetic ones that judge it beautiful, though there may be overlap, just as there may be overlap between the legal and moral realms. But the tension in much good literature depends on not reducing the moral point of view to others, such as law or etiquette. Suggested defining characteristics of the moral point of view include that it is "other-regarding" (it cannot be reduced to self-interest, even enlightened self-interest); it is over-riding (in terms of what one ought to do, it trumps all other points of view); and decisions within it must be universalizable (if you think you are permitted or required to do something, you have to agree that anyone in a relevantly similar situation is permitted or required to do it—you cannot make an exception for yourself). These candidates are widely accepted, though they are debatable: Ayn Rand thought that enlightened self-interest is the only rational game around; Søren Kierkegaard thought that religious obligations can override moral ones; and Friedrich Nietzsche thought that every moral situation was unique and, in any case, that it would be in poor taste to universalize your personal moral judgments. Although some of us regard the above features and necessary elements of the moral point of view, others take the "family resemblances" approach described above, and think of these and the other candidates listed in introductory ethics texts as "morality-making features," without insisting that any of them are necessary or sufficient to define the moral point of view.[36]

Explanation and Justification

You might think it obvious that moral prescriptions such as "Do not murder innocent people," and moral evaluations such as "Terrorism that murders innocent people is a heinous crime," cannot be confused with empirical claims. But sometimes empirical descriptions and scientific explanations are conflated with moral justifications. For example, after the terrorism of 9/11, social scientists raised questions like "Why do they hate us," and they tried to uncover root causes of the despair and resentment that motivates terrorism. Some critics objected that such talk amounted to excusing or justifying the horrible actions, since it made them more understandable. However, these critics are confused: you can understand that an increase in poverty breeds an increase in theft without concluding that the theft is justified. And you may give a true explanation of my believing that abortion is wrong by citing my conservative religious upbringing, but you would insult me if you thought that an *explanation* (even a true one) constituted my *justification* for my belief. I would want you to assess my *reasons* for my continuing to hold the belief, not just understand the *causes* that brought me to it. And even if your altruistic feelings are explained by theories of evolution or theology, you can give an independent justification of their value. So scientific explanations are empirical descriptions of suggested causes of beliefs or actions, while justifications are normative evaluations of the reasons given to claim that the beliefs or actions are acceptable.[37] When one is fighting enemies, it would be foolish to refuse to understand what motivates them; nevertheless, understanding motivations, while it may provide some mitigating considerations about the degrees of evil, does not eliminate agents' responsibility, nor does it negate the reasons for punishing or incapacitating them.[38] Only those who deny all human responsibility—extreme determinists who think that everything we do is completely caused by previous events—believe that to explain all is to excuse all. (Notice that they cannot coherently say that to understand all is to *forgive* all, since forgiveness implies that someone did something wrong, and that implies human responsibility.) However, what a critic of extreme determinism should reject is not a particular empirical explanation, but the metaphysical belief that *everything* we believe and do is explainable without any reference to our responsibility.

Almost everyone who believes in human responsibility—who does not reduce humans to mere products of their genes and environment—believes that there can be many empirical causes for our beliefs and actions. Thus they believe that there can be true—if partial—explanations for them, and that understanding these causes is very important, although they do not eliminate moral and legal responsibility. So even if the perpetrators of the 9/11 crimes were understandably upset over US foreign policy in the Middle East or the laxity of our morals or the depth of our hypocrisy, and even if it is important for us to know their motivations, it remains true that understandable motivations do not excuse crimes, anymore than understanding the hatred behind genocide excuses it. Given that explanations do not absolve responsibility, it is no wonder that many of the moral debates mentioned by Aristotle concern the justifiability of reasons rather than the adequacy of explanation.[39]

All of the Above

In our conversations it is often important to agree on the type of claim we are discussing, since what is relevant to evaluating an empirical claim about terrorism, for example, is likely to be different from what is relevant when we are trying to clarify its definition, or when we debate whether it has ever been justified. The four types we have looked at—empirical, metaphysical, conceptual, and normative—are presented only as a useful map for conversations; there are other interesting ways of classifying assertions, and our own map will sometimes lead to ambiguity, especially for claims that include "weasel words," which can mean different things. To say that human nature is *basically* social, for example, can be treated most naturally as an empirical generalization. Then hermits are regarded as exceptions and "basically" means something like "almost always." But if hermits are regarded as deviants from what God or nature intended, or as deficient examples of human nature, or as not truly human, the claim could be meant as a metaphysical, value, or conceptual one, and a lot of time could be saved by clarifying that before discussing it further. When such clarification is impossible, it can still be conversationally important to notice that very ambiguity.

Also, sharp lines cannot always be drawn between these categories. To say that one is "healthy," for example, is perhaps to bridge the descriptive and value realms. In the history of philosophy, the term "empiricist"[40] is applied to philosophers such as David Hume, who assert that of our four types of claims, only the empirical and conceptual ones have to do with knowledge. In particular, they assert a sharp separation between empirical and value claims—a logical gap between "is" and "ought" often called "the fact-value dichotomy." Some empiricists go so far as to argue that value assertions are expressions of feelings or attitudes rather than "cognitive" claims about what can be known to be true or false. However, many nonempiricist philosophers think it makes sense to talk about goals or functions for organisms. Like Aristotle, they assert a "teleology" (from "telos," the Greek word for "goal") that has values built right into the aims of nature or of God or of human practices.[41] For example, if an organism is not only alive (an empirical issue) but is also flourishing and healthy, it is living its telos in a satisfactory way (a value-laden judgment). Aristotle's example is that if the definition of a "sea captain" includes the goal of getting the ship out of and into the harbor safely, then if we observe that a captain sinks nine out of ten ships we do not need any separate value claims to conclude that we likely have a lousy captain. Even those who have doubts about this sort of teleological thinking should be alert to how claims are sometimes meant as intriguing combinations of our four types. And even those who insist that empirical explanations are not normative justifications should recognize that our language is rich enough to sometimes call the distinction into question.

The above complexities can make our conversations very interesting, even when we are not trying to persuade each other or to justify our views, but simply to explain them to each other or, for that matter, to clarify them to ourselves. Of course, sooner or later we are likely to discuss which views are true, or at least reasonable.

Conversations and Arguments

"Talk shows are proof that conversation is dead," I have heard said, because they reduce conversation to argument and argument to quarreling. But it does not have to be that way. Even when we narrow down to conversations that are arguments we can see the discussants as hearers and givers of reasons, as opinion holders and molders who are willing to examine their beliefs. An argument then can be an effort at least to understand each other's ideas and perhaps to convince each other of their appropriateness.

In an age of negative campaigning and thirty-second attack ads, our "argument culture"[42] gets bad press because debate is so often used as a type of warfare or, less ominously, as a point-scoring game. Arguments are used to try to defeat opponents, if not demolish them. Argument so often reduces to battling or sparring because so much of our culture is adversarial.[43] Indeed, some of us pride ourselves on a legal system in which we seek the truth precisely by having hired guns shoot it out in court, using whatever legal tactics will win the minds of the jury. And political discussions seem to attract the largest television audiences when the opponents heap clever invective on each other rather than reason together. Apart from law and politics, many people tend to associate good debaters with the sophists of ancient Greece, less interested in finding truth or agreement than in playing verbal games and winning a contest. Socrates told the Sophists that they were good at rhetoric but not at conversation; this from one who loved to argue but did it as a mutual inquiry, as a conversation.

Evaluating Arguments

Why is argument so often used to fight each other's thoughts rather than to share them? To understand why it need not be that way, we must consider the nature of arguments. As illustrated by earlier examples, they always consist of more than one claim—whether explicit or implicit—and they always have a logical structure in which at least one claim, called the inference(s), including the final inference or conclusion, is thought to follow from at least one other claim, called the premise(s). What can be challenged in another's argument, therefore, is the truth or plausibility of the premises, as well as the validity of the conclusion—whether it follows logically from the premises.[44] Thus, when arguing about beliefs, we do not merely describe them; we evaluate them. Of course, having an accurate description of another's belief is a necessary condition for a good argument about it. Unfortunately, it is also a condition too often unmet. When I teach students how to argue about social issues, I insist that before they criticize an opponent's view they must be able to describe it so clearly and sympathetically that the opponent can agree to the description. My experience is that the best way to raise the level of a debate is to enhance listening skills rather than speaking skills. Careful listening is also the quickest way to find any possible common ground. Probably this is because in order to understand and describe another's belief, one must interpret it, which requires imagination as much as intellect; one must be able to put oneself in the heads and hearts of others and try to see the issue the way they do. Unfortunately, accurate description of another's view is difficult (and rare) on hot-button issues such as abortion.

Still, debating an issue goes beyond description to evaluation. We often use the term "argument" broadly to refer not just to the premises and conclusions of the debaters, but also to the debate itself. In this sense, an argument consists of the debaters making claims about whether the conclusions of their arguments are justified. As we noted above, to evaluate another's argument is not simply to *explain* why the other holds to it. Of course, if I say that the only reason I have for the belief is that I was raised that way, I have reduced my reason to a cause. But thoughtful people are usually able and even eager to provide the reasons they have for the views they were taught, and the difference between merely inheriting these views and openly debating them is being willing to examine the reasons.

There is no question that arguments and debates generally involve an element of disputation; they are used to see whether reasons can be justified by withstanding careful examination. Does this element imply that their use is inherently adversarial, if not belligerent?

Three Uses of Argument

Argument will not be reduced to fighting as long as we keep some important distinctions in mind. Arguments and debates can be used in at least three ways: to *defeat* others, to *persuade* others, and to *inquire* with others.

Contests can be fun, as when friends score points against each other in a game. Of course, there are still winners and losers, so when a debate is seen as a contest, someone is trying to defeat someone else. Although this can be done in a way that remains fun, it should still be kept in its place. Even if there were a place for eating contests, it would be a shame to confuse them with dining. Moreover, in so much of our media the aim is not just to win a debate and defeat an opponent, but also to humiliate one's opponent in front of an audience. Often the opponent is not even part of one's intended audience; one is not trying to persuade the opponent about the truth, but to persuade the listeners that the opponent is incompetent or worse. Some critics have charged that teaching rhetorical skills of debating and even philosophical skills of analysis consists of training in how to score points and defeat others. Even when this is done fairly—without manipulating the truth or demonizing the opponent—it is hardly geared to help us understand each other or to cope with conflicts in a civil way; indeed, the intent is quite the opposite. So a book on civil disagreement will not appeal to this use of argument. That our politicians too often feel that they have to use it in self-defense is one of the most counterproductive features of politics today. Unfortunately, politicians, or, more frequently, the well-funded committees that support them, have discovered that diatribe often sinks deliberation and logic rarely beats contempt.

Arguments can also be used by debaters to try to persuade each other that one viewpoint is better than the other. Here the audience is the other participant, more in the role of discussants than opponents, since the idea is to change minds rather than score points. So cheap rhetorical tricks will be avoided; when you are debating me you will always try to rebut the most charitable interpretation of my view, since you are seeking an ally, not a conquered foe. Hence you will also listen with an open mind to my criticisms of your view; you cannot win me over unless I am sure you understand both my own position and my view of your position. Done well, this use of argument can be a respectful and effective way of finding common ground or at least agreeing to disagree more respectfully. But it has its limits, since our natural defensiveness about being right makes us wary of agreeing that we were wrong. Socrates thought we should be delighted to be shown wrong; we are then disburdened of useless and possibly harmful intellectual luggage. But he was forced to drink hemlock because few humans can live up to such a standard. I have been a debater on high school and college debate teams, and friends have said that I can be persuasive in argument. But I find that more minds are changed by hugs and handshakes than by arguments. It is a sense of mutuality and common endeavor that opens us up to the give and take of inquiry. Persuasive argument can, of course, have a different audience than the other debaters, and in this way it can play an important role in a pluralistic democracy: Well-reasoned letters to the editor, for example, can have a very productive role in public debates about policies and candidates. But they seem to be most effective when the writers' minds are already made up and they are simply soliciting support. Then writers of different persuasions can counter with arguments that exhibit the features mentioned in this paragraph rather than only those mustered to defeat an enemy. Still, in many one-on-one conversations and small group discussions, the aim is less persuasion than inquiry, which is our third use of argument.

Some people think that mutual inquiry is something other than argument, calling it dialogue, or conversation, and insisting that it has all winners and no losers because it concerns not disagreements over what is a good answer but agreement over what is a good question.[45] There is no point in arguing much about terminology here, but do notice that most of our dialogues and conversations are not about reaching consensus on either answers or questions; few of them are committee meetings. Of course, in this book we are focusing on those conversations that are about disagreements over whether the answers are right and whether the questions are clear. So naturally we are interested in the conversations that examine each others' arguments—making explicit the unstated assumptions, evaluating the plausibility of the premises, assessing the strength of the inferences, and clarifying both the questions and the answers. Obviously we can also do that in the first two kinds of debates, but here we are focusing on the occasions of mutual inquiry, the give and take aimed not at scoring points or even persuading, but at working together to get a better grasp of the truth or, at least, of our differences.[46] Sometimes the aim of the conversation may begin as efforts at persuasion, and then end as clarification of differences, as when diplomats say, after failing to reach agreement, "there was a frank and candid exchange of views." Even when the beginning aim is simply an exchange of views, we can call it argument and debate, realizing that it can be a civil conversation among seekers of the truth rather than a contest among those who think they have found it. I remember a church sign in New England that said, "Unanswered questions have done less harm than unquestioned answers." That is the spirit of mutual inquiry.

Mutual inquiry is for people who are ready to form and give an opinion but also realize they are not omniscient. If we were gods, we could just look at the objective truth and form our opinions accordingly. But, in our honest moments, we are "fallibilists" (chapter two) about many of our views; we admit, at least intellectually, that we could be wrong. As noted earlier, this does not mean that we cannot commit ourselves to them, since we can and must take stands on debatable issues. Still, responsible thinkers want to evaluate their beliefs, especially when they conflict with the views of others whom they have reason to respect. Indeed, the disagreement presents an opportunity; rather than having our beliefs confirmed by those who share them, we can inquire with those who do not. Thus inquiry often works best when conducted with those who are willing to offer contrary positions, as long as they are willing to listen to others.[47]

Civility

The next chapter will explain why mutual inquiry, however carefully and considerately it is done, will not always (or even often) lead to consensus. In fact, in a pluralistic society the purpose of inquiry is less to reach agreement than to understand each other better. Probably many issues fit for mutual inquiry are ones we would not even want to agree on. And even on those moral and political ones where we would like consensus, we cannot expect to get it. This fact alone does not prove that our unresolved differences are irresolvable; we may not have tried hard enough. But life is short and we have lots to do, so if we are going to do things together, we must at some point decide to cope with our ongoing disagreements in a civil way. "Civility" associates with practices and dispositions such as etiquette, manners, politeness, protocol, propriety, and decorum, though it cannot be equated with any of them. The latter categories tend to be culturally relative and in their specific details only sometimes carry moral weight, though I think there are convincing arguments that intentionally violating the accepted norms of politeness, for example, can be morally disrespectful.[48] The Latin root for civility is the same as for city, the place where we meet strangers and cannot rely on friendship or familiarity to do what needs to be done.[49] I like the anecdotal evidence that the handshake originated as a civil way of assuring others that one will not use one's sword on them. Not using one's sword hardly implies back-slapping camaraderie, so civility hardly implies friendliness. No wonder some writers refer to "the ordeal of civility."[50]

Civility is treating others with appropriate courtesy and respect.[51] Much of what civility involves is context relative, and often it is relative mainly to what is needed for a shared task or mutual endeavor. Then the question of what civility requires in a given context or association is related to the question of what we are trying to accomplish together. Notice that the context may well include people who are strangers and even past opponents, so we cannot rely on affection, friendship, or familiarity to set boundaries; civility is something we intentionally bring to the situation, not necessarily something that flows from natural feelings.

Notice also that civility involves patience and *restraints*; it has as much to do with what we will *not* do to each other as what we will do for each other.

When we ask how a couple is getting along, and the answer is, "Well, they are civil to each other," we know that self-sacrificing affection is currently not likely the major motivator in the relationship. That civility has as much to do with *forbearance* as with positive actions does not, of course, undermine its importance, since what we will *not* do or say to each other can be essential to cooperation. As with manners, the restraint is self-imposed, though admittedly with the threat of social sanctions—it is not illegal to be rude or uncivil, but it will invite comment. It is the sort of thing that is noticed more in its absence. In chapter four we will ask what political civility requires when citizens engage in political disputes about candidates and legislation. Here we ask what civility requires in other sorts of conversations.

In his book *Civility*, Stephen Carter says that it was important for him to first write his book, *Integrity*, because we need to have moral selves before we develop tools for interacting well with others.[52] He underscores the point that civil conversation requires participants who are willing to take a stand and to argue for it. In his book *A Civil Tongue*, Mark Kingwell makes it clear that civil *talk* requires, first of all, a civil *ear*—the willingness to listen.[53] He underscores the point that civil conversation requires participants who are able to hear and understand the others' positions in a sympathetic way. Take these two points together and I think we have the essentials of civil conversation: personal convictions plus a willingness to talk about and listen to differences. These may be sufficient for civil discourse, though we should ask if there are some things that simply ought not get raised in an honest but civil discussion.

For example, perhaps we should restrain ourselves from publicly questioning each other's motives—the bane of so many public discussions. On the one hand, it can be healthy for us to submit our motives to examination. On the other hand, when it is done publicly, in committee meetings, for example, it seems so often to waylay the discussion into dead ends that are as heated as they are unenlightening. Probably it is a matter of context, depending (as noted above) on what is the mutual endeavor we are trying to accomplish in the conversation. There may be some things that would always be uncivil or counterproductive to raise,[54] but the list may be shorter or different for intimate conversations, such as those with trusted participants, than for public ones, such as faculty debates about curriculum reform. It may be that in some political situations, hidden agendas should be exposed, greedy motives impugned, and hypocrisy unmasked; and in juridical contexts such pitiless truth may be required. But for most of our conversations, including committee meetings, we can avoid heated and futile digressions by not questioning motives; instead we can simply discuss what interests would be served by a given proposal, for example, and what effects can be predicted if it is implemented. So I think we have both pragmatic and principled reasons for not impugning motives in many public debates: Such restraint helps us accomplish our shared endeavor and it also shows respect toward all participants by not questioning their commitment to the common good. In short, the rule of thumb for conversational civility is that all participants should take turns saying what they think and then listening to others, using self-imposed restraints that are conducive to what is the shared goal of the conversation.

With all this civility and conversation, why would we not reach more and more consensus? To see why civil conversation will lead to civil disagreement rather than consensus, we must consider the dynamics of pluralistic societies and the types of pluralism we find in them.

Notes

1. On the empirical verification of the doctrine of original sin, see Gilkey, *Shantung Compound*, 114–16. He describes his experiences in a prison camp where he says the "unpadded" conditions revealed human nature as it truly is, a fundamental bent of the self toward its own welfare. Gilkey was influenced by the "realist" theology of Reinhold Niebuhr, who is often credited with the line about the empirical verification of the doctrine of original sin, though he himself apparently credited others (*The New Republic*, February 28, 2005, p. 13). The doctrine was emphasized by St. Augustine, who taught that our disordered way of loving ourselves and others confuses our minds. In *Can a Darwinian Be a Christian?* Ruse claims that on this point Darwinian biology empirically supports Christian doctrine: "[A]ll too quickly, self-interest runs into qualities like greed and lust and boastfulness. There are good biological reasons for this. . . . Original sin is part of the biological package. It comes with being human" (210). As we will see in the next chapter, what we will call "the burdens of judgment" implies that even a society of saints or altruists would inevitably have conflicts in pluralistic society. But we begin without assuming pluralism.
2. See Hobbes, *Leviathan* (part I, chapter 13, first published in 1651) (many editions).
3. For Rousseau's rebuttal of Hobbes's view of the state of nature, see Locke, *Discourse on the Origins of Inequality* (part I, first published in 1755) (many editions). John Locke took a mediating position, arguing that people would abide by natural rights and responsibilities, but that the behavior of a few bullies would make it convenient to have police. See Locke, *Second Treatise of Government*, chapter 2, first published in 1690 (many editions). Of course, these different speculations about the state of nature (human nature in the raw—unformed by the influences of civilization) had important implications; they led to significant differences in how Hobbes, Locke, and Rousseau described both the *motivation for* as well as the *content of* the "social contract" proposed by each thinker as the alternative to the state of nature.
4. Nance, *The Gentle Tasaday*, 19.
5. See Headland, "The Tasaday Controversy." The controversy was aired in a 1989 BBC Nova TV production called "The Lost Tribe." Linguistic analysis suggests that they may have been isolated for, at most, hundreds rather than thousands of years. Of course, this point would not undermine and could even enhance the significance of the remarkable social harmony, were it not for the evidence of a hoax. A balanced account is given by Hemley, *Invented Eden*.
6. Clottes, "Chauvet Cave," 104–21. See also Thurman, "Letter from Southern France." The latter article inspired a highly regarded documentary film (released in 2010) by Werner Herzog, *Cave of Forgotten Dreams*.
7. *The Republic*, written around 380 BCE (many editions).

8. *Utopia*, first published in 1516 (many editions).

9. The organization Cultural Survival, with its journal *Cultural Survival Quarterly*, its newsletter *Cultural Survival Voices*, and its website www.cs.org, is an advocate for these threatened groups and an excellent source for information about them. Also, Quinn's books, especially *Ishmael*, and his website www.Ishmael.org, have started something of a movement for what might be seen as Rousseau-inspired advocacy for a preindustrialized way of life. Even those who regard Quinn's prescriptions as unrealistic can imagine that abiding by his "laws of life" would greatly reduce conflicts in and between groups. Estimates of the current population that consists of indigenous people range up to 5 percent. See Miller, *Cultural Anthropology*, 376.

10. Perhaps the survival of indigenous cultures depends on separation even from our Coke bottles, as suggested by the 1981 film *The Gods Must Be Crazy*. Regarding internal as opposed to external conflicts, what Sigmund Freud called "the narcissism of minor differences," as well as what Michael Ignatieff calls "the Cain and Abel syndrome," warn us that it does not require significant cultural differences to elicit hatred and conflict. See Ignatieff, "Nationalism and Toleration," 77, 96.

11. Hanvey, in *An Attainable Global Perspective*, a pamphlet I give to students who go on semesters abroad with me, warns us that the human tendency toward an "us-them" mentality may be innate: "This practice of naming one's own group 'the people' and by implication relegating all others to not-quite-human status has been documented in nonliterate groups all over the world. But it is simply one manifestation of a species trait that shows itself in modern populations as well. . . . It must, once, have been an adaptive trait" (10). Evolutionary moralists tend to agree that in over an estimated 99 percent of our species' history we developed a tribalism that involved suspicion and hostility between groups. See Shermer, *The Science of Good and Evil*; Seabright, *The Company of Strangers*; and Wong and Yuwa, *Genetic Seeds of Warfare*.

12. Skitka and Mullen, "The Dark Side of Moral Conviction," 36.

13. "Conviction" derives from a Latin root meaning "to find guilty" or "to overcome (presumption of innocence)," but it has come to connote beliefs strongly held, including those one might simply have inherited from one's upbringing. "Commitment" derives from a Latin root meaning "to put together," suggesting that one actively decides them; but it now connotes the resoluteness that flows from convictions one can simply find oneself having. Of course, all convictions and commitments have a voluntary element in the sense that one can examine them and then reaffirm, modify, or reject them, though in the next chapter we will note some limits to this voluntariness.

14. Sometimes self-respect is distinguished from self-esteem, the former being my recognition of my status as a person with moral rights and responsibilities, the latter being my appreciation of my talents and achievements (see Sachs, "How to Distinguish Self-Respect from Self-Esteem," 346–60). Respect, then, derives from moral and religious premises: "I am an end-in-myself, not merely your tool," or "I am created in the image of God; this is holy ground." "Pride" is sometimes used to refer to both, though more often to self-esteem. When referred to as one of the deadly sins, presumably pride connotes inflated self-esteem, though Austen's *Pride and Prejudice* captures the rich ambiguity of the term by including an ongoing debate over the appropriateness of pride as opposed to vanity. Keeping one's basic commitments

involves both self-respect and self-esteem, I believe, but for conciseness I'll use only the former term, since they are so often used interchangeably.

15. For integrity, in addition to coherence between conviction and behavior, we probably also insist on a stability condition—the coherence must persist over time—and perhaps on a publicity condition—I must publicly announce my convictions as the reason for my actions (see Benjamin, *Splitting the Difference*, 51). Notice that these are rather formal elements of integrity; a committed Nazi can have integrity so defined. But what I say about the need to maintain our integrity is consistent with building substantive moral conditions into the definition. In any case, the people whose identity-maintaining integrity we want to encourage are those whom we regard as morally virtuous.

16. Following Rawls, *Political Liberalism*, 30–31, I distinguish our institutional identity from our moral identity. The latter involves one's fundamental moral and religious commitments (what Rawls calls "comprehensive doctrines") while the former—institutional identity—refers to the public and political associations we are part of and the legal rights we consequently hold. We can change our fundamental commitments through religious conversion, say, without losing the rights pertaining to our ongoing institutional identity. Rawls notes that the postconversion Paul is the same Roman citizen as the preconversion Saul. We can be born again into a different moral identity without losing the legal rights and responsibilities we had earlier. The next chapter will note that our deep commitments usually include more than simply moral ones and may even include personal projects or attachments that override our moral commitments. Hence there is reason to speak more broadly about "personal identity," but here I specify "moral identity" to underscore the point that it is our moral commitments that seem decisive in our rejecting a generalized broadminded acceptance of all differences.

17. Fish, "Postmodern Warfare," 38.

18. Rorty, *Contingency, Irony, and Solidarity*, 73. Earlier in this book, Rorty discusses a famous quotation from Joseph Schumpeter: "To realize the relative validity of one's convictions and yet to stand for them unflinchingly, is what distinguishes a civilized man from a barbarian." Many philosophers fear that this attitude invites fanaticism unchecked by rational controls, but Rorty interprets it as underscoring how his postmodern ironist can take a firm stand: "[T]he liberal societies of our century have produced more and more people who are able to recognize the contingency of the vocabulary in which they state their highest hopes—the contingency of their own consciences—and yet have remained faithful to those consciences" (46).

19. Lynn McFall makes an affirmative answer to "Is there anything you would never do?" a necessary condition of identity and integrity. Unless we have unconditional commitments that are not defeasible, or overridable, we have nothing we can refer to as "I." She calls this the "Olaf Principle" in honor of the character in an e. e. cummings poem who says "there is some shit I will not eat." See McFall, "Integrity," 85–87. And Harry Frankfurt says that without unconditional commitments we have no fixed or essential identity (Frankfurt, "On the Necessity of Ideals," 108–16). Larry May prefers the metaphor of a *web* of commitments in which there is not an *unshakable core* of commitments, but ones that are more or less central to one's identity. See May, *The Socially Responsive Self*, 24. My use of a spectrum is compatible with both metaphors, as is Charles Taylor's linking of commitment and identity: "To know who I am is a species of knowing where I stand. My identity is defined by

the commitments and identifications which provide the frame or horizon within which I can try to determine from case to case what is good, or valuable, or what ought to be done, or what I endorse or oppose. In other words, it is the horizon within which I am capable of taking a stand." Taylor, *Sources of the Self*, 27. In the next chapter we will see that some value pluralists are suspicious of absolutizing any commitment.

20. "Conditional" commitments are "defeasible" in the sense that they can override each other, depending on context. I borrow in this and the previous paragraphs from Kekes, *The Morality of Pluralism*, 87–88, which distinguishes among loose, conditional, and basic commitments. Conditional, defeasible commitments yield what Ross calls "prima facie" duties , a term that ethicists often use interchangeably with "conditional" and "defeasible"(*The Right and the Good*, 19–21).

21. The twenty-three "moral exemplars" were chosen from a field nominated by others based on a set of criteria developed with a panel of twenty-two ethicists and social scientists. I will quote from the criteria because they underscore the importance of convictions and commitments to personal identity and integrity: "1. A sustained commitment to moral ideals or principles. . . . 2. A disposition to act in accord with one's moral ideals or principles. . . . 3. A willingness to risk one's self-interest for the sake of one's moral values. 4. A tendency to be inspiring to others and thereby to move them to moral action. 5. A sense of realistic humility about one's own importance relative to the world at large . . . " (Colby and Damon, *Some Do Care*, 29). Their commitments were not static: "Many moral exemplars show great capacities for change and growth, even late in life" (167). Yet they so closely associated their commitments with their sense of self that they often felt "they had no choice but to act accordingly" (294). Of course, in some sense, people always have the choice to ignore or violate their commitments. Sartre, in *Being and Nothingness*, predicates much of his existentialist ethics on avoiding the "bad faith" of refusing to admit that one always has the choice to reject one's sense of obligation (56–86). But the feeling that they have no choice is commonly reported by those whom others regard as moral heroes, such as those who risked their lives to save Jews from Nazis (see Oliner and Oliner, *The Altruistic Personality*, 222). What they mean, I think, is that maintaining who they are—their moral identity—requires that there are some things they will (not) do. My colleague Chuck Huff alerted me to the Colby and Damon study.

22. Colby and Damon, *Some Do Care*, 298.

23. From Rest, *Defining Issues Test* (www.ethicaldevelopment.ua.edu [June 9 2012]), designed to determine at what level one is in Lawrence Kolhberg's stages of moral development.

24. Aristotle, "Politics," 509.

25. Unless I indicate otherwise, I use "liberalism" to refer not to the "L" word that American conservatives oppose, but to the political philosophy deriving from the classical liberal thinkers, especially John Locke, Immanuel Kant, and John Stuart Mill, which emphasizes individual rights and freedoms. In this sense, most American politics consists of variations on liberalism, with the "conservatives" and "libertarians" often more classically liberal than those who get called "liberals" by the media. In Europe, which has retained the classical meaning, "liberal" political parties are usually what Americans call conservative. We will return to types of liberalism in chapter four.

26. Mill, *On Liberty*, 36. First published in 1859.

27. Sometimes it is useful to distinguish between a sentence—an oral or written linguistic entity—and a proposition—what the sentence asserts, or its meaning. This distinction enables us to see that the same sentence can assert different propositions, as in "She's cool," and that several different sentences can assert the same proposition, as in "That's red," "It has a red color," and "Das ist rot." When we ask what kind of claim is being made, we are asking primarily about the proposition being asserted, and generally interpretation is required.

28. The theories necessary for indirect empirical verification or falsification are themselves the product of earlier inferences, often using criteria of theory selection, such as simplicity and comprehensiveness, that go well beyond empirical data.

29. Although we argue about empirical claims as much as value claims, with empirical claims we can more often than with value claims decide what kind of knowledge we lack and how to try to get it. But frequently we do not know how to get it, or we know that getting it would be wrong or too costly. Consider the debates over the causes of child abuse or of global warming.

30. The term "metaphysics" originally came from Aristotle's editors when they placed the book in which he discussed such matters after ("meta") his book on physics; it has come to connote matters that are behind or foundational to our experience of the physical world. In his *Critique of Pure Reason* (first published in 1781, many editions), Immanuel Kant famously called these "synthetic a priori" beliefs. Unlike conceptual beliefs, they are not analytic since they do not simply unpack the meaning of the words; "every effect has a cause" is analytically true by definition of "effect" and "cause," but "event" does not have "cause" as part of its meaning. And they are not dependent on experience ("a posteriori") the way empirical claims are; that heat causes metal to expand is empirical; that any expansion of metal must have some cause was perhaps first learned from experience, as was "$2 + 2 = 4$," but, once understood, both beliefs have become independent (a priori) of empirical experience.

31. "Every event has a cause" applies to macro-level events (roughly, the events one can directly sense). At the level of elementary particles things get more complicated.

32. Smith, *Moral, Believing Animals*, 46–53.

33. Van Fraassen, *The Empirical Stance*: "If I am right, then what distinguishes the secular from the religious is not the theories they hold, or beliefs about what the world is like, although these too are often found among the differences. The crucial distinction lies in a certain attitude, in how we approach the world and relate to our own experience" (194). Stances, then, involve a worldview (*Weltanschauung*), which typically includes all four types of beliefs we are discussing, as well as emotional, attitudinal, and spiritual matters. Indeed, believing that there is only one appropriate stance for all human inquiries, or believing with van Fraassen that there are more than one, is part of one's worldview. Sire's *Naming the Elephant* gives an explication of the concept of "worldview" from the standpoint of one who self-consciously affirms a distinctly Christian one.

34. Sometimes social scientists use "normative" to refer to empirical claims about what is typical, or "normal." I will use it interchangeably with "value," which connotes claims that are evaluative or prescriptive rather than descriptive.

35. The categories of "point of view" and "realms of value" come from Taylor, *Normative Discourse*.

36. A good example of a list of defining characteristics of "the moral point of view" can be found in Pojman, *Ethics*, 6–8. In addition to the ones mentioned in my text, Pojman lists as possible "traits of moral principles" those of "prescriptivity," "publicity," and "practicability."

37. In addition to empirical mechanical explanations, there are also empirical teleological explanations ("She opened the window intending to freshen the air"), metaphysical teleological explanations ("God created humans in order to communicate with them"), and perhaps metaphysical mechanical explanations ("The devil made me do it"). Obviously, none of these are, in themselves, justifications for what was done.

38. Staub, in *The Roots of Evil*, provides a useful set of explanations of what causes genocide, but the title itself shows that he does not think that making it understandable makes it in any way excusable or justifiable. In *Greed and Grievance*, Mats Berdal and David Malone assemble an excellent group of articles that show that the "ancient hatreds" explanation for civil wars is less plausible than economic motives. If true, this fact would be very important in deciding how to react to civil wars, but it would not, by itself, excuse or justify them.

39. Notice that there can be normative arguments (from an intellectual point of view) about the justifiability of causal explanations. These are arguments about whether one has given reasons good enough to validate a causal explanation. Such scientific arguments can be at least as heated as moral arguments about values; we already noted that there is more dispute about the causal explanation of child abuse than about its moral justifiability, and the same is true about terrorism. Would a complete explanation eliminate human responsibility? Can reasons be reduced to causes? These questions get us into the ancient and ongoing philosophical and psychological dispute about determinism. "Hard" determinists deny all human responsibility; "soft" determinists, or "compatibilists," assert that determinism is compatible with responsibility, since a decision can be your own choice even if it was determined by features of your character that you did not choose; "free will" proponents, or libertarians, believe that we are responsible for our decisions because they were not determined—we could have done otherwise. My comments in the text are, I think, incompatible only with hard determinism. However, we should note that even hard determinists can insist that we should fight against terrorism and other crimes, since we are determined to be intolerant of what is dangerous to innocent people, even if the issue of responsibility, to say nothing of evil, is out of the question. One need not blame a disease in order to fight it.

40. The most notable 20th-century examples of empiricism are positivism and behaviorism; the former used their "criterion of meaningfulness" to rule out metaphysical and value claims as meaningful, and the latter insisted that psychology could study only observable behavior. Van Fraassen, *The Empirical Stance*, points out how difficult it is to define "empirical" and "empiricist" (117–31). The epistemological commitment to nothing but sense experience or to nothing but the discoveries of physics has all the vagueness and ambiguities of "Sola Scriptura" ("nothing but scripture") during the Reformation. Lots of theory-laden and value-laden interpretation is required, even as one takes a "stance" or attitude toward what to trust in a restricted area of inquiry. Therefore, the question of what one's experience will show or what science will eventually come up with in that area is quite open-ended.

In addition, says van Fraassen, an empirical stance in one area of inquiry is compatible with other stances in other areas.

41. MacIntyre, in *After Virtue*, links teleology to a virtues approach in ethics: Virtues are what enable us to achieve the aims of human practices.

42. See Tannen, *The Argument Culture*.

43. Adversarial tendencies are not particularly American or even Western, of course; many Mediterranean cultures seem to converse through vigorous argument, and I have attended demonstrations in which Tibetan monks showed off their skills at defeating each other in debate. The great Greek tragedies and comedies were entries in drama contests.

44. A sound argument is one that is both valid (the logical structure is such that if the premises are true, the inferences, including the conclusion, must also be true) and also has true premises (so the conclusion is true). This definition applies to deductive arguments, such as the invalid one about egoism that I used as a negative illustration earlier in the text. More common in everyday conversations are inductive arguments, in which the truth of the premises does not *assure* the truth of the inferences but simply indicates that it is likely. Hence we evaluate the inference as strong or weak, depending on how likely is the truth of the inferences given the truth of the premises. "Most people trim the truth on their income taxes when they can get away with it, so they probably lie to their friends" is probably weaker than "Most people lie to their friends, so they probably trim the truth on their income taxes when they can get away with it." Of course, the truth of both beginning premises is questionable, which underscores the point that, in most everyday arguments, we are less likely to ask whether we know for sure that the premises are *true* than to ask how *probable* we think they are.

45. For examples of the view that in conversations, as opposed to arguments, there are no losers, see Marty, *Education, Religion, and the Common Good*, 15–16, and Hinman, *Ethics*, 312.

46. "Yet a very common purpose of moral argument—perhaps so common that it regularly escapes the notice of moral theorists—is simply to gain increased understanding of the person with whom, or the position with which, one disagrees. Moral argument for this purpose will be especially important to the foreign traveler, or the college student encountering unfamiliar habits and practices. . . . Of course, moral debate with those whose moral conclusions one rejects will sometimes yield as great a gain in self-understanding as in understanding of the other" (Moody-Adams, *Fieldwork in Familiar Places*, 111–12). This point is compatible with recent research suggesting that humans evolved using arguments not to search for truth but to persuade others by finding reasons that support beliefs arrived at intuitively. See Mercier and Sperber, "Why Do Humans Reason?," 57–111. Traits that developed for one purpose can be nurtured for another.

47. In his analyses of "discourse ethics" and ideal conversations, Jürgen Habermas calls for argument and debate, as long as everyone is free (and feels free) to participate. Though he may focus too much on the goal of reaching consensus rather than understanding and coping with differences, what I call mutual inquiry includes his prescriptions on discourse. See, among many other writings, "Discourse Ethics" in *Moral Consciousness and Communicative Action* (trans. Lenhardt and Nicholsen).

48. For the moral importance of being polite, see Buss, "Appearing Respectful," 795–826. Of course, that you may have a moral reason to be polite or civil

toward me does not entail that I have the right to demand it; see Pippen, "The Ethical Status of Civility," 106.

49. The term "civil society" entered the Western conversation with Leonardo Bruni's translation of Aristotle's *Politics*, in which Aristotle contrasted the polis (city) with the home, where one could rely on familiarity and affection. See Schmidt, "Is Civility a Virtue?," 17–39, at 27. Notice that "civilization" usually has a normative force, as when we talk about civilized vs. barbaric societies. But sometimes it is used merely descriptively as culture writ large—Western civilization vs. Eastern. "Civil" retains the normative force; perhaps "barbaric civilization" is a coherent descriptive phrase, but not "barbaric civility."

50. Cuddihy, *The Ordeal of Civility*.

51. I say "appropriate" courtesy and respect because others can do or say something that your personal integrity requires not being civil. If someone does or says something that is extremely bigoted or rude, perhaps civility requires your willingness to talk about it, but if the other refuses to listen, giving them a withering look and walking away may be appropriate. In "The Virtue of Civility," Calhoun emphasizes that as a distinctive moral virtue civility requires *communicating* and *displaying* respect and considerateness, which implies that integrity may sometimes forbid such display (255–59). The point about *displaying* the respect is perhaps implied in courtesy; it is hard to *be* courteous toward someone without *showing* that you are (it is from the same root as "courting someone"). That is why in the helpful book *Choosing Civility*, Forni makes the point that it is important, for example, not just to listen to someone, but also to show that you are listening (52).

52. Carter, *Civility*, xii.

53. Kingwell, *A Civil Tongue*, 48.

54. Nagel, in "Concealment and Exposure," gives a surprisingly sizable list of items that he says civil people simply will not discuss, even in intimate conversations (3–30). Saying exactly what we think of each other is only one item on the list.

CHAPTER TWO

Conflicts and Pluralisms

Pluralism is talked about so often and so loosely these days that it has a plurality of meanings. I will distinguish various types of pluralism, but the labels I give them are not universally used; indeed, sometimes the labels are used in contradictory ways. So we should attend primarily to the content of the descriptions rather than to the labels. At one level, pluralism refers to an empirical claim about sheer diversity of beliefs and outlooks: people have different and conflicting beliefs and practices, and increasingly, such diversity is found in the same society. At a second level, pluralism refers not just to what people believe, but also to what really is the case independent of our beliefs. Metaphysical (or ontological) pluralism asserts that there is more than one kind of basic stuff in the universe (mind and matter, for example), opposing "monism," which asserts that there is only one (for example, materialism claims that there is only matter in motion). And value pluralism asserts that there are different and incommensurable sources of our loyalties and foundations of our values, so it is wrong to think that goodness has a basic unity or that the pure in heart desire only one thing. At a third level, pluralism refers to the normative claim that a pluralistic society is commendable because it copes with diversity—especially moral and religious diversity—in a civilized way, one that respects both persons and their differences. This chapter will focus on the first two levels—diversity and value pluralism—and the remaining chapters on the third—acceptable ways of coping with pluralism.

Diversity

The sorts of diversity in beliefs and practices that cultural anthropologists describe for us show that differences and conflicts are found in all four of the types of claims—empirical, conceptual, metaphysical, and value—as discussed in the previous chapter. In fact, the complexities of how these types of beliefs interact sometimes make it difficult to say just what kind of diversity we are encountering. Social psychologist Solomon Asch warned decades ago that what looked like a moral conflict may actually be a very different kind of difference. Discussing the case of some South Sea islanders who kill their parents when their health begins to decline, he pointed out that the difference is not about honoring one's parents but about the belief that they will spend eternity in the physical condition they happen to have when they die.[1] The resulting obligation to strangle one's parents (during a time-honored ritual) is, therefore, in a very different moral boat from killing one's parents in ancient Rome, where parricide was the worst crime one could commit. The same underlying moral commitment to honoring one's parents implies very different practices, given the difference in relevant empirical conditions and nonmoral beliefs. So the wide variety we find in marriage customs, bereavement practices, head-hunting, and witchcraft, for example, do not automatically show differences, much less contradictions, in basic moral convictions. Take the controversial moral judgment that the genital cutting of female infants (clitoridectomy) is not only permissible but obligatory. It is derived not just from basic moral values (do what is in your children's best interest) but also from relevant empirical beliefs (without clitoridectomy, a girl will be promiscuous or shunned) and metaphysical or conceptual beliefs (a woman with a clitoris cannot be a true member of the tribe). Of course, this example shows that differences in conceptual, metaphysical, and, notably, empirical beliefs can be just as disturbing and just as difficult to cope with as are moral differences. But it is important to know what type of disagreement people have, if only to know how to discuss it.

Moral Conflicts

There is no denying that some of our deep differences are *moral* ones. Sometimes the moral differences are due to greedy, even evil, tendencies or influences, as with organized and unorganized crime in the business world; some people simply have bad moral beliefs or motivations. But more often the differences are the sort we find among informed and intelligent persons of goodwill. Indeed, we find it even within ourselves as individuals. We need not go so far as Walt Whitman's claim that "I contain multitudes" in order to feel at times almost like a committee. Interpersonal disagreements occur frequently, but so do intrapersonal conflicts. Sometimes I am faced with what we might call a hard *practical* choice: Perhaps my protecting innocent people by exposing some serious wrongdoing will cost me a friend—or my job. Or sometimes the better angels of my nature are whispering in one ear while my devils are tempting me in the other, and I have to choose between good or greed. Such conflict can make for a hard choice, but at least I know what I morally *ought* to do. Other times I am pulled in opposite directions by deep *moral* convictions: I promised confidentiality to a friend, but now another person will be seriously harmed if I do not break my promise. Rather than an angel and a devil, it seems as if two angels are whispering conflicting advice. Even those who believe that, in principle, there must be a right answer have to admit that not knowing what it is can create a serious conflict.

Moral conflict is sometimes between two convictions or principles, at least one of which is wrong: "Never tell a lie" conflicts with "lie whenever you can to thereby maximize happiness." But other times, especially with internal conflicts, the rub is not, strictly speaking, between your moral principles themselves. "Keep your promises" and "prevent serious harm to innocent persons" are both perfectly acceptable and usually compatible. But a situation can arise when you cannot simultaneously satisfy both of them, even though both are relevant and important. Notice that such moral conflict can extend to conflicts about conflict resolution: Should I simply try to decide which obligation or right outweighs the other one in this situation, or would it be better for me to try to weave a nuanced narrative in which important relationships are least ruptured and diverse caring responsibilities are best nurtured?[2] It is as if the committee that I am portraying as my conscience is not only divided on an issue, but also divided about how to handle divisions.

Moral conflict is part of the experience of anyone living an interesting life. In fact, it is so prevalent that some are tempted to identify this sort of conflict—wrestling with apparent dilemmas—with moral thinking in general. But, as already noted in the previous chapter, it is important to remember that most of our moral life does not consist in our consciously thinking our way through conflicts. Every day we make hundreds of moral decisions on the run; they flow from the dispositions—the virtues and vices—that constitute our character. We do not have to deliberate very often about whether it is morally better to help or to harm someone. But, especially in a pluralistic society, conflicts are what stop us short and make us think more carefully about how to cope with disagreement, whether it be among others or within ourselves.

Reasonable Pluralism

Some of the beliefs we disagree with seem obviously due to ignorance or incompetence; few of us will waste time arguing with someone in our society who believes the world is flat or that germs do not exist, however reasonable those beliefs may have been centuries ago. Other beliefs seem obviously due to prejudice or even immorality, such as various types of racism. But many of our disagreements are with people who seem at least as intelligent, informed, and well-intentioned as we are. Though we think some of their beliefs are wrong, we can see how a reasonable person could hold them. Some of their politics, morals, or religious outlooks conflict with ours, but clearly they have positions we can respect. Instead of ignorant armies clashing by night, we often have informed and intelligent individuals disagreeing by day. To be sure, many of our disagreements are with beliefs that fall somewhere on the spectrum *between* really dumb and highly respectable. One can and probably should be civil in these disagreements, including those involving obvious ignorance. It is true that sometimes stark prejudice may sink to a level where civil restraint is inappropriate, and in the next chapter we will look at appropriate ways to react in such situations. But now let us focus on disagreements that are not the result of inordinate ignorance, stupidity, prejudice, or wickedness—namely, most of them.

Since much of my discussion concerns how to cope with *problems* arising from disagreement, it is worth noting that disagreement also presents opportunities. During a psychological crisis about the meaningfulness of his life, the Russian novelist Leo Tolstoy dismissed the self-importance claimed by the intelligentsia: "We are paid and respected for writing these books and papers, so we must be the most important and useful people. This theory would have been all very well had we been in agreement; but since any thought expressed by any one of us was always contradicted by the diametrically opposed views of another, we should have been forced to rethink."[3] But most of us are amazed at such a sentiment, knowing that it is precisely the dialectic of clashing ideas that *does* force us to rethink or, at least, force observers to examine the strengths and weakness of the various sides of a debate. Many of us worry as much about premature consensus as about ongoing differences of opinion, not just because we enjoy intellectual debate but also because we know that healthy change in both science and culture depends on disputation. So as we examine some of the difficulties in coping with disagreement—whether it is within ourselves or between ourselves and others—we should also celebrate it when it is fruitful.

In chapter four I will describe political liberalism as an effort toward fair political cooperation with compatriots who have conflicting convictions about laws and policies. The late John Rawls is the central figure in debates about political liberalism, and he also has thought carefully about why it is that in a free society we will inevitably have the sort of conflicts on important matters that require us to get along without getting consensus. In this chapter we will discuss his reasons for thinking that we will never have Mill's worry about too much agreement. The more we talk with each other, the clearer it will become that many of our differences, even when every one is being reasonable, are deep and probably irreconcilable.

What Is Reasonable?

How shall we understand "reasonable"? And shall we apply it first and foremost to a belief itself—its content—or to a person holding the belief—the believer? The trouble with applying it to the *belief* is that many beliefs may have perfectly acceptable content, but the way the believer arrived at (or defends) the content makes believing it unreasonable. For example, your horoscope in today's paper may have some very good advice for you. But if the only reason you accept its advice is that you think the astrologer's knowledge of the arrangement of heavenly bodies makes it appropriate, many of us will think you are being unreasonable. Of course, occasional unreasonableness can be one of our charming idiosyncrasies. But it is unreasonable nonetheless. So, perhaps we should first define "reasonable *person*" and then let reasonable beliefs be those held by reasonable persons. The problem here is that persons who are generally reasonable may hold some unreasonable beliefs. Consider the horoscope example. A third alternative is to apply reasonable to the "believing" of the belief, rather than to its content or the intellectual virtues of the believer. The *believing* involves less the content of the belief and more the way the believer came to hold it or continues to hold it. Was it arrived at thoughtfully, weighing evidence, perhaps following the sort of methodological controls we find in good science or in sound argument? Or, since few of our beliefs—especially the moral and religious convictions that shape our identity—are *arrived* at this way, we should ask whether we *continue* to hold them in a thoughtful way: considering objections fair-mindedly, taking into account the alternatives, and so on?[4] But how many people do this with their fundamental religious—or even political—convictions? We could bite the bullet and simply say that only such believings are reasonable, and that there are fewer reasonable believings than one might hope, at least in some areas of our lives. Or, instead of looking at how people *actually* arrive at or defend their beliefs, we could ask whether the belief is one that *could* be arrived at reasonably. Then we could be indulgent about the source or explanation of our beliefs and simply focus on whether they *could* be rationally justified. Some might worry that the latter move is too loose, since it would make your believing the content of your horoscope a reasonable believing just because the resultant belief could have been arrived at in a justifiable way. However, if we include "I should trust whatever my horoscope says" within the overall believing, then we presumably could not arrive at it reasonably. Thus "reasonable" applies primarily to how believers react when their beliefs are questioned. Hence I am inclined to apply "reasonable" primarily to believings, rather than to beliefs or believers, though I admit that there can be legitimate debate about what is and is not included in a given believing.[5]

In the next chapter I will use the term "respectable position" (as in "I disagree with you but you have a position—or believing—that I respect") to refer to those believings that one may disagree with but which one finds reasonable. Notice that we need not completely agree on necessary or sufficient conditions for what makes a *reasonable* way of arriving at beliefs. There likely will be overlap in our lists of family resemblances for what is reasonable, and our lists are likely to include such commonsense criteria as consistency, clarity, comprehensiveness, plausibility given our other well-established beliefs, and practicability. The point is, whatever the details of our notions of reasonable or respectable, we will encounter positions that, on the one hand, we disagree with, and on the other, we respect and see as reasonable. Even if you and I have some differences about specific instances—you see pacifism as wrong but respectable while I see it as dangerously blinded by ideology—we both will encounter plenty of instances where we should combine disagreement with respect.

John Rawls distinguishes between *reasonable* and *rational*.[6] He includes some moral elements in the former; merely rational persons can be very calculating and completely self-interested, but reasonable persons, while rational, are also interested in fair-minded cooperation and reciprocity among persons, all of whom they regard as free and equal. Some of us would broaden the notion of reasonable to include hierarchical doctrines, such as one finds in Thailand—where the royalty and the religious leaders have higher status—as long as such doctrines are consistent with the view that all persons are bearers of certain important rights, including the right to life. Having a broad notion of "reasonable" underscores the fact that reasonable people who have freedom of thought and speech will inevitably find themselves with deep and important differences that seem irresolvable. Why is that?

Burdens of Judgment

An important part of the answer is what Rawls evocatively calls "the burdens of judgment," which simply are common sources of reasonable disagreement. Without claiming that it is complete, Rawls gives a list of six, which I interpret and illustrate as follows:[7]

1. The relevant empirical evidence may be complex, conflicting, and hard to assess. We noted in the previous chapter that relevant empirical beliefs can be the most controversial part of moral and political debates. Consider the debate over global warming. Or consider the empirical predictions used in "slippery slope"[8] arguments about public policy, such as whether to allow active voluntary euthanasia. Would it lead to nonvoluntary euthanasia? Would it put pressure on patients to ask for it in order to save costs? Would it reduce research on terminal pain control? These are empirical issues, and intelligent people tend to differ on how to assess the evidence and even on which evidence is relevant.

2. People can agree on the types of considerations that are relevant and also on specific considerations within each type and still disagree over their relative importance. In the euthanasia debate, we may agree that the slippery slope dangers are relevant and also that fulfilling the wishes of terminally ill patients is relevant, but disagree as to which one is more important.

3. Central concepts in the debate may be imprecise and subject to dueling counterexamples. Consider the above discussion of "reasonable." Consider a debate about whether a patient with "unbearable" pain can be "competent" enough to make an "autonomous" decision about "medical" treatment. Each one of the relevant concepts is vague and ambiguous.

4. We live such different kinds of lives that the totality of our distinctive experiences will lead to very different ways of approaching and considering important issues. Consider a debate on euthanasia between a person who has twice been at the bedside of parents dying quickly and peacefully after a full and rich life and one who has watched parents

suffer dehumanizing indignities while dying painfully over several months or years. And, of course, either experience will be interpreted differently depending on whether one is, say, a deeply religious person or a secular agnostic.

5. Often there are several conflicting norms and several different types of normative points of view (as described in the previous chapter), and it may be difficult for a single individual to weigh them, to say nothing of a group of individuals. In the euthanasia debate, the moral consideration of respecting autonomy can be in tension with the moral consideration of sanctity of life, and both of them can compete with economic and political norms. In values, few people in a given society abhor what others adore, but shared values can be ranked very differently. Indeed, a single individual may have trouble ranking them, as we will see in the next section when we discuss a well-known values survey.

6. Across or between cultures, it is more likely that some abhor what others adore. If you celebrate the warrior virtues of heroic Greek society you might—like Nietzsche—gag on the meekness taught in the Sermon on the Mount. On the other hand, you might see something admirable and courageous in both. Even if you cherish both, however, you can see that a person or a society cannot nurture both at the same time; the psychological and social space is too limited. We may appreciate many features of the simple life chosen by the Amish, but we can also see that if we insist on the level of compulsory education needed for equal opportunity in our society, the Amish way of life may not thrive.[9]

These sources of disagreement would likely exist even apart from differences in race, class, and gender, all of which can cause deep but understandable differences in perspective. Of course, there may be darker sources of disagreement, such as sheer ignorance or foolishness, to say nothing of the influences of sin, selfishness, or false consciousness, which can corrupt our cognition,[10] but the above are enough to recognize that much of the time even intelligent, knowledgeable, and good folks will simply need to agree to disagree. Rawls claims, as part of his definition of reasonable, that reasonable people will accept these burdens of judgment. They will recognize that, due to these burdens, there are deep differences between reasonable people, and that two beliefs that flatly contradict each other can each be reasonably held by different persons. The debate over whether we should allow physician-assisted suicide is a good example of this sort of reasonable disagreement.

Suppose you believe that God or reason reveals the truth about all the above matters to those who are willing to learn: Having deep differences on the big issues shows that some people are not listening with open minds and pure hearts. You would be agreeing with the empirical fact of diversity, but not with the above "reasonable pluralism." However, you would still need to decide how to get along with those with whom you disagree. You would likely have to decide that many of their mistakes are tolerable, if not forgivable or even excusable. The alternative might well require more oppression and coercion than even the most enthusiastic of true believers would want. The point is that even those who reject the burdens of judgment will still need to consider the appropriateness of toleration, which is discussed in the next chapter.

Value Pluralism

Reasonable pluralism is logically consistent with relativism, but also with moral monism and absolutism. I might believe that there is a single true and unified moral framework (monism) and that this framework includes an overriding value or hierarchy of values that, in principle at least,[11] enables those who know about it to reach true and consistent moral decisions (absolutism). However, I could still accept reasonable pluralism if I think it is understandable that reasonable persons make mistakes on complex issues like euthanasia policy, especially in a pluralistic society that I think is thoroughly confused about values. Indeed, what I later call "perspective pluralism" simply combines reasonable pluralism with convictions about who is actually right. If I view the above list of burdens as sources not merely of disagreement but also of error and confusion, I might ask where and when things went wrong for so many people.

Enlightenment Incoherence?

Here is one answer: In the 1980s, Alasdair MacIntyre published his highly influential book *After Virtue*,[12] in which he argues that the 18th-century Enlightenment project of trying to find a new grounding for morality caused the moral fragmentation we see in today's society. As we noticed in the previous chapter, Aristotle avoided any fact-value dichotomy by appealing to the natural ends or goals of human activities and of human life itself. Medieval thinkers such as Thomas Aquinas accepted this teleological outlook, and simply enriched the content of the goals (supernatural happiness in addition to natural happiness), the diagnosis of the human condition (sin in addition to ignorance), and the relevant virtues needed to get us through the human condition to our true end (the theological virtues of faith, hope, and love in addition to the classical virtues of courage, moderation, wisdom, and justice). But, says MacIntyre, the 18th-century Enlightenment thinkers, rejecting the traditional teleology as too metaphysical or theological, tried to carve out a distinctive cultural space for morality, and to give it a new grounding by appealing to something universal in human nature. The problem was that they appealed to different universal features, Hume choosing feeling, for example, and Kant choosing reason, and they were much more persuasive in showing the others wrong than in showing themselves right. Then, Kierkegaard decided that the only grounding for the moral realm was the sheer decision of the individual to live a coherent life, one with moral commitments. So far everyone retained conventional notions of the content of the moral life, but soon Nietzsche announced that the conventional content of the moral life consisted merely of arbitrary taboos that people happened to feel strongly about. And ever since then we have had a fragmented and incoherent moral language. We borrow words like "obligation" and "right" from an earlier context in which they made sense, but we reject the teleology central to that context and replace it with our modern way of using moral language—shrill expressions of strong emotions, used mainly to manipulate each other's feelings and unmask each other's motives. So, according to MacIntyre, the fragmentation of values is a modern disease brought on by the loss of a normative coherence we enjoyed before the disaster of the Enlightenment. No wonder reasonable persons end up with irresolvable disagreements.

One can wonder about the historical accuracy of MacIntyre's above scenario. As he himself is aware, a reading of some of the medieval tales such as *The Song of Roland* and *Beowulf* suggests that there were medieval efforts to combine the heroic warrior ethos with the Christian humility ethic as well as with the classical virtues. And many critics argue that such efforts were more a matter of juxtaposing a potpourri of values than of integrating them into a coherent system.[13] MacIntyre himself underscores the tensions involved in combining a variety of outlooks during the Middle Ages, but he thinks that the ongoing teleological outlook gave the virtues approach enough coherence for moral guidance. However, his critics assert that moral fragmentation is simply a feature of the human condition quite apart from Enlightenment upheavals.

Fragmented Morality

Thus, in addition to the issue of historical accuracy, a related criticism of MacIntyre's diagnosis is that the fragmentation of values is not due to history as much as to the nature of value systems. This is the view we will call "value pluralism" or, when it is restricted to moral values, "moral pluralism." The claim is that value conflict is not merely the result of not *knowing* which decision is in harmony with all our values; there *is* no such harmonious decision to be known, because conflict is inherent in any value outlook that is rich enough to be adequate for the human condition. In his widely read article "The Fragmentation of Value," Thomas Nagel[14] claims there are at least five fundamental and distinct sources of our loyalties and normative commitments, and we often find ourselves in situations where they conflict and when we cannot satisfy all of them at once.

Consider first just the secular moral principles that are common in Western ethics.[15] The main division we find in moral debates—such as those in hospital ethics committees—is between those who focus entirely on the morally relevant consequences of our actions or policies, and those who worry more about respecting the morally relevant rights and obligations involved. Thus the "consequentialists" usually argue for some version of utilitarianism, the view that we have the single fundamental moral duty to maximize good consequences for everyone affected by our actions or policies. There is much debate over what is the good that should be maximized. Typically, appeal is made to some nonmoral good or goods, and moral goodness becomes a function of maximizing it or them. So what is morally "right" to do is derived from what is claimed to be the nonmoral good(s) that everyone should pursue. "Hedonists" are those who say that pleasure or happiness is the only good that should be maximized. The 19th-century economist and philosopher Jeremy Bentham is famous for devising a "hedonic calculus"[16] for scientifically calculating how to maximize pleasure. However, his disciple John Stuart Mill, who rescued himself from depression by reading the Romantic poets, was upset by Bentham's purely quantitative approach, especially his claim that if the numbers added up, the game of pushpin was as good as poetry for maximizing happiness. Mill thought that a careful use of the calculus would add up the quantities in favor of poetry, but he also argued that one could just as well take into account higher and lower *qualities* of pleasure. This would greatly complicate the calculus, of course, even if Mill were right that informed folks would agree in their rankings. Meanwhile, other utilitarians argued that there were more intrinsic goods than merely pleasure. For example, many people think that freedom and knowledge are intrinsic goods even when they do not lead to pleasure. The seemingly impossible task of calculating just the pleasures, to say nothing of the types of pleasures and the other types of intrinsic goods, has led to the most common form of utilitarianism today—preference satisfaction. Estimate the number and strength of the preferences of all those affected by your action or policy, and choose the one that will maximize preference satisfaction. This version of utilitarianism is thought by many economists to be a powerful tool for deciding social policy, such as using it in environmental impact statements and institutional review boards. But before relying on it in cost-benefit analysis they should admit not only the practical difficulties but also the moral controversies associated with it.

Utilitarians recognize the practical difficulties of calculating precisely the maximum outcome, but perhaps too optimistically believe that fair-minded estimates can usually provide enough guidance. However, those who focus on rights and obligations—often called "deontologists," from the Greek "deon" or "what is required"—fear that deciding actions or policies by maximizing good consequences could sacrifice the rights of minorities. We may not treat the body politic the way we treat our own bodies, sacrificing a limb for the good of the body as a whole. It is conceivable, for example, that enslaving a small minority would maximize pleasure or preference satisfaction, even when one weighs in the balance the strong objections from the minority. And if the utilitarian reply is that a careful calculation will show otherwise, the deontologist objects that calculating pleasures or preferences is simply a morally offensive way to decide about the protection of fundamental rights. Of course, there is plenty of room for intramural debate about the source, content, and ranking of those rights. The 18th-century philosopher Immanuel Kant argued that treating persons as ends-in-themselves—respecting their autonomy—was a categorical imperative that could serve as a foundation for deciding about rights, though other deontologists think it is too slim a foundation to account for all rights.

Another way that some Western deontologists use to ground rights and obligations is the "social contract" approach. We need not argue about which rights are to be discovered in natural law or human nature if we can simply decide which ones to promise each other. Since there are few actual social contracts to be found, and none that we have all signed, we must ask about contractual promises that are implicit in our social practices, or ones that a suitably informed and reasonable person would accept. Obviously there will be plenty of room for intramural debate about details of this sort of contractual thinking.

The nature and grounding of human rights will come up again in the following chapters, but given the above brief sketch of utility and rights, it should not be surprising that most people feel the moral pull of considering both good consequences and relevant rights in their moral thinking. Thus two of the five sources of fundamental values discussed by Nagel are "general rights that everyone has" and "utility. . . . the effects of what one does on everyone's welfare." He lists a third category: contractual moral considerations—namely the "specific obligations" to other people or institutions that one incurs just by living a social life and recognizing the obligations that bear down on us. We can have obligations to our parents or children or employer or employee that are not generally owed to everyone but which may be some of the strongest obligations we have. Nagel adds two more types of fundamental values that seem to be nonmoral ones. There are what he calls "perfectionist ends," or the value of certain achievements or creations, such as scientific or mathematical discoveries or works of art, that have intrinsic worth quite independent of their instrumental value to individuals or society. And then there is the "commitment to one's own projects or undertakings," such as writing a book or climbing mountains, projects that can acquire remarkable importance to us and to what makes our lives meaningful. Nagel notes that all of these commitments are distinct from self-interest. Although the pursuit of the above five values might overlap the pursuit of one's self-interest, self-interest could be thought of as a sixth fundamental source of our loyalties.

Principlism

We noticed earlier in this chapter that moral principles can come into conflict in the sense that in a given situation one cannot simultaneously satisfy all of the relevant principles. The term *prima facie* is often used to refer to moral duties that sometimes override and sometimes are overridden by other moral duties. One of the most respected and widely used textbooks in biomedical ethics is coauthored by a utilitarian and a deontologist. They agree on a short list of "middle principles" that are relevant to most moral decisions and that are derived in different ways from the authors' respective theories.[17] Not surprisingly, these principles include ones, such as "respect autonomy" and "do no harm," that sometimes conflict, as when a minimally competent patient requests a course of treatment that doctors think will do irreversible harm to the patient. The authors must and do say something about how to cope in a nonarbitrary way with such conflicts. The key is to recognize that the middle-level principles are all prima facie ones and that, when they conflict, those responsible for the decision can generally raise the relevant issues, talk things through, and reach a workable consensus. This approach has come to be called "principlism"; it is the approach used in most of the increasing number of ethics workshops that help serve the continuing education needs of the professions. Critics of principlism sometimes accuse it of advocating merely a mantra of principles, with no objective way of resolving conflicts among them. Notice that if the authors could give some sort of algorithm or clear-cut decision procedure, then they would have a system of prima facie principles that does not, finally, contain conflicts. But moral pluralists insist that there are genuine tensions between the moral considerations that are relevant in a given case.[18] If so, the question is whether pluralism reduces to subjective arbitrariness or to some sort of relativism. We will consider this question, but first we should look at a wider version of pluralism.

Moral and Nonmoral Values

If the moral pluralists are right, there are genuine and ongoing conflicts among moral principles, in the sense that one cannot simultaneously satisfy all the principles, and there is no algorithm for deciding which one overrides the others. But if the moral point of view were to override all other ones, then there would be a quick way to resolve any conflict between the moral values that Nagel lists and the nonmoral ones. However, what is often called "value pluralism" or "normative pluralism" holds that there can be genuine conflicts between our moral convictions and our other loyalties, such as those to our own projects, and it holds that moral obligations do not always override. Complicating this view is the fact that it is difficult to draw a sharp line between moral considerations and other normative ones, including prudential and religious considerations. This point becomes clear when we look at what has been one of the more frequently used instruments for ranking values: the Rokeach Value Survey.[19] Consider its list of eighteen "desirable end-states of existence" (both personal and social end-states) and its list of eighteen "desirable modes of conduct" (both moral and competence modes):

> *Desirable end-states:* a comfortable life; an exciting life; a sense of accomplishment; a world at peace; a world of beauty; equality; family security; freedom; happiness; inner harmony; mature love; national security; pleasure; salvation; self-respect; social recognition; true friendship; wisdom.

> *Modes of conduct:* ambitious; broadminded; capable; cheerful; clean; courageous; forgiving; helpful; honest; imaginative; independent; intellectual; logical; loving; obedient; polite; responsible; self-controlled.

Consider freedom, mature love, self-respect, wisdom, as well as being cheerful, forgiving, helpful, responsible, and self-controlled. Can you divide them cleanly into moral and nonmoral categories? And whether or not you can do that, can you rank them in importance? When the Rokeach Value Survey is given, these values are listed on removable labels, and you are invited to rank the values within each set by reordering the labels as you prefer. This can be a difficult and frustrating job; it is hard enough to decide how to rank comfort and excitement, but then to compare them with freedom and friendship and all the others can be mind-boggling. A hedonist would rank happiness first, thinking of all the others as means to it, but even the hedonist would have trouble ranking the rest in terms of their contributions to happiness. And, of course, nonhedonists are likely to view freedom and wisdom as intrinsic goods independent of happiness. In the second list, maybe most of us would rank honest over obedient, but where do loving, courageous, and cheerful go?

My aim is not to bedevil you with the problems of ranking Rokeach's values; they might not even include the values you are most concerned about. But notice five things about these lists: First, they include much of what most people think of as living a good life; second, it is hard to decide whether some of the values are moral or nonmoral ones; third, rarely, if ever, can we pursue or aspire to all of them at once; fourth, when we have to choose among them, they are very difficult—or impossible—to compare; and finally, it is not obvious that the ones that seem (more or less) to be moral values should always trump those that seem (more or less) to be nonmoral ones.

Incompatible, Incommensurable, and Incomparable

Consider the problem of comparison: Many of the Rokeach values seem incommensurable in the sense that they cannot be measured by a common scale of units of value.[20] Of course, many things that seem quite different are, in fact, commensurable in important ways; apples and oranges, for example, can easily be measured with respect to calories or protein content. But for the sort of values listed by Rokeach, a claim to have found a common measuring rod such as the hedonic calculus is simply incredible to most of us. What is the common unit to be measured in beauty and freedom, for example, or honesty and cheerfulness? Probably we should try to compare specific instances or bearers of these values rather than the abstractions themselves but that simply makes the problem more specific rather than more solvable. What would be the measure used to decide between my becoming more courageous or more cheerful? The measurable amount of happiness they would bring me seems an implausible candidate, and it is hard to think of any more plausible ones.[21]

Maybe we are making the comparison more difficult than it need be; it seems that things can be ranked in importance even if there is no common scale of units to measure them. We already noticed that Mill thought we could agree on our rankings of different qualities of pleasure, for example, even though they could not be quantified on the same measuring scale. I would not know how to measure the relative worth of a good book and a good friend, but if I had to compare them I would have little difficulty ranking them.[22] In the sense of being rankable, some incommensurable things can be compared. Perhaps they can have some "covering value" that they share without that value being measurable. For example, friends and books can both be entertaining—or provocative—and there are any number of other values in terms of which they might be ranked. Of course, if one tries to make the comparison into something commensurable, it can become incoherent or offensive: how many good books is a good friend worth, or how much money? And even when one avoids commensurability, some comparisons seem more fanciful than rankable: "Shall I compare thee to a summer's day?" Perhaps such evocative comparisons suggest that poets can sometimes find so many comparisons that an overall ranking is not worth attempting. The important question is whether the types of values listed by Nagel and Rokeach are comparable such that, when they conflict, they can at least be ranked.[23]

Probably we have to ask whether values can *reasonably* be compared. The 1970s Ford Pinto case, in which the Ford Motor Company knew that greater protection of the gas tank would save lives but decided that the saving was not worth the cost, reminds us that economists seem to price life when asking whether a safety measure is affordable. More precisely, they price things such as lost earning power and costs of traffic delays when asking how much money should be put into preventing fatal accidents. We use terms like "sanctity of life" or Kant's distinction between price and dignity to suggest that some things cannot or ought not be compared to certain other things. Of course, economists can claim that all they are doing is trying to find a rational substitute for the actual pricing of a human life. Life may not have a price but lots of things do that are necessary for it, and those costs can be added up. Still, it seems inappropriate to balance a quantity of an instrumental value, such as money, with a value like life itself. And it is not just that life might be thought to have intrinsic value; so does beauty, but whatever difficulties there are in pricing art, it does not seem morally offensive.[24] Notice that to say one *ought not* price life does not entail value pluralism; indeed, it gives a clear-cut ranking of types of values. Even to say that one *cannot* price life would imply value pluralism only if choosing between life and money is something reasonable persons are sometimes forced to do. If economists think we are forced to do that, and they simultaneously agree that life and money are incommensurable and cannot be systematically compared, then they are value pluralists. A similar point can be made about comparing, say, the value of an endangered species with the value of jobs.

Nagel's list of fundamentally different sources of loyalties suggests that sometimes commitment to your own projects can conflict with your moral obligations. We noticed in the previous chapter that moral saints sometimes go light on family obligations, but this would likely be simply a conflict between specific versus general *moral* obligations, as with Jean-Paul Sartre's famous example of the young man who must choose between joining the French underground or staying home to take care of his mother. Such examples might show something about moral pluralism, but not about the more radical value pluralism that includes conflicts between morality and other values. Consider the conflict between one's projects as a dedicated artist and the obligation to provide for one's family. The example need not be as stark as Paul Gauguin's decision to abandon his family for Tahiti to pursue his distinctive style of painting. Let us just say that nontrivial but not life-threatening aspects of the family's welfare are sacrificed for significant artistic achievement. I think we could fill in a thick description such that, even if there are some covering values such as pleasure and pain, they are not relevant or, at least not sufficient, to reach an unambiguous judgment of what one ought to do, all things considered. Attendance at how many of your children's soccer games is worth how much dedication to a major project? This likely is not merely a case of *incompatibility*; we noted earlier that when saints find their projects to be incompatible with their family obligations, they often neglect the family. But such incompatibility is quite consistent with comparability and even commensurability. You may have to choose between a vacation on the beach and one in the mountains; you cannot have both and it may be a tough choice, but they are comparable in many commensurable ways (cost, pleasure, book-reading opportunities, and so on). When you must choose between moral obligations, they might be incompatible but comparable, as when you must choose to break a promise to one person in order to help another. That they are comparable, of course, does not lessen and may even increase the difficulty of deciding what to do (when they compare quite evenly). However, your commitments to your art and your family may be both incompatible and extremely difficult to compare. If so, we may have an example of a problem that cannot be resolved by systematically ranking or measuring values. And that is the essence of value pluralism.

I certainly have not shown that either value pluralism or moral pluralism is true. But I hope I have explained it enough that one can see it as a reasonable position, even if mistaken. At a minimum, it is an important part of the reasonable pluralism—not merely the diversity—that we find in a pluralistic society. For that reason we should ask whether it implies skepticism, subjectivism, or relativism. It clearly does not imply nihilism, which is the view that there are no values. If there is a problem with value pluralism, it is not that it teaches the lack of values; it acknowledges many values along with the lack of an overriding covering value that would adjudicate value conflicts. But does that leave us without guidance other than subjective preference? We will return to this question later in this chapter, after we look at ways of coping with religious diversity.

Religious Pluralism

Debates about how to respond appropriately to differences have a longer and more heated history in religion than in most other aspects of our lives. Probably this is due not only to the vast diversity we find in religious beliefs, but also to how central they are to our identities and to what gives our lives meaning and significance. Moreover, some of the major religions are mission-minded, believing they have a message that everyone should hear and believe. Anyone who wants to share good news about religion with those who do not know about it cannot escape implicit or explicit answers to deep questions about the plurality of religions. Before discussing what is commonly referred to as religious pluralism, we should briefly consider what it sees as its two rivals—religious particularism and religious inclusivism.

Religious Particularism

Much of the motive for missionary work derives from the attitude toward religious diversity that is often called "religious *exclusivism*," though "religious *particularism*" is a friendlier label. This is the view that my religious commitments are true and that any beliefs and practices that contradict them are false and wrong. (The latter is sometimes specified as *doctrinal* exclusivism.) A particularist need not claim that there is no truth in other religions; Jews can agree with Muslims that God is one while disagreeing about God's character or will. Generally, however, particularists believe that whatever truth there happens to be in other religions, it is not enough for salvation (sometimes called *soteriological* exclusivism), though not all of them claim that the only alternative to salvation is damnation.[25] As the Christian version has it, "No one comes to the Father except through me" (Jesus, John 14:6). Because of this sort of exclusivism, particularism is sometimes associated with spiritual and intellectual arrogance, with the attitude that I have nothing to learn from others and everything to teach them. But, in fact, it is quite compatible with listening to and learning from other faiths, and with a desire to have genuine dialogue with them. For one thing, particularists can see erring religions as having special insight into aspects of faith that they overemphasize, in much the same way that neuroses can provide genuine insight into the human condition.[26] In addition, particularists can believe that God has revealed truths to other faiths; the other faith may incorporate them into an outlook that is wrong, but there they are, and the orthodox can learn from them.[27] Another point, which we will underscore in the next chapter, is that particularists, even given their exclusivisms, can be very congenial toward religious toleration; although they have been responsible for much religious persecution, particularists can agree that the latter is not justified by the mere belief that others are religiously wrong.

Religious Inclusivism

"Religious *inclusivism*" is the view that other religions may well have truths that can lead to salvation, though when they do, it is because they implicitly are on the way toward the true religion. The Christian version is that, although no one comes to God except through Christ, the latter is the savior of more people than those who believe it. So inclusivists can think of their own religion as the true religion intended for everyone and still recognize saving truth in other religions, often in the context of seeing the other religions as implicit or incipient forms of their own. To quote the Catholic Christian Karl Rahner: "Christianity does not simply confront the member of an extra-Christian religion as a mere non-Christian but as an anonymous Christian."[28] Perhaps one has to have this attitude applied to one's own religious outlook in order to feel the ambivalence of being thought of as an embryonic member of another's religion. The Christian students with whom I traveled in the Middle East discovered this when Muslims ecumenically assured them that Christianity was not so much false as an incomplete form of Islam. One of their pamphlets said, "Welcome to your own religion!" and quoted the Prophet Mohammed as saying, "Every child is born in a state of 'Islam,'" and concluded with the reminder that "All who embrace Islam actually 'revert' to their original religion."[29] Such attention helped some of them realize how Jews sometimes feel when they are proselytized by Christians. As it is sometimes drolly put, inclusivists believe that they have the only true religion but they are not the only ones who have it.

Religious Pluralism

Recognizing that others are not flattered when they are told they are implicitly or incompletely believers of someone else's religion, religious *pluralism* teaches what it regards as a more respectful attitude toward religious diversity: Many religions, including the major religions, are alternative and effective ways relating to God (or the sacred) or achieving salvation (or liberation).[30] The qualifications in the parentheses are needed because pluralists want to respect those nontheistic religions that have ideas about the goal of human existence other than salvation and eternal life. Pluralists need not claim that *all* religions are effective, since of the thousands of different outlooks that could plausibly be called religious, there have been and continue to be some very dark and dangerous ones, such as the Heaven's Gate suicide cult or the Aum Shinrikyo sect that gassed people in a Tokyo subway train. But then religious pluralists need something like the notion of "reasonable" in "reasonable pluralism," discussed earlier, as applied to religions.[31] Allowing the pluralists some minimal rational and moral threshold for religions to be considered effective paths is simply to think of them as reasonable pluralists. However, as we will see, if they build in substantial religious standards for the religions they include, they run the risk of begging the question when they say all and only these are effective paths to the goal(s) of religions. We should notice that pluralism is not eclecticism or syncretism, which involve picking and combining agreeable parts of various religious traditions, as "new age" religions tend to do; a pluralist insists that each religion has its own distinctive integrity.

Sometimes religious pluralists say that the religions they have in mind are *equally* effective routes to what religious people are seeking. But here they must be careful. If they mean it as a presumption, it is probably a version of relativism, which we will discuss later. It would then also be a claim that is denied by most of the believers of the religions they are trying to respect. And to say that most religions will eventually mature into this sort of relativism looks more like some sort of higher-level inclusivism than pluralism. On the other hand, if the equal effectiveness of religions is treated as something like a discovery, pluralists must use some sort of yardstick or criteria for effectiveness. "Effective" is one of those goal-oriented words, like "healthy"; it can seem like an empirical discovery that something is healthy, but only if one is presupposing some value-laden or goal-oriented criterion that enables one to see that something is not just alive, it also is flourishing. What might be the goal or the criterion for effectiveness that a pluralist uses when deciding that religions are equally effective? Let us look at one well-known answer.

Pluralist Theology

The English philosopher of religion John Hick, widely recognized as a leading pluralist theologian, suggests that the goal of religion is salvation or liberation in the sense of transformation from self-centeredness to Reality-centeredness, especially as expressed in unselfish regard (love, compassion) for others.[32] Hick uses the singular—religion—because he thinks that, rather than seeing mutually exclusive systems, we can see the religious experience and the religious life of humanity as a dynamic continuum, one with various upheavals from time to time as prophets and founders introduce new ways of interpreting the experience of the sacred. In some traditions the experience is interpreted as relationship with a personal, sacred deity; in others it is interpreted as contact with an impersonal, sacred dimension. The difference suggests to Hick that the various traditions are all in contact with a mysterious and ultimately unknowable Real. Given the different cultural factors and spiritual needs, these traditions construct alternative names, faces, and ideas about the Real, and about how we relate to it. The crucial distinction is between reality in itself, uninterpreted and thereby unknown, and reality as it appears to us, interpreted using the cultural categories that organize how we perceive, feel, and think about things. Physicists need a similar distinction when they say that light photons sometimes appear as waves and sometimes as particles; to ask what light is in itself, uninterpreted, is to ask what cannot be answered. What we must do is appeal to something like the principle of complementarity, asserting that although the two models of light seem contradictory, at some level that we do not and perhaps cannot know, they are expressions of a harmonious reality. If something as ordinary as light is experienced in what looks like contradictory ways, it is no wonder that something as mysterious as the Real gets interpreted in the "contradictory but complementary" modes of personal and impersonal. "If we suppose that the Real is one, but that our human perceptions of the Real are plural and various, we have a basis for the hypothesis that the different streams of religious experience represent diverse awarenesses of the same limitless transcendent reality, which is perceived in characteristically different ways by different human mentalities, forming and formed by different cultural histories."[33]

Hick's account may remind us of the story about the six blind men and the elephant. The man in contact with a leg says that an elephant is very much like a tree, the one grabbing the tail says it is like a rope, the one feeling the ear says it is like a fan, the side feels like a wall, the trunk like a snake, and the tusk like a spear. We know that they are all saying something true but limited about the elephant, and where they go wrong is when they deny the truth of what the others are saying. Similarly, there are different paths up the same mountain, but all of them reach the top.

The problem with interpreting Hick's religious pluralism in this way is that we never see something analogous to the whole elephant or the top of the mountain. Of course, the six blind men could talk with each other, and if they did so carefully and open-mindedly they might speculate that their seemingly incompatible descriptions could be partial truths about a single reality. But this thought would hardly be a valid inference; it would need some further substantive assumptions or revelations. So maybe thinking in different ways about the elephant are equally effective ways to get to the top of the same mountain. But even mixing in a different metaphor just pushes the question back: If we never see the top, how would we know that each path is equally effective in reaching it? How can one be sure that a given path does not lead to a dead end or to a cliff? Analogously, how would we know that the different religious interpretations are equally effective ways of encountering what seems to be an ineffable or indescribable divine dimension? Hick appeals at this point not to accuracy of theological descriptions but to the spiritual fruits of the traditions that construct the divine in different ways: Do they equally effectively attain the salvific goal of transformation from self-centeredness to Reality-centeredness, as expressed in love or compassion for others? Of course, if we look at how people in the various traditions have actually behaved, taking into account religious wars and oppression of the poor, we see a very mixed bag indeed. So Hick reaches "the modest and largely negative conclusion that, so far as we can tell, no one of the great world religions is salvifically superior to the rest."[34]

The conclusion of Hick's approach seems modest and ecumenical, but is it pluralistic? Notice that he refers only to "the great world religions," leaving us to wonder about more recent but significant religions such as Baha'i or the Latter Day Saints (Mormons). Since they are related to one or more of the traditional religions, perhaps they are included. But then so would Christian Science and the Unification Church. In any case, it seems that the religions included are those that can be measured by Hick's yardstick of salvific effectiveness. We noted earlier that all pluralists will need something like the "reasonable" in "reasonable pluralism," but "salvific effectiveness" seems to come with a rather specific and controversial religious content. Notice that it is not just the non-major religions that will wonder about it. Probably most believers in the major religions would regard his explanation of their beliefs as misleading and reductionistic. He reduces what many of them regard as a special revelation from a personal deity to a human cultural construct based on a mystical experience of an indescribable Reality. And many believers would find his description of the essential goal of their religious life misleadingly narrow.

This objection in no way implies that Hick's understanding of religion is ignoble or false; it only objects to thinking of it as truly pluralistic, since its ecumenical openness comes from interpreting the huge variety of religious ways of life in a religiously specific and controversial way.[35] I examine Hick's view in particular, partly because he is a pioneer in ecumenical theology who is perhaps the most respected Western writer on religious pluralism, but also because his sophisticated appreciation of diversity can serve as a general caution about pluralism. When he uses a particular kind of transformation as his "covering value" in comparing religions, he runs the risk of coping with religious plurality by introducing another religious outlook, albeit a very ecumenical one. It is true that anyone thinking about pluralism will do so from a unifying perspective, a conceptual horizon within which one tries to organize one's thinking about the diversity.[36] But when pluralists make religiously substantive and controversial claims about the essence of religion, they risk narrowing down religious diversity to what their yardstick (about the essential) can measure. So the question is whether there is an outlook on religious diversity that itself does not make religiously substantive assumptions.

Plurality of Truths

One route to take is the postmodern one of insisting that there is no "meta-narrative" about religion in general, there are only local narratives about each religion and a true pluralist simply accepts that all (or, at least, most) are true.[37] This view can insist that the particularities of religions include different goals and not merely different paths to the same goal. Not only is our experience filtered differently, the central categories for each tradition are incommensurable with those of others, and therefore they cannot be translated into each other (even to show contradictions), though dialogue can be fascinating and useful, as we see how interestingly different our outlooks are. There is much more that can be said about this approach, but here I note only that it flirts with and perhaps is married to the sort of relativism about truth discussed later. Most religious believers are not relativists in this sense, since they think that religious beliefs apply rightly or wrongly to a reality that is independent of their own beliefs. So the question is whether there is an approach to religious pluralism that avoids this type of relativism, one that allows and even invites inter-religious dialogue while maintaining with integrity one's own distinctive religious convictions.

Perspective Pluralism

What we need is a reasonable viewpoint about the plurality of reasonable view-points, one that respects the integrity of each view while admitting any con-tradictions between them, and does so in a way that avoids implying that all reasonable views are equally acceptable or true. I think a good way to provide this is to recall Rawls's burdens of judgment, especially the fourth one, and recognize that our having lived different lives—how we were raised and the experiences that have shaped our character and thinking—often gives us dif-ferent perspectives about what makes sense. So any number of claims, theories, and ways of life, including moral and religious outlooks, will be judged right or wrong—or reasonable or unreasonable—depending on our respective perspec-tives. Moreover, we can recognize that many of the perspectives from which others judge our own views to be wrong are themselves reasonable perspec-tives, as justified for them as ours is for us.[38]

At this point someone might say, "And that is why we should not call one another wrong, just different." But this move is not a valid inference. A perspec-tive pluralist[39] can just as well say, "From my perspective, I think you are wrong, though I understand that from your perspective, you think you are right. More-over, I think your perspective is a reasonable one, even though I think it is false insofar as it disagrees with mine." This view combines the attitude that I think I am justified in believing I am right with the realistic recognition that some of those who disagree with me are justified in thinking they are right. This is not a relativism of what is true or right, but a relativism of justification—of being justified in believing that one is right. At no time in history was the belief that the sun orbits the earth a true belief, but for most of human history it was a reasonable belief, and people were justified in believing it.

One's perspective can change, of course, including one's religious outlook. There can be Damascus Road types of conversions; alternatively, there can be gradual shiftings as one encounters other perspectives, perhaps broadening one's own. Sometimes encountering difference simply stimulates a deeper and more informed reaffirmation of the essentials of the views with which one was raised. If we think of our perspective as a web of beliefs, commitments, and attitudes, we can make changes to it that are peripheral and minor, or ones that are central and major.[40] Most of us wisely tend to be what I call "epistemo-logical conservatives"; when we encounter challenges to our beliefs that force us to make some changes, we usually make the changes that require the least repairing of our cognitive web. Even these changes can add up, and they some-times become or precipitate significant revisions. But no matter how broad or different my perspective becomes, I will still have one, it will still be different from others, and it will still influence how I judge things. Not being God, we cannot rise above all perspectives and check out reality independent of our per-spective. And, of course, we cannot incorporate all perspectives into our own since, even if that were logically possible, it would still make our perspective a different one from those that we are combining.[41] Notice that doubts about one's perspective, or reduced confidence with which one holds it, or modesty about asserting its truth over that of others, become automatically part of one's distinctive, overall perspective. Analogously, perspective pluralism itself can become part of our overall perspective.

Does perspective pluralism incline one to say that, since each perspective *seems* sound to those who hold it, every perspective should be thought to *be* equally sound to everyone? Not from my perspective. I recognize that other perspectives are reasonable for others, and therefore it is reasonable for them to act on them, but where they disagree with mine I think they are wrong. For example, the perspective of some tribal women in Senegal may make it reasonable for them to practice clitoridectomy on their daughters.[42] I see that the practice is reasonable to them and for them, but it does not seem reasonable to me, and I think my perspective is right on that issue and theirs is wrong. In the next chapter I will discuss appropriate ways to react to this disagreement, but here we can underscore that it is indeed a disagreement between perspectives, each of which is reasonable in its own situation. Of course, not every perspective need be judged as reasonable for those who hold it; as we discussed earlier, reasonable pluralism is not the same as sheer diversity. Paranoia may be reasonable *to* paranoid people without being reasonable *for* them.[43] That many conflicting outlooks can simultaneously be regarded as reasonable does not imply that all outlooks, including those due to sheer prejudice or stubborn ignorance, must be regarded as reasonable.

Nicholas Rescher argues for the above view, calling it "contextualistic rationalism" or "orientational pluralism."

> Confronted with a pluralistic proliferation of alternatives, you have your acceptance-determination methodology and I have mine. Yours leads you to endorse *P*; mine leads me to endorse not-*P*. Yours is just as valid for you (in your methodology validity principles) as mine is for me. The situational differences of our contexts simply lead to different rational resolutions. And that's just the end of the matter.[44]

Well, it is not quite the end of the matter, since we still have to figure out how to get along. But at least we see a way of asserting our own convictions as true while recognizing that other obviously reasonable people are justified in contradicting them. We see that the justifiability of our beliefs is not so much a function of their truth as it is of what logically follows from our perspective, from what we might call our "evidential set" of beliefs, and—within reasonable limits, of course—reasonable people can have different and contradictory evidential sets.

Does perspective pluralism reduce our confidence in the truth of our own perspectives? Does recognizing that other reasonable people are justified in saying we are wrong make us wonder who is right? Does it reduce our willingness to take a stand based on our own convictions? Does it tempt us toward skepticism, relativism, subjectivism, or other worrisome isms? Not to any worrisome extent, as long as we remember some important distinctions.

Pluralism and Other Isms

The variety of pluralisms examined above is complicated, and things would get more complicated were we to take into account differences in the terminology of different writers. My only defense is to cite the admittedly self-serving adage that, as the alternative to obscurity, sometimes clarity requires complexity rather than simplicity. So far we have discussed diversity (sheer plurality), reasonable pluralism (the diversity among reasonable outlooks), value pluralism (irreducible diversity of basic sources of our values), moral pluralism (a value pluralism restricted to moral values), religious pluralism (reasonable diversity of paths to religious goals), and perspective pluralism (reasonable pluralism combined with convictions about who is right). Perspective pluralism entails reasonable pluralism, but neither of them entails value pluralism, since the former two can deny that nonmoral values can legitimately override moral ones. Of course, value pluralists can readily accept reasonable pluralism and perspective pluralism, and people who accept the latter two can grant that value pluralism is reasonable, even though some of them think it is false. We noticed earlier that value pluralism does not lead to value nihilism (the view that there are no values) because it asserts not the lack of any values but the presence of many and conflicting values. Sometimes people fear that diversity and conflict in religion may tempt us to *religious nihilism*; if people disagree so deeply and passionately, maybe there is nothing there. But I think that heated disagreement is more likely to lead us to think that there is something there, but nobody knows what it is, which is *skepticism* rather than nihilism. An alternative to such skepticism is to think that everybody knows what the truth is, but truth and the knowledge of it are relative to each perspective. When the perspective referred to is that of each individual, such relativism is usually called "subjectivism." One type of subjectivism is to reduce values or religion to sheer individual preference. Value pluralism, with its irresolvable conflicts, sometimes leads people to assert the latter kind of subjectivism; we cannot rationally calculate what to do, so we simply let our strongest preference decide. If the preferences even out, we toss a coin or simply decide in some other arbitrary way. The view that all our values require this sort of unguided choice is sometimes called "decisionism."

Fallibilism

I hope to show that none of the above isms are valid inferences from any of the pluralisms we have discussed, but there is an ism that may be a reasonable reaction, namely "fallibilism." To be a fallibilist about your belief is to go beyond the intellectual humility of admitting you might have more to learn; it is to admit that your belief might actually be wrong. Some of us are fallibilists about all or most of our beliefs, others are fallibilists about only some.[45] Sometimes fallibilism is purely academic: I can admit that, in the abstract, I might be wrong, say, about my own name, or whether I had breakfast this morning, but in practice I am certain I am right. René Descartes's famous experiment in methodological doubt tried to convince us that, in the abstract, you can doubt the truth of every belief except that you exist (even doubts require a doubter). But fallibilism in the abstract is not our issue. What many people think pluralism reasonably elicits is genuine doubts about any number of beliefs, including moral and religious ones. If you accept value pluralism, for example, and you have to decide whether to break a promise to one person in order to help another person, it does not take much intellectual humility to admit that just maybe you could have made a better choice. Sometimes such doubt about the choice arises precisely because you do not doubt the importance of either of the principles. But what if you recognize that reasonable people disagree with the principles? Does reasonable and perspective pluralism—recognizing that there are any number of reasonable conflicts on almost any kind of belief—automatically persuade us that we could be wrong about those beliefs? It probably does about many of them, especially those on complicated scientific issues such as global warming, or empirical predictions about slippery slopes in the euthanasia debate. And, of course, doubts here can affect the certainty with which we hold beliefs about related social policies. To pursue the implications of this fact, we must ask about the amount of control we have over our beliefs, convictions, and commitments.

Control over Beliefs

Do we have control over our beliefs such that we can decide what to believe? Not direct control, at least not usually. You cannot grit your teeth and decide to believe that the temperature around you is twice what you think it is. And it is hard to know what you could do to change your mind about beliefs based directly and obviously on reliably functioning physical senses, such as your belief that there is a printed page in front of you. These are among the beliefs that we simply find ourselves having. Of course, we find ourselves having all kinds of beliefs, including moral and religious ones that we were raised with, existentially important ones such as "my mother loves me," and also scientific ones such as those about global warming. Over many of these beliefs we can have some indirect control by deciding which books and news sources to read and listen to, whom to talk with and, importantly, which ones not to read and listen to, or whom not to talk with (or what not to talk about). The internet provides easy ways for us to broaden our sources of information and opinion but it also makes it easy for us to restrict them. If we have the confidence to be teachable— that is, the intellectual humility to truly listen to and have genuine dialogue with those who think differently from us—we likely will find ourselves raising reasonable doubts about many beliefs. The choice to be open to discussion is the choice to give up some control over which doubts we will find ourselves having. The willingness to be teachable will not always lead to doubts, as my earlier example of clitoridectomy illustrates; we can listen carefully to the considerations that make it reasonable for some people to do it and not be swayed at all from the strength of our conviction that it is wrong. This point brings up an important distinction: In raising questions about the truth or reasonableness of our beliefs we can ask whether we accept the *truth* of their content, but we can also ask about the level of *confidence* with which we accept their truth. As with deciding the truth of a belief, we generally do not have direct control over the level of confidence with which we hold it, though we can have some indirect control through the measures mentioned.

Conviction, Commitment, and Skepticism

In the previous chapter we referred to *convictions* as those beliefs that we hold firmly, including those that shape our moral and religious identity. Even if perspective pluralism does not change the content of our convictions, does it tend to change the degree of confidence with which we hold them? This is an empirical issue, and not one that is easily answered. Notice that the change in confidence could go either up or down; I've noticed that sometimes reasonable opposition to one's convictions creates the sort of cognitive dissonance that actually results in an increase in confidence. The important question for us is whether reasonable pluralism *should* change the level of confidence with which we hold to the central convictions that give our lives meaning and structure, and provide our sense of identity. Here we should recall the distinction mentioned in chapter one between conviction and commitment; convictions are those important beliefs that associate with attitudinal commitments, with resolutions to live and act in certain ways. Often there is a positive correlation between the level of confidence with which we hold a conviction and the degree of resoluteness with which we commit ourselves to act on it. But sometimes—maybe many times in a pluralistic society—our commitments must and do exceed our confidence in the truth of the associated convictions. For example, if global warming seems to constitute an extremely dangerous risk to the world, it may be reasonable to commit ourselves to combating it before we are completely confident that the risk is extremely high. How much we should combat it before how many more studies are completed, and how strong and costly a commitment we should give it are important additional questions, but the main point holds: It is sometimes reasonable for resoluteness of commitment to exceed confidence of belief.

Similarly, two sociologists exchanging wedding vows can know that their marriage has a nontrivial chance of ending in divorce, but their knowledge that acting on such doubts tends to be self-fulfilling can motivate a level of commitment to the marriage that simply ignores the possibility of divorce. Faithfulness in a marriage can and should be pledged at a level of commitment that exceeds the caution with which a fully aware person these days might rationally believe that only death will end it.

Likewise, a religious commitment can (and sometimes probably should) ignore the intellectual recognition that one might be wrong. Billy Graham was once quoted as saying that he never had a doubt in his life about his religious faith. Perhaps so, but it is possible that what he meant is that he never wavered in his religious commitment. The recently published letters of Mother Teresa indicate that sometimes her level of confidence in her Christian convictions was vastly lower than the degree of resoluteness with which she committed herself to her Christian way of life.[46] This underscores different dimensions of what we call faith. Theists, for example, distinguish between religious faith as *belief*, or assent to theological propositions, on the one hand, and, on the other, faith as *trust* in God and *commitment* to live according to God's will. Of course, these dimensions are closely related, but pluralism probably requires us to think about our religious beliefs more intensively and extensively than our grandparents had to, which can raise doubts about our convictions. But that is compatible with a trusting commitment, perhaps one that is even richer for being more self-conscious. Peter Berger, a sociologist who has specialized in the effects of modernity and pluralism on religion, argues that pluralism causes "a gigantic movement from fate to choice in the human condition."[47] And the choice, which incorporates doubts, allows for authentic faith rather than naïve belief precisely because it is made in the context of reasonable alternatives.

Of course, we can think too much; daunted by all the reasonable alternatives, we might back off making commitments until we are sure we are right. But perspective pluralism can also have the opposite effect; knowing that beliefs about what is true can be justified only within a perspective, we can avoid trying to hover over a multiplicity of perspectives. Realizing that there are many reasonable perspectives, we can commit to what seems best, even if we have some lingering doubts. Firm commitment without complete certainty is simply the reasoned recognition of our finitude. Besides, the making and living of the commitment will often help us appreciate its appropriateness; thus, as long as we remain teachable, we can combine reasonable pluralism with commitment and conviction.[48] So I do not see that reasonable or perspective pluralism implies skepticism.

Socrates and the Courages of Conviction

Would such pluralists be willing to go to the stake and become martyrs for commitments they make while admitting there are reasonable alternatives? Or, to look at the other side of the coin, would they be willing to make martyrs of others? The remaining chapters will discuss the issue of when coercion is justified in a pluralistic world, but the question raises the broader issue of what it is to have the "courage of one's convictions." The phrase usually links courage with convictions, but we can now see that it could just as appropriately link courage with the commitments that we base on our convictions.

Socrates certainly had the courage to *die for* his commitments. His life was put on trial for, among other things, corrupting the youth of Athens by encouraging them to question authority. And in his *Apology*, or defense, at his trial he pointed out that he was willing to *kill for* his commitments when he fought wars against the enemies of Athens. But he also thought that a rarer courage is the courage to *live for* one's commitments, since that can involve ongoing ridicule and opposition, and not just from one's enemies. And he thought that the rarest courage with respect to convictions and commitments is the courage to *examine* them. That is why he said that the characteristic philosophical virtue is not an intellectual one but a moral one—courage. A true philosopher realizes that one should not have the courage to live one's convictions, or die for them, and certainly not kill for them, without first having the courage to examine them and see if they are worthy of killing, dying, and living for. That is why he famously said, "The unexamined life is not worth living."

This claim is probably arrogant when generalized to everyone; we all know people who have lived very worthwhile lives without examining their deepest convictions. Many people have the good fortune to be raised with a healthy perspective that nurtures a worthy life without a lot of introspection. And, as Woody Allen quipped, the examined life is no picnic either. Apart from any pain involved in challenging one's dearest beliefs, people can get so engrossed in self-analysis that courage turns to narcissism, and we want to tell them that the unlived life is not worth examining. Balance is required, though it would be paradoxical to prescribe for everyone the appropriate degree of intellectual humility and openness to other perspectives.[49] In nonpluralistic societies and homogeneous subcultures such openness is rare, and sometimes the willingness to die and kill for honor and commitments—admirable in some ways—makes us wish for a stronger inclination to examine the commitments. In short, perspective pluralism may reduce the readiness to become a martyr or make one of another, but the life of Socrates shows that it is compatible with willingness to do both and also that any reduction in willingness can be the result of a wider and more responsible courage about one's convictions and commitments.

Subjectivism and Practical Wisdom

Reasonable pluralism, as discussed earlier, admits a variety of reasonable outlooks, many of which contradict features of other reasonable outlooks. Moral pluralism asserts that, within a single moral viewpoint, the moral values can conflict with each other in such a way that there are no covering values sufficient for adjudicating the conflict. Value pluralism asserts that nonmoral values can conflict with moral ones and that the moral ones do not always override. Perspective pluralism allows a variety of outlooks, each of which can be justified from its own viewpoint, and the viewpoints can be justified to reasonable people even when other reasonable people disagree with it. Does all this reasonable variety imply the subjectivism of simply letting our strongest desires rule, or the arbitrariness of impulsive decision making? In "The Fragmentation of Value," Nagel calls such subjectivism "romantic defeatism," the opposite of the "exclusionary over-rationalization" that would try to find a single covering value or an algorithmic method to solve all problems. Instead, for anyone confused by any of the pluralisms we have discussed, he recommends the sort of judgment that Aristotle called "practical wisdom."[50] For example, when we ask about what is the best social policy on abortion, euthanasia, or gay marriage, we will encounter conflicting considerations within our own minds, to say nothing of conflicts within the body politic. But notice that such conflicts also arise when we ask less morally loaded questions, such as who is the best architect, or president, or comedian. That there are a number of reasonable answers, even in our own minds, and that there are relevant considerations that cannot be measured with the same (type of) yardstick, do not mean that we cannot reflect and debate reasonably about it. We can rule out lots of bad answers and narrow down to a number of reasonable answers without having a way to settle the single truth of the matter.

Sometimes, when the remaining options seem equally reasonable, going with one's strongest impulse, or relying on a vague intuition, or even flipping a coin may be a reasonable way to decide. But usually we resort to such methods only after ruling out many of the available options as unwise.[51] Although value pluralists insist we do not have an algorithm for straightforwardly narrowing down the reasonable choices, like other pluralists they can appeal to such ideas as that of "leading a life"[52] and that of living your life as a narrative.[53] Our lives move along, sometimes in several directions at once, and we seek a reasonable balance between "going with the flow" and "taking charge." In so doing we can think of our lives as narratives in which we are both authors and critics, and in which many of our lines are reactions to coauthors or to changing stage settings, over whom and over which we have limited control. Sometimes things happen or we do things that force major rethinking about how (or even whether) to make sense of it. Through it all we ask what are the "fitting" decisions to make. There is no mechanical way of deciding what "fits" in the unfolding of our lives, but we can usually make some narrative sense of them by using our practical reason to discern what is going on and what are the more or less responsible ways to react and to improvise. Of course, sometimes we wish we could have a chance for a second draft or a dress rehearsal, but perhaps the closest we can come to that is engaging ourselves in good novels, plays, biographies, and so on, which can heighten the sensitivity with which we interpret what is going on in our lives as well as the discernment of responsible choices. And it is this practical discernment that pluralists say can help us avoid arbitrariness as we live without consensus on algorithms or absolutes. Thus pluralists, including moral and value pluralists, need not believe that their views entail mere subjectivism or sheer decisionism.

Moral Complexities

In the previous chapter we noticed that when we set priorities among conditional commitments, it often involves "moral traces" of regret and loss. When goods collide and when not all evils can be avoided, the best thing to do is often the least bad thing, and its being *bad* can haunt us more than we are comforted by its being *least* bad. The above discussion of moral and value pluralism underscores the potential for tragic choices in the midst of ambiguity. Of course, ambiguity about what is the right thing to do is not necessary for a choice to be difficult, hard, or even tragic. We can know exactly what we ought to do and still hate to do it, as when we must hire the better qualified candidate and disappoint a friend. This tough decision would not even be a moral choice, though it could become one when the less qualified candidate is qualified enough to be hired plus he or she needs the job more. Even when one is hopelessly conflicted about what to do, the tragic choice may not be a moral one. In a *Sophie's Choice* situation, when a Nazi told her to choose just one of her two children to save or he would kill both of them, one could be firmly convinced that she is morally obligated to save one child or the other rather than have both perish, but still find it horribly difficult to choose between them. Even when it is moral principles that I must choose between, I can be sure that I am choosing rightly but still feel terrible about choosing what is morally necessary. For example, I may firmly believe I am obligated to make a deal with wrongdoers in order to prevent something terrible from happening but still feel guilty, as in the movie *Schindler's List*, when Schindler cooperated with Nazi killers in order to save his workers. In a widely cited article, Michael Walzer says of such cases, "We know he is doing right when he makes the deal because he knows he is doing wrong. I don't mean merely that he will feel bad or even very bad after he makes the deal. If he is the good man I am imagining him to be, he will feel guilty, that is, he will believe himself to be guilty. That is what it means to have dirty hands."[54] If it is true, as Walzer says, that he *knows* he is doing wrong, then he not only *feels* guilty, he *is* guilty of wrongdoing. This would be a controversial claim quite apart from moral or value pluralism, because it would imply that when I decide that one prima facie moral consideration is outweighed by another, I risk inescapable wrongdoing. It is not just that I get my hands dirty by allowing or causing something *bad* to occur; many moral perspectives imply that sometimes one must balance some evil against a greater good. But utilitarians, for example, would deny that one does *wrong* by obeying the fundamental rule of maximizing good over evil. They could admit that it is natural to feel queasy or unclean at such times, and they might even think that Walzer's considerations make such compunction a useful feature of moral psychology. But regrets and guilt *feelings*, even if useful for controlling the human tendency toward getting nonchalant about necessary evil, do not entail that one *is* guilty of wrongdoing. One might even assert a residual obligation to mitigate the evil one does without agreeing that there was a *violation* of a moral obligation.

If I break my promise to help you prepare for an examination because another friend needs my help in a serious emergency, at a minimum I may owe you an explanation and apology.[55]

So there can be significant complexities and psychological ambiguities in the moral life even for those who reject moral or value pluralism. It is true that moral pluralism, with its variety of logically independent moral considerations, adds the potential for deep ambiguity over how to juggle incommensurable but relevant factors. And value pluralism adds the possibility that a nonmoral consideration may override a moral one.[56] But complexity and ambiguity are part and parcel of a rich moral life, and they do not require surrender to arbitrariness or subjective whim.

Relativism

Relativism of truth is the view that what is true or false and what is right or wrong are relative to individuals or groups (and, by extension, often relative to geographical location and historical period). It is not simply the empirical diversity claim that what people *believe* is true and right is relative, and it is not simply the claim of perspective pluralism that what people are *justified* in believing to be true and right is relative. It does not deny that there is truth and value, as does nihilism, nor does it deny that we can know what is true and valuable, as does skepticism. Asserting relativism is not the same as asserting the sociological point that there are no universally accepted truths, or the rhetorical point that nobody can convince everybody of any interesting truth claim. Relativists can and generally will accept both those assertions, but so can those who believe they are fortunate enough to know the truth that many do not know. Also, relativism is not the view that differences are simply partial understandings of the truth, the way the blind men grasping different parts of an elephant say different things about what an elephant is like. Relativism need not deny a deeper compatibility in differences, but it asserts that even when there is deep incompatibility between claims, such as those of theism and atheism, both are true in the different contexts of theists and atheists. Implied in the above is the relativist's belief that there is no nonarbitrary way to accept one context as cognitively superior to another.

All reasonable people are relativists about some values. It is wrong to slurp loudly while dining in Minneapolis, whereas it is fine in Tokyo. So when dining in Rome, do as the Romans do. On many matters of taste and etiquette, on marrying and burying customs, and on what is good to eat, we let a hundred flowers bloom, and we should. But there are other matters on which some of us think there is an objective truth; these include not just scientific matters but also values: slavery violates fundamental rights and is objectively wrong even in those places where and times when people were or thought they were justified in practicing it. Some of us think clitoridectomy is objectively wrong, even as we think that some people may be somewhat justified in practicing it, or, at least, some people may have been justified in practicing it. In other words, the important distinction between relativism of justification and relativism of truth cuts across what is called moral relativism; as I will underscore below, we can admit the former without sliding into the latter.

Whether general relativism is reasonable or even coherent is an ancient debate in philosophy. A practical difficulty is that it makes the acceptability of terrorism a matter of opinion, and some of us see that result as a *reductio ad absurdum* of the position—that is, as a logical implication that is so unacceptable that it shows the unacceptability of the position. And when applied to itself, one can wonder if it is self-referentially consistent; if relativism is true as a universal generalization, then it seems that it is false. Even what some see as the social and political advantage of relativism, namely that it promotes tolerance, is problematic at best; it seems to imply that intolerance is permissible, perhaps obligatory, wherever it is sincerely believed to be. Anyone asserting that we all ought to be tolerant of certain differences seems to be implying a nonrelative duty. I should note that relativists have given thoughtful answers to these objections, which is why I think that at least some versions of relativism are reasonable perspectives, even if I think they are wrong.[57]

Our main question is whether any of the types of pluralism we discussed above imply general relativism. I claim that they do not. Remember that most of the pluralisms we have discussed imply the relativity of justification. We noticed earlier that whether it is reasonable for you to believe something is a function of your "evidential set" of beliefs, which will depend on your "plausibility structure" and thereby it is a function of where and when you live, the perspective with which you were raised, and the course of your life. As we will notice in the next chapter, when we discuss positions we can respect, perspective pluralism puts some imprecise restrictions on our evidential set of beliefs; for our perspective to be reasonable, it must avoid beliefs that are inordinately stupid or selfish, or the result of self-deception or wishful thinking, or, given your historical and social context, inexcusably ignorant. Even this restriction will have some relativity built into it, since our implicit criteria for intellectual adequacy, while overlapping, will vary somewhat, at least in their application. The point is that a perspective pluralist will be fairly broadminded about what constitutes a reasonable position that others are justified in holding. But this openness toward what people are intellectually entitled to believe does not imply that what actually is true or right is relative to any reasonable perspective; people can be reasonably wrong. Of course, if you think I am reasonably wrong and I think that about you, at most only one of us can be right, and we reasonably disagree about who it is. Moreover, since each of us is coming from our own perspective, neither of us has unbiased access to the truth, and it may be that neither of us knows what it is. But that is just to say that truth and right is objective and does not share the relativity of reasonableness.[58] So even those who reject the notion of objective truth or right can agree that general relativism is not implied by reasonable or perspective pluralism. That inference would need some additional premises, ones that those who believe in objective truth might accept as reasonable but not as true.

To assert that there are *objective* values is not to claim that any of them are *absolute*. An absolute value would be one that overrides all others, and that is precisely what value pluralism denies. But in denying that there is some universal covering value by which all others can be compared, such as pleasure or preference satisfaction, one does not imply that the incommensurable or incomparable values are not objective. To claim that a value is objective is to say that it is true or appropriate independently of what people believe or say about it,[59] but that does not imply that it can never be overridden by another value. Indeed, we noticed that some of the poignant—even agonizing—decisions that confront pluralists are precisely due to their not being able to simultaneously satisfy all of the relevant principles that they regard as objectively important.

If I am right so far, perspective pluralism is a reasonable view that avoids most of the isms that many regard as worrisome. But we still must confront very important problems about how a pluralist with integrity copes with many of the conflicts in a pluralistic world. For example, when your perspective implies that certain practices are harmful to innocent people, but you can also see that the practice is justifiable to reasonable people, then what should you do? This is the problem of appropriate toleration and appropriate use of coercion in a pluralistic world, the subject of the remaining chapters.

Notes

1. Asch, *Social Psychology*, 481–82. Asch argues that differences about infanticide can be another example of a basically nonmoral dispute, as when the infant is not yet thought to be a person: The difference is real, yet it is not about the acceptability of murder but about some conceptual and metaphysical issues connected to personhood. The case of the Inuit who, when they became old and fragile, would be expected to leave the tribe and die, is even more complex: The empirical conditions were that if the tribe slowed down for them, everyone would die, and the metaphysical belief was that they live after their death as long as their descendants do. In this situation, to voluntarily starve has very different moral meaning than it would in most societies. This is not to deny that people can have conflicting moral beliefs about euthanasia; it is simply to say that sometimes what looks like a moral difference is a different difference.

2. The famous Heinz dilemma mentioned in the previous chapter, where Heinz must decide whether to steal a drug to save his wife, is part of the *Defining Issues Test* designed by James Rest to determine at which stage people are, given Lawrence Kohlberg's stages of moral development. Carol Gilligan, a student of Kohlberg's, noted that the stages seemed to be linked to an ability to think legalistically about ranking rights as justice requires. Gilligan claimed in *In a Different Voice* that some people, especially women, think more contextually about caring relationships and responsibilities. This is a difference in everyday moral decision making, but obviously it is also a difference in conflict resolution.

3. Tolstoy, *A Confession and Other Religious Writings*, 24–25.

4. On the difference between evaluating how we *arrive* at our beliefs and how we *justify* them, see Wolterstorff's interpretation of Thomas Reid, in "Can Belief in God Be Rational If It Has No Foundations?" (163): "The deliverances of our credulity disposition are innocent until proved guilty, not guilty until proved innocent." Wolterstorff points out that we can cultivate non-innocent belief dispositions from perverse motives, but one would need reasons for suspecting such motives.

5. John Rawls goes in various directions, defining "reasonable doctrine" as well as "reasonable person," and specifying that reasonable persons affirm only reasonable doctrines, and that the latter are ones that *can* be affirmed in a reasonable way even when they happen to be affirmed in an unreasonable way. Rawls thinks of a "comprehensive doctrine" (similar to what in the previous chapter I called a "worldview" or "*Weltanschauung*") as an organized set of beliefs, especially moral and religious ones, that provide persons with their moral identity and guidance and structure for their lives. There are many reasonable ones that differ from and contradict each other. See Rawls, *Political Liberalism*, 50, 59–60. If "reasonable" applies primarily to believings, as I suggest, then whenever we do not know how persons would defend their beliefs, we cannot know whether we can respect their believings as reasonable. But then we could give the benefit of the doubt and say that it could well be reasonable.

6. Ibid., 48–54.

7. Ibid., 56–57. I state Rawls's "burdens of judgments" largely in my own words and I use my own examples; he is not responsible for my exposition.

8. Slippery slope arguments (also called "wedge" or "domino" or "camel's nose in the tent" arguments) are very common and can be used well or poorly. Usually they involve *empirical* predictions that (given what we know from history or psychology) if we accept a proposed practice, such as physician-assisted suicide, we will end up accepting one that is bad, such as nonvoluntary euthanasia. But sometimes the alleged slippery slope is a *logical* one, as when one argues that a particular justification of a policy or action also justifies something that is bad. For example, some people claim that if the prevention of suffering is justification enough for allowing people to die, it also justifies mercifully killing them. There may be psychological differences between allowing to die and killing, such that people who practice the former will not practice the latter. But the point of the latter type of argument is that we have to accept the logical implications of our arguments. These two types of slippery slope arguments should not be confused, since the evidence relevant to one of them will be irrelevant to the other. For example, one cannot rebut the claim that a particular justification of one practice also justifies the other simply by noting that physicians practice the one but not the other. And one cannot rebut the claim that voluntary euthanasia will lead to nonvoluntary by noting that one can justify the former without justifying the latter. The empirical prediction is about what people will slide into doing quite apart from beliefs about what is justifiable. Both of these arguments should be distinguished from "negative fallout" arguments of the form that part of the package of a proposed policy is a feature that is bad. For example, part of a liberalization of euthanasia practices is that patients would necessarily have available a new option that some of them probably would rather not have to think about.

9. Rawls gets his notion of limited social space from Berlin, *The Crooked Timber*, 13: "Some among the Great Goods cannot live together. . . . We are doomed to choose, and every choice may entail an irreparable loss." The desire not to choose is what motivated accommodation to the Amish in the *Yoder v. Wisconsin* Supreme Court decision, which gives the Amish a waiver on the level of compulsory education. As a result, it is debatable whether Amish youth have a substantial "right of exit," an issue we will discuss in chapter four. See Kraybill, *The Riddle of Amish Culture*, 184–87.

10. In the introduction to the paperback edition of *Political Liberalism*, Rawls cites differences in comprehensive doctrines as well as differences in race, class, gender, and occupations as two sources of conflict in addition to the burdens of judgment (lx), and in the original edition he makes a point of noting that "prejudice and bias, self- and group interest, blindness and willfulness, play their all too familiar part in political life" (58). Rawls would not be surprised by the growing literature on "confirmation bias," the human tendency to notice and highlight evidence that supports one's prior opinions while not noticing or ignoring evidence against them, but most of the burdens of judgment would hold independently of this frustrating, if not corrupting, feature of human nature. Relevant here is the theological dispute over the degree to which sin perverts our cognition. We noted previously (chapter 1, n. 1) that there is a parallel secular debate about the role of selfishness in human nature. Some thinkers seem to imply that sin or selfishness renders most of our beliefs guilty until proved innocent, while others think that God's providence or human decency implies that most disputes are more likely attributable to the burdens of judgment than to corruption. Those impressed by Rawls's list of the ways that well-intentioned and intelligent people inevitably disagree can be realistically suspicious about human nature and still agree that many or most disagreements in a pluralistic society are due to reasonable differences.

11. The "in principle" qualification covers a variety of possibilities when claiming that we can, in principle, use a unified moral theory to reach mutually consistent decisions. Plato thought that the form of the Good was available to the few philosophers who, through intellectual conversion and rigorous education, escaped the cave of shadows and illusions where everyday experience prevents clear perception of the Good. Ignorance is the problem, and knowledge of the Good is rare and difficult. Others might add sin as part of the problem; our own selfishness blinds us to the truth. Or, according to Thomas Aquinas, our own sinful decision can put us into a predicament where there no longer is a morally good way out, as when I make a bad promise. The point is that I can affirm that there is or was a true answer in principle, but that for a variety of reasons we do not know what it is or it is no longer available. Of course, practical dilemmas resulting from our ignorance or past folly can be just as difficult as those that would result from genuine and deep inconsistency in our value system.

12. I cited MacIntyre's *After Virtue* in the previous chapter when I discussed MacIntyre's rebuttal of the fact-value dichotomy. MacIntyre is not a monist or absolutist, but his historical account is sometimes used as an alternative to what I will call moral pluralism. I describe his historical account without endorsing it.

13. "The pot-pourri sometimes called western civilization has always contained conflicting values. Greek, Roman, Christian and Jewish traditions each contain distinctive goods and virtues that cannot be translated fully into the ethical life of

others. The notion of a 'western tradition' in which these irreconcilable elements were once fused cannot withstand philosophical—or historical—scrutiny." Gray, *Two Faces of Liberalism*, 12.

14. Nagel, *Mortal Questions*. Other moral pluralists who have written recent and very accessible books include Isaiah Berlin, John Kekes, and John Gray, cited earlier; Galston, *Liberal Pluralism*; and Hampshire, *Justice Is Conflict*. Rawls says that Nagel's value pluralism is consistent with his own reasonable pluralism, but he thinks that Nagel's view is more controversial than is needed for political liberalism (Rawls, *Political Liberalism*, 57). To say with Nagel that people will have deep conflicts even apart from the burdens of judgment is sometimes called strong or ontological pluralism as opposed to Rawls's weak or epistemological pluralism, but these terms are used in various ways.

15. In discussing moral principles, referring to *secular* ones already narrows things down considerably. I have mentioned the teleological ethics of Aristotle, which takes a virtues approach rather than a principles approach to ethics, focusing first on dispositions of character (on what we ought to *be*) rather than on rules for actions (on what we ought to *do*). Typically the virtues approach tries to articulate the natural or proper ends of human existence or human practices and to cultivate the virtues and character conducive to these ends. Of course, there is plenty of room for intramural debate over what these ends are or which virtues are conducive to achieving them. Both the virtues approach and the principles approach can be situated in a religious or theological context. Theological ethics need not claim a distinctive content; it can claim simply that theology provides ethics with either the necessary *foundation for* or the *motivation to act* (or both) on the same or similar virtues that God or nature reveals to everyone. The theological foundation can ordinarily be out of mind and out of sight, as foundations frequently are. And the motivations can range from crude (reward and punishment) to sophisticated (gratitude for our lives and opportunities), but can apply to the same natural law that St. Paul says is written on everyone's heart (Romans 1). However, theological ethics can also claim additional, special, revelation about ethics. When it does, there is intramural debate over whether God reveals specific moral *rules* (sometimes called legalism), or basic *principles*, or basic *virtues*. And, of course, given the ambiguities in the Bible, there is plenty of room for debate about the details of those rules, principles, and virtues. So a full description of Western ethics would show even more diversity than we discuss in the text. It is important to note that such diversity in foundations and basic principles is quite compatible with a fair amount of agreement on particular moral decisions; people using different reasoning can converge on a decision. Indeed, in hospital ethics committees, there is often consensus on what should be done even when there is no consensus on basic principles. In the last chapter we will see that widely different religious and philosophical foundations allowed agreement on a universal declaration of human rights. In his recent book, *The Righteous Mind: Why Good People Are Divided by Politics and Religion*, Haidt argues that what more often divides us is not principles but our putting different emphases on the sources of our moral feelings, sources that include feelings about fairness, care, liberty, loyalty, authority, and sanctity.

16. In Bentham's "hedonic calculus," one considers the pleasures that would result from the various options available and then calculates their intensity, duration, certainty, nearness (as many economists do, Bentham thought that promises for the far future

had to be appropriately discounted), purity (to what extent are pains part of the package?), extent, and fruitfulness. Purity and fruitfulness are important because, although pleasure is good in itself (an intrinsic good), it can lead to pains and thereby simultaneously be instrumentally evil; and other goods, such as knowledge, though not intrinsically good, can lead to pleasure and thereby be instrumentally good. In fact, "no pain, no gain" reminds us that the intrinsic evil of pain can be an important instrumental good. Therefore fruitfulness sometimes requires forgoing an immediate intrinsic good for painful but rich instrumental goods.

17. Beauchamp and Childress, *Principles of Biomedical Ethics.* The four middle-level principles are respect for autonomy, nonmaleficence (do no harm), beneficence, and justice. The authors include advice about how to specify and balance these principles in specific cases, but they believe that it is impossible to provide a clear algorithm for reaching a decision. Notice that if opposing considerations can be weighed or balanced in some formal or informal way, then one can reach a decision. Of course, even then it may be psychologically difficult to carry out the decision, since one would be overriding some important moral values. On the other hand, if the considerations are incommensurable or incomparable in the senses defined later, they by definition cannot be weighed or balanced, even if in some way one can arrive at a considered adjudication analogous to an overall aesthetic judgment.

18. Tensions and conflicts might infect even moral theories that try to avoid the ambiguities of principlism. Sometimes a theory can look monistic and absolutistic because it seems to have a single, overriding principle, but the application of it may require specificatory principles that are independent and possibly occasions for conflict. Donagan's *The Theory of Morality* claims that a single principle—"It is impermissible not to respect every human being . . . as a rational creature" (66)—is the single guide for all moral decisions. Apart from such problems as moral duties to animals, Brody's *Taking Issue: Pluralism and Casuistry in Bioethics* points out the wide variety of ways one can disrespect persons (and the difficulty of simultaneously avoiding all of them) and raises the question, "Is there then a single property of failing to show respect which has several different subproperties, each a type of failing to show respect, or are there different and independent properties which are just being artificially lumped together under the predicate 'failing to show respect for a human being as a person'?" (33). Notice that sometimes the problem with a moral system might be one of gaps rather than inconsistencies; the principles cohere but they do not cover all the moral problems we encounter. Gaps may be less of a philosophical problem than conflicts, but the practical difficulty can be just as intense.

19. Rokeach, *The Nature of Human Values.*

20. See Chang's introduction to the book she edited, *Incommensurability, Incomparability, and Practical Reason,* for definitions of and distinctions between "incommensurable" and "incomparable." "Common scale" actually involves two elements: something shared in common and something that can be measured. It is possible for two works of art to share beauty as a common characteristic without its being measurable. A variety of definitions of these and related terms are discussed in Hsieh's "Incommensurable Values."

21. Incommensurability of values seems a serious problem for any ethic that claims one should maximize some good, as we noted utilitarianism does. A popular version

of the latter—preference satisfaction—has the additional problem that maximizing preference satisfaction will work only if all relevant preferences are included in the weighing, even the "bad" preferences. But it seems implausible to decide whether oppression is wrong by seeing if the preferences of the oppressed are outweighed by the preferences of the oppressors. And efforts to screen out certain preferences will likely require moral beliefs that are independent of utility. Whether comparability (without commensurability) is sufficient for maximizing goods is a debatable issue that we cannot pursue here.

22. Martin Buber says that in his early youth he preferred books over people, but toward the end of his life he said, "Here is an infallible test. Imagine yourself in a situation where you are alone, wholly alone on earth, and you are offered one of the two, books or [people]" (Buber, *Autobiographical Fragments*, 71–72). Notice that if he had specified books or *friends*, the choice would be even easier. Notice also that commensurable things can be cardinally ranked; comparable but incommensurable things can, at best, be ordinally ranked. Chang argues that any comparisons must involve some sort of covering value, even comparisons between morality and prudence (119), but this is controversial. Larmore, for example, argues in "Pluralism and Reasonable Disagreement" that "sometimes we can find a solution to such a conflict, not by appealing to a common denominator of value, but simply by recognizing that one consideration carries more weight than the other" (61–79). Value commitments may be, in other words, *comparable* without being *commensurable*, "rankable without appeal to a common standard providing the reasons for the ranking" (65). And Galston, in *The Practice of Liberal Pluralism*, argues that we often make plausible comparative judgments (for example, between endangered birds and lumber jobs) without employing a covering value (15). In *The Good in the Right*, Audi boldly claims, "If there is incommensurability, in the sense of the absence of a common measure for all moral considerations, there can nonetheless be *comparability* in the sense implying the possibility of a rational assessment in the context of the relevant facts" (65). Factors that can be ranked in some instances may not be rankable in others; generally one would prefer pain over death, but how much pain and for how long a life? We will return to this issue of rational assessment.

23. If one cannot find a covering *value* to resolve a conflict, perhaps one can find a covering *rule* such as that suggested by Lockhart, *Moral Uncertainty and Its Consequences* (26): "In situations of moral uncertainty, I (the decision-maker) should (rationally) choose some action that has the maximum probability of being morally right." The question, of course, is whether this can be plausibly calculated in all situations of uncertainty.

24. Notice that applying the categories "sanctity" or "dignity" to human life does not mean it is infinitely valuable; that would imply a measuring rod, and one that would make it irrational to take any risk to life, however small, for any finite benefit, however large. One would not know how to live.

25. One can be motivated to share the good news that God loves you without thinking that if you do not believe it God will punish you eternally. This point is important whether or not Jean-Jacques Rousseau is right in claiming, "It is impossible to live in peace with those one believes to be damned" (Rousseau, *On the Social Contract*, 226) (first published in 1762).

26. Mouw and Griffoen, *Pluralisms and Horizons*, 108. The point about neurotics providing genuine insights they take from Paul Tillich.

27. Adeney, in *Strange Virtues*, teaches a version of exclusivism, or particularism, with epistemological humility. He is a missionary who thinks he should listen as well as talk: "It may be that God wishes to speak to *you* through the other, rather than vice versa" (189). Epistemological or intellectual humility, whose patron saint is Socrates, is not timidity, but rather the confidence to be teachable. And spiritual humility simply recognizes that one is the recipient of a gift rather than one who is better or more worthy of salvation than others. A clear-headed and fair-minded defense of exclusivism is Plantinga's "Pluralism," 173–92.

28. From "Theological Investigations," 326. Rahner did not direct his "anonymous Christian" comment to non-Christians; he meant it as a way for Christians to think about others.

29. It turns out that this claim sometimes trades on the ambiguity of "islam" or "submission" as a feature asserted to be part of all true religions and as a proper name for one religion.

30. For reasons that will become clear, it is hard to define religious pluralism in a way that captures what different religious pluralists teach. My definition is consistent with most of what Eck says in *Encountering God*, chapter 7. She gives one of the most widely read defenses of pluralism, and also discusses exclusivism and inclusivism. She associates pluralism with active engagement and dialogue with other religions, but I noted that the latter can also be associated with exclusivism and inclusivism.

31. Pluralists prefer terms like "genuine" or "authentic" or "major" or "traditional" rather than "reasonable" when discussing the religions they have in mind. But such terms turn out to be as normatively loaded as "reasonable" when they are used to focus on acceptable religions. Of course the concept of religion is itself very open-ended. As with so many of the categories we use in this book, we are likely to have a list of family resemblances rather than clear-cut necessary or sufficient conditions. Most pluralists want to include Confucianism, Buddhism, and Taoism, so their notion of religion must be broader than theism. I do not see how the concept of religion itself can be uncontroversially defined in a way that narrows down the referents to those that some pluralists claim are effective routes to the sacred.

32. Hick, "Religious Pluralism and Salvation," 365–77. See also Hick, *God Has Many Names*, and Hick, *An Interpretation of Religion*.

33. Hick, *Philosophy of Religion*,117. In this defense of theological pluralism, Hick appeals to Kant's distinction between things in themselves (noumena) and things as we experience them given our physiological and psychological makeup (phenomena). Kant thought that humans all use the same categories of interpretation of the physical world, which is why our empirical experience is so similar. To account for the dramatic differences in religious experience, Hick adds historical and cultural differences to how we experience the Real, which introduces a level of relativity that we do not find in Kant's epistemology.

34. Hick, "Religious Pluralism and Salvation," 369.

35. Similar objections to Hick can be found in Griffiths, *Problems of Religious Diversity*, and Netland, *Encountering Religious Pluralism*. Another criticism of Hick is that he sometimes uses "interpretation" and "construct" rather loosely. Are religious doctrines *shaped* in some way by *how* we experience the Real, or do we have

an essentially ineffable experience and then *construct* doctrines that are completely shaped by our cultural perspective?

36. Twiss, in "The Philosophy of Religious Pluralism," 67–98, correctly notes that any explanatory interpretation of religions is likely to use a higher-order scheme that will not be accepted by the religions it tries to explain. This is true, and it shows that, at the level of theories, even pluralists are exclusivists, since they think that their theory is right and that those who disagree with it are wrong. But I think Hick's "salvific effectiveness" criterion is less an explanatory theory than an assertion about the true essence of all religion(s). The latter seems more a religious claim than a scientific claim about religion; for example, if it were true, it would challenge substantive religious beliefs of many people about salvation.

37. A fine survey of a range of postmodern views regarding religious plurality is Knitter's *Introducing Theologies of Religions*, part IV. What I describe as religious particularism, religious inclusivism, and religious pluralism largely overlaps what Knitter calls (respectively) the Replacement Model: "Only One True Religion," the Fulfillment Model: "The One Fulfills the Many," and the Mutuality Model: "Many True Religions Called to Dialogue."

38. On something as complex as an overall perspective that includes moral and religious beliefs, it is hard to compare degrees of justifiability. At a minimum we can say that quite likely the internal and mental markings for thinking one is right are at least as clear and persuasive to the other as mine are to me. Beyond that, we can sometimes understand another's perspective well enough to appreciate it as reasonable, even though we disagree with it. When I studied and taught in Thailand for several months, I learned to appreciate the Buddhist karma doctrine as reasonable for those raised in that intellectual and spiritual environment. Moreover, that environment seemed to be scientifically informed and no more infected by noetic vices such as false consciousness or stubborn bias than the one in which I was raised. Is it coherent to say that your perspective seems at least as justified for you as mine does for me, and yet I think you are wrong? Feldman, "Plantinga on Exclusivism," 85–90, gives a counterexample involving a medical researcher who decides she is justified in believing that drug A works best against a disease (87). Can this researcher believe that another researcher is *as* justified (not just justified) in believing that drug B or C works best, and still believe that she is right and he is wrong? I am not sure how to answer except to say that fairly straightforward factual issues, especially scientific ones, seem to me to be in a different cognitive boat from broadly perspectival ones. There may be a spectrum here on which some types of contradictions cannot be handled as "pluralistically" as others. Even if Feldman's point were generalized, however, perspective pluralists could amiably say that a perspective they disagree with is reasonably and responsibly justified for another without saying that they believe it is *as* justified for the other as they believe their own is for themselves. So the relativity of justification would still hold. Some *internalists* in epistemology believe that justification of beliefs requires only internal, introspective markers of justifiability. In this theory, paranoid persons might be justified in thinking you are out to harm them even when that belief seems clearly unjustified to everyone else. *Externalists* believe that at least some of the factors that justify a belief are external to the believer's introspective cognitive perspective, factors such as the reliable functioning of one's cognitive faculties. So externalists say that if paranoids' cognitive faculties are not working in a reliable way, their belief that you are

out to harm them is not justified. Clearly some internalists can agree that another's perspective is justified even when it contradicts one's own. And, given the "burdens of judgment" discussed earlier, I believe that externalists can also accept this relativity of justification, at least with respect to many of the problematic issues we are discussing. What I say is partly inspired by Nicholas Wolterstorff's notion (interpreting Thomas Reid) of "situated rationality": "Rationality is always situational, in the sense that what is rational for one person to believe will not be rational for another to believe. Thus in general we cannot inquire into the rationality of some belief by asking whether *one* would be rational in holding that belief. We must ask whether it would be rational for *this particular person* to hold it, or whether it would be rational *for a person of this type in this situation* to hold it" (Wolterstorff, "Thomas Reid on Rationality," 65). In *Divine Discourse*, Wolterstorff uses the categories of "entitlement" and "doxastic obligations" rather than that of "justification" to claim that our entitlement to believe something is linked to whether we have fulfilled our obligations, and that the latter is "a function of various aspects of the particular situation . . ."(272). Others use the categories of "warrant" or "epistemic desiderata." I retain the more commonly used notion of "justification" even though I cannot justify my usage without going into more details of issues related to virtue epistemology.

39. Instead of "perspective pluralist," one can use "perspectival pluralist." The adjective would be grammatically preferable to the noun, but my experience is that not very many people will use it. "Perspectival" is sometimes used as a synonym for "orientational" or "outlook." Perspective pluralism as defined refers to differences *among* people, but it is worth noting that a given person can adopt different perspectives when trying to make sense of experience. For example, we can adopt an "actor" perspective when we are engaged in pursuing our goals, but we can also stand back and adopt a "spectator" attitude to our own projects, as when we evaluate them and even call them into question (see note 49 in this chapter). The human condition allows and perhaps requires this movement between passionate engagement and critical self-reflection. If one thinks of this fact as a "perspectivism" (as does Palmquist in *The Tree of Philosophy*, 177), it should be distinguished from the "perspective pluralism" that refers to the justifiability of contradictory perspectives held by different people. In either case, perspective pluralism is only one part of an overall worldview (*Weltanschauung*); the latter would include one's substantive moral and religious beliefs. I believe perspective pluralism can be part of an outlook that includes strong and conservative religious beliefs, including those of Adeney (discussed in note 27 in this chapter), which combine particularism (or exclusivism) with appropriate intellectual humility. Even if we thought that the cognitive effects of sin interfere with our ability to appreciate important truths, we could at a minimum agree that error can *seem* reasonable, which would enable us to say, "I can understand how you see it as reasonable." This is simply to admit that some of our better beliefs are due more to grace or luck than to our superior cognitive skills. Beyond that, we could agree that at least some, maybe most, of what we see as error is largely the result of the sort of burdens of judgment we discussed above in connection with reasonable pluralism. In short, we could see them as mistaken but reasonable, wrong but justified for those who hold them. Thus perspective pluralism is reasonable pluralism with an attitude, an attitude compatible with particularism.

40. The metaphor of "web of beliefs" comes from Quine and Ullian, *The Web of Belief.*
41. One can appeal to what "an ideal observer" would do, as a way to acknowledge that there may be an objective truth about which perspective is best. Indeed, an "ideal observer" can function as a regulative ideal to help guide our decisions. But modesty forbids us from elevating our situation to that of an ideal observer.
42. Schweder, *Why Do Men Barbecue Other Men?*, is just one of the anthropologists who remind us to take seriously the outlook of those supporting clitoridectomy; those who believe, for example, that it is barbaric not to cut off at least part of an unwelcome vestige of the male organ. A perspective pluralist can take this thinking seriously even while believing that it is seriously wrong from what she thinks is a better perspective.
43. You can agree that something is justified *to* me if I merely think it is; for you to think that something is justified *for* me, you must agree that, in my situation, it is *reasonable* for me to believe it justified. The case can arise in which there *are* good reasons available to one in my situation that are sufficient to reject my belief, but I do not *have* those reasons in my viewpoint. Then my view is justified to me but not for me. For example, given what I care about, something can be important to me because it is a means to what I care about. I may have a deep desire for health but deny the obvious fact that exercise will promote it. Then, in an important sense, I *have* a reason to exercise, but I cannot *give* the reason; a policy is justified *for* me, but not *to* me.
44. Rescher, *Pluralism*, 116–17. For orientational pluralism, see also Rescher, *The Strife of Systems*. Heim has applied Rescher's view to religious diversity in "Orientational Pluralism in Religion," 201–15. Heim sees his own orientational pluralism as a type of inclusivism that is more respectful of particularity in religion than are most versions of pluralism. See Heim, *Salvations*. Perspective pluralism is, I think, consistent with the essential claims of a number of authors I have referred to, including Berlin, Kekes, Gray, Galston, Hampshire, Mouw and Griffoen, Adeney, and, probably, Eck. The adjectives for pluralism are diverse: Rescher refers to conceptual, substantive, logical, methodological, ontological, axiological (evaluative), and practical; Mouw and Griffoen refer to directional, associational, and contextual, with descriptive and normative versions of each of those three; and McLennon in *Pluralism* adds such categories as critical, legal, interpretive, and sociocultural pluralism. Most of these overlap and reflect different ways of classifying human thought and practice. All of them distinguish between plurality as diversity, which is largely descriptive, and pluralism as a way to cope with plurality, which is largely normative.
45. Intellectual humility by itself does not entail fallibilism, because you can think that others can teach you more about what you believe without thinking that they can teach you something that contradicts what you believe. But fallibilism is a reasonable extension of intellectual humility. Notice that you can be a fallibilist about each of your beliefs without falling into a general skepticism: "About each of my beliefs, I might be wrong" does not entail "I might be wrong about all of my beliefs," since we cannot even challenge a given belief without relying on many other ones.
46. *Mother Teresa* by Kolodiejcuk and Mother Teresa.
47. Berger, *A Far Glory*, 89. For the link between doubt and faith, see also Berger, *The Heretical Imperative*. The root meaning of heresy is "individual choice," which Berger links to authentic faith, in distinction from naïve belief.

48. That one can combine reasonable pluralism with conviction and commitment is the main conclusion of Perry's *Forms of Intellectual and Ethical Development in the College Years*, cited in my preface: I can believe my deepest values to be true yet I can be willing to learn more. As we will see in chapter four, it is possible to be a fallibilist about many of my beliefs without being a fallibilist about my deepest values. It is sometimes said that doubts unite us while convictions divide us. But sometimes convictions unite us, and raising doubts can be divisive. In any case, making commitments can be a human way of combining convictions and doubts. Whether and how acceptance of pluralism affects the quality of one's convictions is helpfully addressed in McKim's *Religious Ambiguity and Religious Diversity*.

49. Thomas Nagel in "The Absurd" notes that we can alternate between leading our lives with intensity and standing back as spectators (11–23). From the latter perspective we can always ask one more question, which leads some to think our lives are absurd but leads Nagel to say that having both the actor and spectator perspectives make our lives all the more interesting. Perry, *Forms of Intellectual and Ethical Development*, 38–39, shows how students have to work out their own sense of balance: "In these records the students speak often of such inner balances as those between action and contemplation ('I've come to learn when to say to myself "well, now, enough of this mulling and doubting, let's do something"'); permanence and flexibility ('Sometimes you have to go into something with the feeling you'll be in it forever even when you know you probably won't be' or 'I used to think that I had to finish anything I started or I'd be a quitter; now I see it's a nice point when to stop something that may be unprofitable and put the effort in more hopeful directions'); control vs. openness ('Well, you have to let experience teach you; it's good to have a plan, but if you insist on following it without a change ever—'); intensity vs. perspective ('That's the trick, I guess, you have to have detachment, or you get lost, you can't see yourself and your relation to what you're doing, and yet if you stay detached you never learn from total involvement, you never live; you just have to do it by waves, I guess')."

50. Nagel, "Fragmentation of Value," 135.

51. Raz, in "Incommensurability and Agency" (Chang's *Incommensurability, Incomparability, and Practical Reason*), distinguishes two conceptions of agency: rationalistic and classical. The former makes a decision a matter of taking the option supported by the strongest reason, whereas, in the latter, "reason does not determine what is to be done. Rather it sets a range of eligible options before agents, who choose among them as they feel inclined, who do what they want to do or what they feel like doing" (127). Raz also points out that our desires are not brute urges, cravings, or impulses (117). Many philosophers and psychologists have noted that, unlike other animals, we have not just desires but also desires about our desires. Second- and third-order meta-desires so often involve reflection that Smith (*Moral, Believing Animals*) wonders why they should not be called judgments or evaluations (9). In *The Reasons of Love*, Frankfurt argues that clarification of what we have reasons to do comes only from finding out what we most care about and doing enough reflection to be "robustly confident" (28) in caring about it. In this book and in his earlier presidential address to the American Philosophical Association (Frankfurt, "The Faintest Passion"), Frankfurt underscores the value of being "wholehearted" in one's commitments rather than having divided loyalties. Value pluralists, of course, insist that ambivalence due to divided loyalties is simply part of the human

condition and that integrity is as compatible with conflicted complexity as with neatness. Purity of heart could be complicated. In addition, as we have noted, a perspective pluralist can make whole-hearted commitments even when there is room for doubts. I can decide to *will* one thing even if I find that I *want* more than one.

52. For a discussion of how a pluralist might avoid skepticism, relativism, and arbitrary decisionism, see Taylor's "Leading a Life" in the Chang anthology *Incommensurability, Incomparibility, and Practical Reason* (170–83). Taylor credits Wollheim's *The Thread of Life*. In "What Is Morality?" (Rasmussen, *Universalism vs. Communitarianism*, 237–64), Dreyfus and Stuart argue that moral decision making is a *skill* that develops with practice. Robert Audi, in *The Good in the Right*, appeals to morally mature intuition: "Perhaps I simply see that I must do what is called for by my job, even where I have reason to relieve a friend's distress instead. My final duty can be obvious to me even if I make no comparison to ascertain that I am not missing a better alternative. This is part of what it is to have moral maturity" (64).

53. MacIntyre's *After Virtue* revived the "narrative" approach to ethics. A good anthology of articles on the advantages and disadvantages of narrative ethics is Lindemann, *Stories and Their Limits*. Smith, *Moral, Believing Animals*, chapter 4, discusses how living our lives as narratives is simply part of the human condition, and that, postmodernism notwithstanding, we all use metanarratives in making sense of our lives. Of course, we should remember the point that novelists often make: The difference between reality and fiction is that fiction has to make sense. Unlike good novels, our lives have lots of meandering dead ends and undeveloped characters that make unexplained appearances; we *construct* our stories as we *interpret* what is going on in our lives, and much *editing* is needed to make narrative sense of them. Does this mean that such narratives embellish, deny, and falsify, as in Tim Burton's 2003 movie *Big Fish*? Here is where such virtues as honesty, humility, and courage can provide authenticity to the stories of our lives.

54. Walzer, "Political Action," 166. Walzer has been quoted as saying that he thinks this article has been so frequently reprinted because many teachers like to use it as an example of an incoherent position.

55. Santurri carefully argued in *Perplexity in the Moral Life* that there are genuine moral dilemmas such that one must inescapably violate an obligation, but allows that sometimes causing pain or other harm to fulfill one's duty can result in some residual obligations. One of his examples is an army medic who is forced to operate with insufficient anesthetic: "It is certainly reasonable to suppose that the medic is morally obliged at some point to . . . provide an explicit justification for the action, and to express her deep sorrow and regret over the fact that the action had to be performed" (55). Another example is a person who must break a promise to fulfill a greater moral obligation: "we may speak of these residual obligations as the outcome of agent contribution to the loss of moral value signified by the broken promise without implying thereby that a moral wrong has been committed" (56). Opposing Santurri, Gowan's *Innocence Lost* asserts that "[o]n the face of it, this is a perplexing idea. Ordinarily when we speak in moral contexts of it being obligatory to render an apology or to pay compensation, we assume that what is being apologized and compensated for is a moral wrong. . . . [I]t must have been in some way wrong to break the overridden promise; and if it was wrong, the wrongdoing was inescapable" (112). One can deny the existence of "hard moral dilemmas" of

the sort that require one simultaneously to fulfill incompatible moral obligations of equal stringency and still, like Gowan, assert that overriding an obligation of lesser stringency involves (inescapable) wrongdoing. Others, like Santurri, assert that the complexity of the moral life can involve tragic choices, ones that appropriately elicit both regret and obligations for compensation without involving moral wrongdoing. In the latter case, guilt feelings can be understandable and maybe even useful without being morally justified. The line between deep regret at doing what is bad and appropriate remorse at doing what is wrong may seem erased by Walzer's saying that the man with dirty hands will not merely feel very bad, he will believe himself to be guilty. The line may be psychologically thin but still philosophically important. In *Walking the Tightrope of Reason*, Fogelin argues that morality and law are just two examples of rule-governed activities that most people must engage in but, given the complexity of our lives and the need to accept intuitions that can come into conflict, we cannot escape contradictions unless, in the interest of rationalistic consistency, we accept loss of plausibility (66). This point seems to me to be compatible with either Santurri's or Gowan's claims about guilt feelings.

56. Kekes, *Morality of Pluralism*, is willing to say that when moral values conflict with nonmoral ones a person can act *immorally* but *reasonably* (178). This combination jars many of us, which is why Kantians and others, including most moral pluralists, claim that, for a reasonable person, moral considerations override nonmoral ones. Many value pluralists, in opposition to Kekes, say simply that the good life involves comparing moral and nonmoral commitments, and that immorality occurs only when nonmoral considerations override in a way that violates practical reason. Adams, in "Vocation," discusses the Gauguin case along with others that raise the question whether a sense of being "called" to a particular life project can justify serious costs to others affected by one's decision (448–62). The hands of even saints can look dirty to those who are short-changed by a saint's single-minded commitments. Schuurman's *Vocation* has an insightful discussion of how weighing the costs to others—as well as advice from others—should influence one's decision about whether a "call" is from God. The problem of comparing moral obligations with the importance of pursuing one's distinctive and identity-defining projects can be as difficult in a religious context as in a secular one.

57. The literature on relativism is vast. For an orientation, I recommend Moser and Carson, *Moral Relativism*; Fogelin, *Walking the Tightrope of Reason*; Melchert, *Who's to Say*; and Elgin, *Between the Absolute and the Arbitrary*.

58. Among the ethicists who defend relativity of justification while denying relativity of truth is Stout, *Ethics after Babel*, 25–31. Santurri, in "Nihilism Revisited," 67–78, argues that asserting this distinction does not avoid relativism or nihilism unless one explains how truth and justifiability are connected (71), and he suggests that the latter requires some sort of moral realism (the view that there are objective moral truths independent of our beliefs and languages). Stout is content to appeal simply to how we use words like "truth." I wish to note only that perspective pluralism is consistent with moral realism.

59. Objectivity of belief is not the same as universality of belief. Beliefs are intersubjective when they are shared, but their being universally shared does not show that they are true or that they would not be true even if nobody believed them. There may well be mathematical and other truths that nobody will ever believe, and it is

conceivable that there are (almost) universal beliefs that are false. Even those who believe in an absolute value or hierarchy of values, one that provides the single right answer for any moral decision, need not assert that it is universally accepted, though they may believe that it is universally accessible to sincere seekers. Those who maintain that there are some universally accepted moral values are usually moral pluralists, allowing that the goods associated with these values can come into tension with each other. Bok, for example, in her *Common Values*, plausibly claims that certain basic or minimal values are necessary for the very existence of societies. These include positive values such as mutual support and reciprocity (130), negative ones such as not harming others (15), as well as rudimentary fairness and rules for conflict resolution (16). She allows that there may be some amoralist individuals who reject these values, but they will be parasites on societies that cannot exist without the minimal values (18). Bok also points out that, while they are *necessary* for group life, they are not *sufficient* for flourishing; we also need maximal values: ideals and virtues usually linked to religious and cultural convictions and commitments (20). She does provide something of a value hierarchy by claiming (controversially) that minimal values should always be a check on maximal values, but insists that the minimum values themselves are not absolute; lying, for example, is generally incompatible with group life but exceptions have to be made (19). Of course, while raising children, the maximal and minimal values generally are thoroughly integrated, as in the Ten Commandments. It takes the value conflicts we find in a pluralistic society to try to tease them apart, as we will see in the next chapters.

CHAPTER THREE

Toleration and Respect

Our story so far is that in a pluralistic society we can and should engage in open-minded conversations during which we listen as much as we talk, engage in sincere dialogues during which we try to see the issues the way others do, and engage in mutual inquiries during which we patiently and fair-mindedly examine each others' arguments. However, we cannot expect that these well-intentioned efforts will bring consensus. Given the burdens of judgment, such discussion, rather than bringing agreement, will instead often clarify the depth of the differences and the sharpness of the conflicts. This is still a helpful result, especially since the pluralisms we have discussed show that such differences and conflicts are quite compatible with reasonableness all around. But we must now consider whether all the differences we encounter in a pluralistic society are tolerable. Of course, even a pluralistic society finds itself with crimes and other forms of behavior that no civil society can endure, so appropriate intolerance will always have its place. Indeed, moral progress in history is often marked precisely by civilized societies' becoming *in*tolerant of oppressive practices such as slavery and various forms of unjustified discrimination. Intolerance is often appropriate even if we appropriately tolerate many types of irrational behavior, such as bad eating habits. A more interesting question is whether all the reasonable differences are tolerable. Can I be reasonably justified in thinking that my behavior is permitted, even obligatory, and yet you are reasonably justified in thinking that I should be prevented from doing it? Yes, this sort of conflict is possible, as shown in American history by such controversies as those over polygamy, euthanasia, prohibition, and mandatory participation in social security. Such examples motivate us to clarify the concept of toleration, as well as examine the debate over the criteria for when toleration is appropriate and when it is not.

Toleration and Tolerance

The concepts of toleration and tolerance are used in many different ways, making it impossible to legislate how to use them. I suggest, however, that clarity is best achieved if we keep in mind some important distinctions, even if we disagree somewhat on precisely how to label them. In particular, we should distinguish toleration from indifference, resignation, timidity, and approval. "Toleration" is derived from the Latin *tolero*, which primarily connotes the enduring of something. So first we must ask what are the types of things endured and then ask what it means to endure them.

Objects of Toleration

We endure pain; indeed, we sometimes talk about having a high or low tolerance for pain, or having a stoic attitude toward pain. So *conditions* might be the sort of things we tolerate. Notice, however, that if we freely choose the pain, as an athlete does under the motto "No pain, no gain," we are pushing the limits of language to say that we tolerate it. Toleration connotes that we would prefer not to have to endure what we are enduring. Of course, we can choose to endure the pain of a medical treatment because it is the least bad option open to us; there is an element of choice, but it is important to notice that the choice is only within a tight limit of options that we did not and would not choose. There may be any number of personal and social conditions that we choose to endure: The human condition itself is something that an unhappy person might endure, given the alternative. So there may be a legitimate sense in which we can be said to tolerate various types of conditions. However, this chapter will focus more on human *actions* and *practices*, which are the usual sorts of things we can be said to tolerate, actions such as someone's interrupting you or practices such as your neighbor's habit of playing loud music late at night.

Do we tolerate *persons*? Persons obviously can be the objects of toleration in one sense, since it is their actions and practices that we tolerate. But, strictly speaking, the alternative to enduring persons themselves would be eliminating or banishing them. There were times in history and there are places today where people were and are killed or banished just for what they *are*, as the horror of ethnic cleansing demonstrates. Discriminating against persons because of features (largely) outside their control, such as skin color, racial features, sexual orientation, and religious upbringing, could be called intolerance toward persons. It could also be called intolerance toward whatever actions or practices the discrimination forbids, such as getting a particular type of job, renting an apartment, or going to the public school of one's choice. Also, it seems that the opposite of discrimination against persons is not mere toleration of them; it is acceptance of and respect for them. In any case, the typical object of toleration is less what people *are* and more what they *do*, though sharp lines probably cannot be drawn here. Given the way some court systems actually work, it would be naïve to think that people are judged to be criminals and then executed or imprisoned only for what they do, not what they are.

Can we tolerate a person's beliefs or, more precisely, a person's belief in something? The alternative would be brainwashing (or worse), which also is generally not an option today in our society. Admittedly, there are sometimes thin lines and mere matters of degree between persuasion, indoctrination, manipulation, and brainwashing. If we say that any effort at changing a person's mind through rational persuasion is intolerance of their beliefs, I think we stretch the meaning too far, and we risk making education a matter of intolerance rather than liberation. One can claim that truth is intolerant of error[1] without implying that trying to teach the truth is being intolerant toward another's holding a wrong belief. As long as one uses acceptable pedagogy, one that respects intellectual freedom, it seems counterintuitive to classify teaching as intolerance toward beliefs or believings. But if someone wants to say that teachers are intolerant of ignorance, I would not so much object as point out that we at least need to distinguish acceptable pedagogies from overly coercive ones, as well as from manipulation and brainwashing.

In short, though there may be senses in which we tolerate persons and their believings, the usual objects of toleration and intolerance are the behaviors and practices resulting from persons' acting on their beliefs.[2] For example, today in most of our societies, debate over freedom of thought is largely debate over freedom of speech.

Not Indifference

John Stuart Mill claimed that intolerance comes naturally to people on things that they care about. In fact, he claimed that intoleration comes so naturally that religious toleration is realized only when "religious indifference . . . has added its weight to the scale."[3] One difficulty with evaluating this claim is that there are many behavioral overlaps between toleration and indifference. If I simply leave you alone to worship as you please, you might not be sure whether I am enduring something I find disagreeable or whether I just do not care about how you worship. In spite of this overlap, Mill does notice the distinction. It may be easier for you to tolerate my strange religious practices when you care only a little about such matters, but if you could not care less about them you are hardly enduring them—you are more likely ignoring them or are merely curious about them. Some philosophers go so far as to say that you cannot be tolerant about something unless you are inclined or tempted not to be[4]; I claim only that you must find it disagreeable, though the degree of discontent can range quite widely—from mild discomfort to shocked abhorrence.

Must the discontent involve some degree of *moral* disapproval? There is debate about this issue. Some writers seem to claim that we *cannot* tolerate actions that we regard as morally wrong,[5] whereas others suggest that toleration applies *only* to matters involving moral disapproval.[6] Perhaps both sides are right, depending on the culture; it has been remarked that the genius of American politics is to treat matters of principle as if they were merely conflicts of interest, whereas the genius of French politics is to treat even conflicts of interests as if they were matters of principle.[7] However, I agree with those who argue that we probably cannot draw a sharp line between what we dislike and what we disapprove[8] and that, in any case, the issue of toleration can arise whenever there is disagreement about any matters regarded as important, be they mores or morals. The point to underscore is that toleration is to be sharply distinguished from indifference. Toleration involves refraining from trying to prevent something that is disagreeable, something that one cares about.

Not Resignation

If we are unable to stop something, it seems a stretch to say that we are tolerating it; we do not tolerate earthquakes, we resign ourselves to their inevitability and to our powerlessness at stopping them. To tolerate something is to refrain from using power in an effort to prevent it; to decide to refrain from using that power, we must believe we have it, that we could do something about preventing what we are instead tolerating. Sometimes we may not have the power to prevent it directly; a single individual cannot do much about people smoking in restaurants. But individuals can work to get laws passed that would mandate others—the police—to use direct power to prevent it. To promote making something illegal is indirect rather than direct intolerance, but it is real intolerance.

Of course, sometimes we may decide that we could prevent something, directly or indirectly, but that the prevention would come at too high a price, as when we decide that wiping out all crime would require something too close to a police state. Hence we begrudgingly tolerate a certain level of wrongdoing. In 1968, NATO decided not to risk nuclear war by militarily intervening when the Soviet Union invaded Czechoslovakia. The Western powers reluctantly decided to tolerate the invasion, given the cost of doing otherwise. One might object to the use of "tolerate" here, since NATO said that the invasion was *intolerable* (as we might say of even a low level of crime), though it quickly added that it would rely on diplomatic opposition rather than military power.

Two questions emerge at this point. First, does it make sense to talk about our putting up with something "intolerable," when we could stop it at a cost we think is too high? We sometimes talk about intolerable pain for the terminally ill, for example, when they in fact endure it, perhaps because illegal mercy killing would come at too high a cost. I think clarity is enhanced by our saying that if we put up with something that we could directly or indirectly prevent, we are tolerating it. When the toleration is due to our decision that intolerance would come at too high a cost (and *risk* of a great harm is a cost), it means only that our toleration is reluctant, that it comes with regret or even guilt feelings, not that it is something other than toleration. There may be good rhetorical reasons for the Western powers to say that the Soviet invasion was "intolerable." But, in my suggested sense of the term, they reluctantly tolerated it; if there was resignation, it was not to helplessness or inevitability but to the wisdom of caution.[9]

The second question is whether we should distinguish levels or types of intolerance. Perhaps rhetorical opposition is a type of intolerance, even when one does not threaten physical force: "One can express one's intolerance in many ways: facial expression, body language, words, laws, economic pressure, imprisonment, torture, mutilation, and death."[10] I claimed earlier that a teacher's words against an ignorant belief should not be thought of as expressing intolerance, but this last quotation shows how widely the term is used. I suppose that when I wrinkle my nose at a political argument from my brother-in-law there are people who would call that intolerance. But the kind that we must focus on in this book is coercive intolerance; my brother-in-law is not even intimidated by my gesture, much less coerced by it.

Coercion is another concept that is used very loosely. We will focus on coercion that involves serious harm, or the threat of it, be it physical, economic, or psychological harm. One reason I think good teaching is tolerant is that it does not involve threats of significant harm,[11] though it certainly can involve psychological pressure. It is difficult to draw the line where pressure becomes coercion, but we can agree on paradigm cases: The power of the police and others who legally are *in authority* is generally coercive, since it is backed up by threats to life and liberty. The power of an advisor or a doctor or a lawyer or anyone who is *an authority* is generally noncoercive when it is not abused. We "follow doctors' orders," not because they have the right to command us, as do the police, but because we think that, given their expertise, their "commands" are right. Should we cease to see them as competent authorities, their orders would carry no weight. The "soft" power of persuasion may generate even more influence than coercive power, but it does not involve the threat of physical or psychological harm. Mill took seriously Alexis de Tocqueville's warning about "the tyranny of the majority" in *Democracy in America*, because he thought that expressions of disdain could easily become morally coercive.[12] Mill's usage may be stretching the term a bit, but probably we have to agree that there are degrees and levels of what we can call intolerance. However, we should be leery about letting all types of opposition be called intolerance. We can admit that some types and degrees of pressure are morally inappropriate without putting them in the same boat with the sort of intolerance that our legal system can enforce, or that the strong can inflict on the weak.

So I think clarity requires that we limit the concept of intolerance to situations where one person or group directly or indirectly coerces another person or group from doing something. The coercion is done *directly* either by physically intervening or by threatening harm; it is done *indirectly* by working to make something impermissible and leaving the direct coercion up to those with the authority for enforcement. The point at which words and gestures become intolerance is the point at which they become coercive, which is context relative and allows for borderline cases. Under this way of understanding things, most cases of using strong moral rhetoric to oppose an action or to try to change another's mind are not coercive and are not examples of intolerance.[13] Surely telling the Soviets in 1968 that they were being bad global citizens by invading Czechoslovakia was not coercive; threatening economic reprisals could be, depending on context; and threatening military action would be, as long as it was credible. The Western powers decided that a credible threat of military action would risk a preemptive nuclear strike, so they held off. Even if Western economic and diplomatic threats showed some degree of intolerance, it seems clear that the Western powers decided against being as intolerant as they could have been.

In summary, toleration and intolerance are matters of degree.[14] There are borderline cases where it is hard to say whether the harm that is threatened is significant enough to make it a coercive threat; a gesture that says, "I will be very disappointed in you" is quite different from one that says, "You will go to jail," and only the context can tell us how much harm is being threatened. In a pluralistic society, the most socially pressing questions of appropriate toleration or intolerance are often questions of whether certain behaviors or practices should be illegal, so the issue can arise whenever we think we *can* make or keep something illegal—say, physician-assisted suicide—but wonder whether we *should*. We are not resigned to its inevitability; instead, we are asking about the justifiability of preventing or allowing it. Of course, in addition to legal toleration, we confront questions of toleration in most of the other organizations prevalent in society. What are the limits on membership in my church? In my Boy Scout troop? Can we tolerate behaviors by members of these organizations that we should not tolerate in their leaders? Obviously, ecclesiastical denominations face such issues. And, of course, similar questions arise in any number of the relationships in which we are involved. Parents, for example, must be intolerant of some behaviors in their children that strangers can and should endure.[15] Sometimes we will be tempted to confuse toleration with resignation. Especially in delicate relationships, we may too quickly decide that something disagreeable is inevitable and then tell ourselves that we are resigned rather than tolerant. In any case, when reacting to disagreeable differences, we should distinguish toleration, including reluctant toleration, from resignation at what cannot be changed.

Neither Timidity nor Arrogance

Sometimes we put up with stuff that we should not tolerate just because we are moral cowards. Or, at least, we are too timid or shy to take a stand against something we should. If we refuse to be intolerant when we see harmful abuses at our place of employment, we should not pat ourselves on the back for being tolerant; we are simply being wimps. Or if we do call it reluctant toleration—the self-interested cost-benefit analysis came out too high—we should at least distinguish it from the principled toleration that is the main subject of this chapter. Prudent people sometimes take refuge in what might correctly be called silent toleration, but that merely shows that toleration strictly defined can be motivated by darker dispositions than our moral virtues.[16]

An interesting debate has emerged about the opposite of confusing toleration with timidity, namely confusing it with arrogance. The 18th-century

Prussian Emperor Frederick the Great was one of the "enlightened despots" who tolerated a variety of religions. Immanuel Kant praised him for rejecting the "haughty label" of "tolerant," because, in Kant's view, Frederick had a moral duty to allow religious freedom, and therefore no moral right to be religiously intolerant.[17] Thomas Paine, in his discussion of the French Revolution and Edmund Burke's rejection of it, made a similar point: "Toleration is not the opposite of Intolerance, but is the counterfeit of it. . . . [O]ne assumes to itself the right of with-holding Liberty of Conscience, and the other of granting it."[18] If Kant and Paine are right, then my explicit decision to be religiously tolerant is like my decision to tolerate your breathing the air; neither of them are something I should even think about interfering with. If kings had no moral right to be religiously intolerant, it would be arrogant and inappropriate for them to tout their toleration. This point is also made by those who worry that toleration is too often the arrogant stance of the powerful toward the powerless, as when a society decides to tolerate interracial marriages, for example.

However, a counter-consideration to Kant and Paine's complaint is that much of the history of the human race is progress in recognizing previously unacknowledged rights. So pioneers in recognizing human rights do make a new—sometimes radical and courageous—judgment about them, and they should be praised for being humble enough to be tolerant in a new way. One need not have a moral right to intervene in order to think about whether to be tolerant; some paradigm cases of toleration are when people have the wisdom to decide that they do not have such a right. We are tolerant when we think we could stop something disagreeable but refrain from doing so, whether out of mere prudence or out of moral principle. People never had the moral right to persecute others for heresy, but we can still tip our hats to those who first recognized this. Perhaps sometimes our tolerance of something that should be none of our business shows an unattractive side of us, but it is toleration nonetheless, and it is more praiseworthy than intolerance toward it.[19]

Not Approval

Toleration is not acceptance in the sense of approval or endorsement. You can tolerate my behavior by accepting my *right* to behave in a certain way without finding that behavior acceptable or agreeing that it is right for me to do it. In contrast, broadminded approval of differences does not endure them; it celebrates them. Also, on the theory that we should hate the sin but love the sinner, you can be very accepting of me as a person while disapproving of what I am doing.[20] So when we merely "put up with" others' *actions*, we need not convey that we are merely enduring their presence or persons. Reined-in contempt is rarely appropriate toward persons, even if it is toward their behavior. *The New Yorker* once printed a cartoon of a man wearing a sandwich board saying, "Put up with thy neighbor."[21] This collapses the distinction between people and their behavior, but it also underscores the point that toleration can vary in tone. On a spectrum, it can range from hostile forbearance to respectful open-mindedness. However, even the latter is not broadminded approval. The latter point prompts some writers to suggest that toleration is an interim value, "serving a period between a past when no one had heard of it and a future when no one will need it."[22] Will the agreeable openness that Western liberalism cultivates toward differences make toleration unnecessary, even offensive? Some authors have suggested that we use "tolerance" to refer to the agreeable acceptance of differences, and reserve "toleration" for enduring the disagreeable, noting that as we become more tolerant in attitude we will need less toleration.[23]

The ambivalence in liberal attitudes toward toleration was underscored for me a few years ago when I served on a "Cultural Diversity Task-force" for the local public schools. Our mandate was to develop a plan "to ensure that all students will have an appreciation for cultural diversity and global interdependence." A strategic planning retreat, which had earlier produced the mandate, provided us with ten basic beliefs, including John Stuart Mill's belief that "diversity enriches society." It became clear that much of the positive attitude toward diversity derived from the "inclusive education" approach that the State of Minnesota emphasizes in all of its school districts. Students should be affirmed rather than discounted because of differences in age, wellness, ability, social and economic class, sex, physical and psychological characteristics, color, race, religion, and so on. Although most of these sorts of differences can be found in even a homogeneous society (so they can hardly be construed as cultural diversity), many of them do involve differences that should be celebrated rather than endured, and not only because of political correctness. Thus, those at the strategic retreat agreed on something like Mill's "diversity enriches society" thesis, and it is not surprising that this attitude was generalized by some educators to almost all differences, including genuine cultural differences. Indeed, the pedagogy with which the teachers on our task force seemed most comfortable stressed the importance of being nonjudgmental when encountering customs that conflict with one's own.

Sometimes "nonjudgmental" simply translated into the wise policy of being very careful about making judgments and very judicious about expressing them. But more often, those who stressed a nonjudgmental attitude wanted students to avoid negative evaluations, and they felt that the best way to teach this was to nurture an open and affirming attitude toward cultural differences. Thus they agreed that "nonjudgmental" really meant "positive-judgmental." It should not be surprising that many parents oppose such pedagogy. One does not have to be a fundamentalist to worry that this is a way to teach empathy by implying that one religion, morality, or practice is as good as any other. If students think that they have no grounds to believe that others are wrong, they might eventually infer that they also have no grounds to think anyone is right.[24] When such relativism gets too closely associated with liberal tolerance and public school pedagogy, one can expect trouble. A better pedagogy is that we cultivate not just the disposition to approve what is acceptable but also the disposition sometimes to endure what one disapproves. Then we can nurture strong convictions about right and wrong—even local loyalties and parochial solidarities—and still avoid dogmatic intolerance by teaching the appropriate role of sometimes tolerating the disagreeable. We should teach toleration precisely because we should teach how to disagree.

For reasons we discussed in the previous chapters, I think that the need for toleration will not go away. Sometimes talking with each other will reveal common ground, but often we will simply become clearer about our disagreements and our lack of prospects for consensus. It is true that "tolerant" is sometimes used to describe a person or a society that gladly accepts differences, but I think clarity is enhanced if we use it simply to describe a person or society that is disposed toward tolerating what is disagreeable. In a pluralistic society this is generally a virtue, though we have noted that a civilized society must be intolerant of many types of harms. And we should not be surprised that sometimes in nonliberal societies tolerance is associated with moral slackness. So I suggest that we use "tolerance" and "tolerant" to refer to the attitude of being disposed toward toleration, and "toleration" to refer to the action or practice of enduring disagreeable behavior and practices by refraining from trying to coercively prevent them. "Intolerance" is the linguistic opposite of both tolerance and toleration ("intoleration" is rarely used), so "intolerant" also does double work.

History of Toleration

The history of toleration in the West, especially religious toleration, is often associated with the history of classical liberalism and its three philosophical saints—John Locke, Immanuel Kant, and John Stuart Mill. This association gives an incomplete view,[25] but the consensus[26] history is as follows. When humans thought that the gods were local and that gods' concerns were provincial, we could worship our gods while allowing and encouraging others to worship their gods. Polytheism was quite compatible with religious toleration or, at least, indifferent to what others worshiped. (Of course, religious differences could still pump up the intensity with which cities and states fought over economic and political issues.) When the Jews thought their god was the most powerful—and jealous—among the gods, they did not expect or even desire others to agree. Even when the most powerful god was revealed as the One Creator God, giving this monotheism universal implications, God's call was directed toward a chosen people. Although priests and prophets debated whether the call was to a *most-favored* nation or to one with *added responsibilities*, the call did not always require intolerance toward other religions (though, again, theology could pump up the intensity of territorial disputes).

Christianity and Islam

However, when God was thought to reveal to Christianity or Islam a universal doctrine of exclusive salvation, mandating them to make disciples of all the nations, unbelief and apostasy took on new and troubling meaning, especially when the coercive power of the state was informed by theological concerns. Here emerges a historical difference between Christianity and Islam. The former was an oft-persecuted minority for its first several hundred years, so it developed an ecclesiastical hierarchy separate from the state, one that invited a division of labor between Caesar and themselves, though there was always room for disagreement about overlapping responsibilities. So the Christian New Testament did not imply anything like an intolerant theocracy; indeed, any later tendencies in that direction came in *spite* of rather than *because* of the church's sacred texts and early history. Islam, on the other hand, did not confront even the question much less the answer of distinguishing church and state, because for several hundred years, at least, separate institutions simply did not exist. As Islam spread its message, it also set up social structures involving tribes and caliphs that appealed to a religious law (Shari'a) that did not distinguish religious, moral, and political responsibilities.[27] And Christianity also began to blur these boundaries after it became the official religion of the Holy Roman Empire.

The question about toleration became one of why we should let pernicious error create confusion and disorder and lead the gullible to perdition. Human rights were seen as matters of what God declares right, and even compassion required us to consider the eternal destiny of those in the wrong or, at least, the souls of those who might get corrupted if we maintained a *laissez faire* attitude toward religious error. Hence, once monotheism became not just universalistic but also expansionistic and exclusivistic, religious intolerance was seen as both pious and reasonable. When the fighting was at the borders, citizens could still thrive at a distance from the infidels, but when religion turned the religious wars upon themselves, as Christianity did with the Reformation, life became uncertain, nasty, and too often short. Even theists who were inclined to be lenient toward unbelievers, on the grounds that they were generally inculpable for their ignorance (they were also useful trading partners), could become brutally intolerant toward apostasy, on the grounds that once one knows the truth, only inexcusable corruption could cause one to reject it.

Locke

Terror and exhaustion, if not prudence, motivated Europe to heed calls like Locke's *Letter Concerning Toleration*,[28] which stressed the irrationality of coercing beliefs that must be voluntary, as well as the rationality of accommodating certain types of religious differences. He argued that what we know about history and human nature shows that toleration is necessary for civil peace.

It is not the diversity of Opinions, (which cannot be avoided) but the refusal of Toleration to those that are of different Opinions, (which might have been Granted) that has produced all the Bustles and Wars, that have been in the Christian World, upon account of Religion. The Heads and Leaders of the Church, moved by Avarice and insatiable desire of Dominion, making use of the immoderate Ambition of Magistrates, and the credulous Superstition of the giddy Multitude, have incensed and animated them against those that dissent from themselves; by preaching unto them, contrary to the Laws of the Gospel and to the Precepts of Charity, That Schismaticks and Hereticks are to be outed of their Possessions, and destroyed.

Locke was not one to celebrate diversity; he merely insisted on the imprudence of not enduring it. Even then he is notorious for not extending toleration to Catholics and atheists, on the grounds that they threatened harm to the state, the former because they pledged highest allegiance to a foreign prince and the latter because they were not motivated to keep their pledges. Anglican and Puritan practices could be tolerated because, although one or the other of them was terribly wrong, they could be endured without undermining civil order. But enduring them was a far cry from appreciating them.

Mill

With Mill's *On Liberty*, a new element was added.[29] Mill did defend toleration of diversity on the prudential ground of its leading to truth and on the moral ground of a utilitarian right to liberty. But, in addition, he supported measures that would *nurture* diversity, not merely endure it. Mill himself may have had a personal taste for the eccentric, but he also argued that everyone should see human diversity as the means for human progress. Thus he listed public opinion, and not just legal coercion, as undesirable constraints on natural human growth. Indeed, he was fond of comparing the use of such traditional constraints to the Chinese practice of foot binding. Not only did normal adults have the moral right to freedom, but encouraging them to pursue diverse visions of the good life was both necessary and sufficient for the ongoing improvement of society.[30] Therefore, as long as people were not allowed to harm each other, society should encourage and not merely allow diversity. It is clear that Mill's liberalism advocates a pluralism whose broadminded *acceptance* of diversity renders toleration (in the sense of enduring the disagreeable) of most cultural differences quite unnecessary.

Justifications: Prudence and Principle

Locke's appeal to the prudence of toleration, however reluctant, was probably the most persuasive justification to an England that had just lived through Cromwell's battles, the beheading of King Charles I, and the Protestant-Catholic uncertainties of the Restoration. England was ready for Locke's pragmatic argument about how to stabilize the peace of the 1688 "Glorious Revolution" of William and Mary. But Locke spent more space in his *Letter* on "the *principal Consideration*," a point of rational (rather than specifically moral) principle, namely that true religion requires "inward persuasion" of the mind, which made "Penalties in this case absolutely impertinent; because they are not proper to convince the mind." The need for "inward Sincerity" made coercion irrational, and not just imprudent: "I may grow rich by an Art that I take not delight in; I may be cured of some Disease by Remedies that I have not Faith in; but I cannot be saved by a Religion that I distrust, and by a worship that I abhor."[31] This argument, interestingly, was also accepted by Catholics such as Thomas Aquinas, Reformers such as John Calvin,[32] and also by the *Qur'an* ("There is no compulsion in religion," 2:256). The problem with this "inward persuasion" argument is that it ignores what we noticed in the previous chapter—that we can have indirect control over our beliefs. This fact provides an opening for effective coercion by controlling what people hear and do so that, quite apart from crude brainwashing, people might eventually see the light. Besides, those using coercion might well be less concerned for the soul of the heretic and more concerned for the souls of those who should be shielded from pernicious error.

If coercion regarding which religious teachings people hear and practice is not always irrational in its aims, then for principled arguments against such coercion that go beyond prudential ones, we need to move to moral and religious grounds. We already noticed that Mill argued on utilitarian grounds that we should respect persons' autonomy, which includes their rights to freedom of speech and worship. Those with a high regard for rights are often leery of utilitarian justifications, since they depend on the very sort of considerations that the prudential arguments use—how to maximize happiness or preference satisfaction. Hence another major philosophical argument for toleration came from Kant's categorical imperative, in particular the version we discussed in the previous chapter: We ought to treat persons as ends in themselves. Treating persons as ends does not mean merely taking into account their interests; we do that with our pets. Moreover, the Inquisition sincerely believed that it was in the interest of heretics to use torture on them so that they could see and say the truth. But persons are the sort of beings that deserve *respect*, Kant thought, and the respect was toward their autonomy, their ability to decide for themselves what they should believe and do. So the principle of respect for autonomy became the main philosophical moral justification for religious toleration.

A theological justification that overlaps respect for autonomy was longer in coming but has the potential to become highly significant, since American popular culture is so much more influenced by religious considerations than philosophical ones.[33] The biblical doctrine of being created in God's image requires Jews and Christians to recognize that every person deserves the sort of love and respect due imagers of God. This doctrine has rightfully been called "the democratizing of the image of God,"[34] since it makes a radical move: The high status that until then in the Middle East had been claimed only by royalty, was now applied to all persons. The implication is that some of the awe we feel toward God we should also feel toward all persons who image God, both as "mirrors" who have some of God's characteristics, such as creativity, and as "representatives" who have the privilege and responsibility to make stewardly decisions about how to live and act in God's world.

Religious believers can argue that this awe toward imagers of God calls for a reverential and diffident love, one that incorporates a "stand-back" element and not just an urge to love, nurture, or value: it "eschews domination"[35] and fans both a reason and a passion for seeing individuals as "exalted" and as ends in themselves.[36] Some religious thinkers argue that this reverence toward the sanctity of persons provides a firmer ground for toleration than do appeals to utility or to a secular notion of universal dignity.[37] Even if liberty is not a religious value in itself, it is such an important aspect of accepting other important values that we must take a "tragic view of liberty" and admit that the theological requirement to grant it to fallen people, while an act of hope, does make a possible way for sin.[38] Normal, adult persons must be addressed as hearers and givers of reasons, not just as followers of orders, even of orders that are in their own interests. This justification for religious toleration from theological principle need not agree with Kantians that autonomy is the highest-ranking norm, but it does provide even socially conservative believers a powerful motivation for not using coercion against what they see as religious error.

A Paradox of Toleration?

So we can take religion very seriously, believe that we are right and others are wrong on matters of great and holy significance, and still tolerate their propagation of error. This point pushes what has been called "the paradox of toleration."[39] If you are sure that something is wrong, you are committed to believing the world would be better off without it. Then it seems you have a moral obligation not to allow it. This inference is what has motivated so much principled intolerance. The resolution of the paradox is that the obligation is a *prima facie* one; you should not allow the offending practice unless there is a stronger moral reason to tolerate it, such as respecting autonomy. Another way to put it is that you are committed to believing the world is better off without the wrong, all other things being equal. But the duty to respect autonomy means that the world would be better off without it only if its absence were assured in the right way. And when it is persons or imagers of God that are doing tolerable wrong, it is worse to coerce them than to endure the wrong.

Does this mean that people have the right to do wrong? Well, we certainly have a legal right to do what we think is wrong, unless it harms the innocent or meets some other criterion that justifies legal intolerance.[40] But do we have a moral right to do what is wrong? It seems contradictory to say we have a moral right to do what we *know* we have no moral right to do. But this truism does not cover most cases of tolerable wrongdoing, because usually people think that they are morally permitted or even obliged to do what *they* think is right but what *others* think is wrong. And for the reasons given above, sometimes the others have the moral (and often the legal) obligation to tolerate what they, but not the agents, believe is wrong.

This point underscores how toleration is logically independent of skepticism. It is true that, usually,[41] if you are quite uncertain that something is wrong, you probably should not try to stop others from doing it. But you can also be very sure that something is wrong, such as certain types of sexual activities, and still believe that you have powerful moral or religious reasons to respect autonomy and therefore to avoid using either direct or indirect coercion to prevent it.[42] Notice that such toleration is very different from refusal to blame and from forgiveness toward the blameworthy. We can be intolerant of the behavior of Christian Scientist parents who, on religious grounds, refuse necessary medical treatment for their children and, at the same time, either refuse to blame them or, if we do blame them, to forgive them. And we might blame and refuse to forgive pornographers while tolerating (within limits) their behavior. Similarly, empathy and sympathy[43] cut across toleration and intolerance. A religiously orthodox physician who is sympathetic with the idea of using scripture to guide important decisions can empathize with the Christian Scientist parents and still seek a court order that overrides their decision.

Cooperation and Compromise

We noticed at the beginning of this chapter that "toleration" is derived from the Latin *tolero*, which primarily connotes "endure" in the sense of "put up with." But some writers claim that a secondary connotation is "bear" in the sense of "sustain."[44] I have objected to suggestions that toleration in some full or deep sense connotes agreement or acceptance, but I believe that we can go beyond toleration and actually cooperate with practices we disagree with. Cooperation helps others carry out disagreeable actions, implying "sustaining," though I still think clarity is enhanced if we do not call it toleration but indicate that it is a sustaining support that goes beyond toleration.[45] It is a stance that says, in effect, "I disagree with you on this matter, but I will help you do what you think is right."[46] And an uncooperative stance says, "My disagreement is such that I refuse to help you do what you think is right." An uncooperative stance can range from passive lack of help, such as that of nurses who refuse to assist during abortions, to active disassociation, such as public resignation. The latter is not necessarily intolerance, which would include steps to interfere coercively with the action or practice. Borderline cases include threatening to resign and thereby publicly expose a disagreeable practice.

As is the case with toleration, sometimes we are too eager to be cooperative. Sometimes we are so quick to please or to avoid controversy that we go along to get along, cooperating with actions we find reprehensible. To avoid taking an uncomfortable stand, we become alienated from our own integrity and complicit in wrongdoing. At the extreme are moral cowards too timid to resist pressure to conform. And there are opportunists who sacrifice whatever principles they have in order to get ahead. All of these will go beyond toleration to cooperate with what they find disagreeable but do so out of the sort of timidity that we distinguished earlier from principled toleration.

Of course, we can also cooperate with the disagreeable out of moral or religious principles or, at least, pragmatic considerations that take into account the general good. *Compromise* is a type of cooperation because one side helps the other achieve part of its aim as long as the other reciprocates. Compromises can be examples of cooperation with the disagreeable, as long as we distinguish compromise from reaching a new viewpoint as a result of consensus-building deliberation. If you and I are initially at loggerheads but then we talk things through and mutually reach a third position that both of us regard as better than our earlier ones, we might be tempted to call that a compromise, or attribute the new agreement to a cooperative attitude, but notice that we no longer have to cope with what is disagreeable. Instead, we have reached common ground, an agreed-on consensus. The sense of compromise I have in mind involves doing something that I would not do except for the opposition of another to what I think is best.

In the winter of 1943, Langdon Gilkey found himself herded with two thousand other foreigners into Shantung Compound, one of the internment camps set up by the Japanese to guard the non-Chinese who were caught by the Japanese invasion of China. The inmates had to set up their own committees and government to handle such survival necessities as assigning housing and preparing food. As the head of the housing committee, Gilkey had to find room in the already overcrowded accommodations for forty newly arrived Belgians. Clearly, the least bad route was to move thirty young bachelors from their rooms into a dorm. The only alternatives were to let the Belgians freeze or to move thirty single women, who tended to be older and much more frail than the men. But the men refused to move, and it was clear that bringing in the Japanese guards to move them forcibly would result in chaos and unacceptable harm. So Gilkey moved the more compliant women. He felt very bad about this, but "[t]o refuse to move the women on idealistic grounds would not have been just; it would merely have resulted in the irresponsible—and much more unjust—political act of leaving the Belgians homeless. In this case, compromise of one's moral principles appeared to me to be morally necessary."[47]

The phrase "compromise one's moral principles" is sometimes ambiguous between allowing immoral considerations to override moral ones, on the one hand, and, on the other, allowing some moral considerations (or, for a value pluralist, legitimate nonmoral ones) to override other moral ones. The former *betrays* moral considerations but the latter *ranks* them. In the above episode, Gilkey did not, for example, let bribes from the men determine his decision; rather, he made a decision that he thought would minimize the injustice. As we noted in the previous chapter, moral pluralists such as principlists believe we

cannot avoid such tough decisions. Notice that even this sort of internal compromise can be seen as a type of cooperation; brute reality insists on our giving
up something that is dear to us, reciprocating only by letting us keep something
even more dear. Gilkey felt bad about his decision because the "moral traces"
of the overridden ideal made him feel like he had "dirty hands" as he tolerated
and cooperated with the immoral refusal of the men, knowing that not doing
so would generate moral dirt to an unacceptably high level of harmful injustice.

In a pluralistic society that requires professional teamwork, it probably is
impossible to avoid occasionally cooperating with decisions that one regards as
wrong. Some of my nursing students told me about instances when they were
ordered to give medicine by injection to patients who, for a variety of good
reasons, should have received it orally, even though the clinical effectiveness
would have been slightly reduced. The orders were given by young interns who
did not know the patients, who went strictly by the numbers, and who were
jealous about their professional authority. The nursing students did explain why
they disagreed with the order, but were told to follow it anyway. The question
they faced was how far to push their reluctance to do what they thought contradicted good medical practice. Since the foreseen harm was relatively small
and reversible, since they were almost as inexperienced as the interns, since a
cooperative team spirit was important for the welfare of everyone, including
future patients, and since an uncooperative stance would jeopardize their professional future, they decided not to pick this battle. Depending on the relative
weights of these considerations, this can be interpreted as the sort of principled
cooperation with the disagreeable that is morally permissible and possibly even
obligatory. But I suppose it could also be interpreted as illustrating the thin line
between principled cooperation and mere timidity or self-interest.

"I'm a man of fixed and unbending principles, the first of which is to be
flexible at all times," Everett Dirksen, United States senator of Illinois, once
famously said.[48] We are not sure whether to applaud or hiss: Compromises
in politics can range from unprincipled calculation of political self-interest,
through pragmatic "splitting the difference" to get as much as one can for one's
vision of the common good, to highly principled cooperation with opponents
out of respect for their vision of the common good. All of these can look like
"flip-flopping" to those unwilling to bend, for whom the best becomes an ob-
stacle to the better. But we have learned that the latter can lead to legislative
stalemate, which itself can have morally harmful consequences. The tough-
est decisions about political compromise involve hot-button issues such as
abortion, stem-cell research, and gay marriage, as well as perennial disputes
such as those over taxes. With respect to gay marriage, for example, agreeing
to allow "civil unions" without calling them marriages can look like spineless
compromise to both sides—to one side because homosexual unions would still
not receive recognition equal to that of heterosexual unions, and to the other
side because recognizing these unions would grant legal benefits to what some
think is sinful abomination. Were one to argue for compromise here, it could

be interpreted as a pragmatic splitting of the difference that nobody celebrates but to which most can grudgingly acquiesce. But it could also be interpreted as the outcome of both sides' recognizing that the conflicting convictions involve reasonable commitments that should be accommodated to avoid threatening important shared values.[49]

Of course, there are some matters on which our integrity forbids compromise or other forms of cooperation, and it may call for intolerance as well. We must weigh the relevant moral duties as well as the morally relevant consequences of the available options, and then make a decision about which consequences we are willing to take responsibility for, given the undesirable circumstances. The weighing need not consist of a utilitarian calculation regarding the balance of pleasure and pain or how to maximize preference satisfaction. Although the moral considerations might involve the latter, they could also involve categorical duties that one feels morally constrained to honor.[50] "Here I stand, I can do no other" is Martin Luther's famous appeal to conscience, and it reminds us of the moral limits on flexibility.[51] But the importance of principled cooperation with some of the views we deny reminds us that we should not confuse having conscientious spine with merely being bull-headed.

Respect

I have urged that toleration and even some types of cooperation be associated with actions and policies that we find disagreeable. And my advocating perspective pluralism in the previous chapter implies that disagreeable actions and policies can be based on positions (or what I called "believings") that we can recognize as reasonable, even if wrong. Hence, in addition to toleration and cooperation, there is a third category, which I call "respect," as in "I disagree with your view but it is one that I respect." This type of respect is not the same as when we say, "I disagree with you but I respect you as a person." Respect for persons can take at least two forms. One is sometimes called "recognition" respect, and is owed to all persons by virtue of their having human rights. The other is sometimes called "appraisal" respect, which is elicited by their notable achievements or high character.[52] Respect for another's position is a type of appraisal respect, elicited by one's evaluation that the position is reasonable.[53] In the previous chapter I favored a somewhat broader notion of "reasonable" than does John Rawls, who seems to build commitment to egalitarianism right into the concept. The category of respect can be used by people who have somewhat different (though likely overlapping) criteria of "reasonable." The point is that we need not commit ourselves to broadminded or indulgent agreement with others' positions in order to be open-minded enough to recognize that positions we think are wrong can be wrong in a reasonable way. We can endorse their justifiability without endorsing their truth.

The criteria that we use—often implicitly—for deciding which positions we can respect are different from those we use to decide which actions and practices we can tolerate. For toleration and cooperation (and their opposites), the considerations are primarily moral ones, especially the morally relevant consequences of the various alternatives available to us. For respecting positions as reasonable, even though we disagree with them, our criteria are largely intellectual, though not without some moral bite as well.[54] Obviously we will also come across positions that we cannot respect, positions that seem silly, inordinately ignorant, unintelligent, depraved, or the product of a corrupted consciousness.[55] Of course, not all silly positions are unattractive; sometimes little irrationalities can be seen as charming idiosyncrasies in persons we love. And to be unable to respect persons' positions does not prevent the entirely different kind of respect for them as persons.[56]

As with toleration of and cooperation with disagreeable actions and practices, respect for disagreeable positions can be a matter of degree, and there may be borderline cases about which we are unsure how to think and feel. Still, in a pluralistic society, it is important to know that one can take a firm stand on controversial issues and yet have a high regard not only for the people with whom we disagree but also for their arguments.[57]

Variations on Civil Disagreement

Given all the sources of possible disagreement among people, we should think carefully about when various combinations of the above attitudes are appropriate. Since our integrity—as well as logical consistency—forbids broadminded approval of all the various positions we will encounter, in our disagreements we must be open-minded enough to ask whether we can respect the disagreeable position and whether we can tolerate or even cooperate with the associated actions or practices. Such open-mindedness[58] is a matter of civility in a pluralistic society, and it enables people of strong conviction and integrity to live together with mutual respect along with their differences.

Six combinations[59] of the above attitudes are possible and, I think, often exemplified in social interaction. First, I could disagree with you but decide that I should tolerate and even cooperate with your decision, which is also based on a position that I respect. It can be both an easy and a pleasant decision to contribute toward your carrying out what you think is a religious duty and what I think is misguided (but not harmful to others). So I contribute to your pilgrimage to Mecca. In other cases this combination can be more difficult, as when I am asked to help you spread the news about what I regard as a wrong but reasonable doctrine.

Second, I could disagree with you and furthermore decide that I should try to stop you from doing something or, at least, try to make it illegal (and certainly not cooperate with it), also thinking that your position is unreasonable. This combination can be easy when it involves the sort of behaviors that are crimes in civilized societies, such as murder or theft. The decision can be more difficult when it involves personal matters, such as when a friend asks you not to report the cheating that you noticed.

If the only combinations were the above two, life would be less complicated, which is perhaps why some people act as if all disagreements are either benign or nasty. But more complex situations call for more nuanced combinations. A third type of case is when I decide that your position is one that I disagree with but respect and, on the one hand, I will not interfere with it but, on the other, I will not cooperate with it either. Our earlier example of a nurse who tolerates but refuses to participate in abortions can illustrate this combination, assuming that she believes that there is a reasonable, albeit wrong, case to be made for having the abortion. If she believes there is no such case to be made, believes in fact that, while abortion is not murder, she is uncertain whether it is justified, then her stance may illustrate a fourth combination: I cannot respect your position as reasonable, and I will not help you carry out your decision, but I will not try to stop you either. Conscientious objectors to violence could illustrate either of these combinations, as could those of us who do not try coercively to prevent others from satisfying some addiction while refusing to be active enablers. As noted before, I specify "coercively prevent" because, given the earlier definitions of toleration and intolerance, one can argue vigorously against the wisdom of a behavior while tolerating it. Also, whether one can tolerate behavior that one cannot cooperate with may depend on role responsibilities: Parents must be more tolerant of some and less tolerant of other behaviors from their children than must others, and professionals must be intolerant of colleagues' gossiping or deceiving their clients, even when the same gossip or deception might be tolerable among those without the special role responsibilities. Professional ethics sometimes calls for strict, legally enforceable, whistle-blowing duties where common moral sense calls at most for persuasion.

A fifth combination involves allowing and even helping with behavior that is based on a position one regards as unreasonable. Sometimes friendship or other types of solidarity permit one to go along with silliness that is not harmful. Certainly parents must sometimes help children—and teachers help students—make their own mistakes even as part of an educational agenda. And, quite apart from an agenda, parents who refuse to take their kids to see "wasteful" fireworks should perhaps lighten up. When disagreement is civil, the fact that one thinks a view is dumb, ignorant, or greedy does not automatically settle how one should respond to it.

The sixth and final combination is one that may seem counterintuitive at first. Should we sometimes be intolerant of—and thereby uncooperative with—actions and practices that we agree are based on a position we respect?[60] Yes, as illustrated by our earlier example of parents who, on religious grounds, avoid giving their children medically indicated treatment. A religiously devout physician who appreciates using scripture to help make important decisions can respect as reasonable the decision of Jehovah's Witness parents to forbid a blood transfusion for their small child who may need one during a life-saving operation. But the physician will regard the decision as not only wrong from her own perspective, she also will decide that she should not tolerate, much less cooperate with, the parents' decision, even though it validly flows from a reasonable perspective. Instead, she should get a court order that makes the child a temporary ward of the state, and override the parents' decision. Similarly, prolife advocates can respect the view of at least some prochoice opponents, recognizing that some reasonable people do not share their religious or philosophical grounds for believing that the rights of personhood begin at conception. But, given the amount and type of harm they believe a prochoice policy would involve, they may try to make such a policy illegal, which is indirect intolerance.[61] A similar point could be made about prochoice advocates and, for that matter, for advocates on both sides of any number of hot-button social issues, such as euthanasia and gay rights. Indeed, the civility of national debates could be greatly enhanced without reducing the strength of advocacy if people would explicitly recognize that others can be thought wrong without being thought unreasonable. We should recognize that principled intolerance can be combined with principled respect, not only for one's opponents as persons, but for their positions as well.

One of the most troublesome issues in a pluralistic society has to do with whether hotly disputed practices should be *legally* tolerated or not. Also, in a pluralistic society, what are the implications of civil disagreement for groups that sharply and deeply dissent from popular consensus or majority decisions? To these issues we now turn.

Notes

1. For the claim that truth is intolerant of error, see Nasr, "Metaphysical Roots of Tolerance and Intolerance, 43–56: "Truth remains always intolerant of falsehood and good of evil" (44). In the same book, Barker, in "Socratic Intolerance and Aristotelian Toleration" (246–55), does not hesitate to talk about Socrates' opposition to mistaken ethical conceptions as "philosophic intolerance" (254), illustrating how broadly the term is sometimes used. Even when we restrict ourselves to verbal efforts at persuading others to change their minds, we find a wide spectrum from sweetly reasonable arguments on one end, through rhetorical appeals in the middle, to abusive browbeating on the other end. Although it is difficult to draw sharp lines here, it is implausible to put the entire spectrum into the category of coercive intolerance. One of the few recent dissenters from my view is Erlewine, whose *Monotheism and Tolerance* argues that bearing witness is not tolerant because it seeks the conversion of the other (132).

2. Toleration can probably also apply to mere physical movements of humans or, for that matter, of animals; I see no reason to think of it as applicable only to freely chosen actions.

3. Mill, *On Liberty*, 8. First published in 1859.

4. Raz, *The Morality of Freedom*, 403.

5. Midgley, *Can't We Make Moral Judgements?*, 70.

6. Raphael, "The Intolerable," 137–53.

7. Wolff, *A Critique of Pure Tolerance*, 21. This observation was made before our politics became so polarized (by confusing interests and principles) that compromise is rare.

8. Warnock, "The Limits of Toleration," 123–39. One can *dislike* something, such as making puns, without implying that it is anything other than a matter of taste. But to *disapprove* of something, such as eating meat, suggests a moral objection. The phenomenon of "guilty pleasures" suggests that we can sometimes like things we disapprove of, which in a backhanded way underscores the distinction. That toleration implies disagreement is widely accepted in the literature; a recent dissent is from Dees, who in *Trust and Toleration* claims that toleration is about accepting a way of life different from one's own even if you approve of it (5–6). I think it is helpful in a pluralistic world of conflicts to have a word that connotes the enduring of the disagreeable.

9. Oberdiek, in his helpful book *Tolerance,* disagrees with me somewhat about the role of cost-benefit analyses in toleration. He thinks there is a sense of "put up with" that should not be called toleration, namely, when the risks associated with physical interventions are too high (66). He also thinks that cautious cost-benefit analysis, like cowardice, is only "a pale imitation of toleration" (95). I agree with Oberdiek that sometimes overly cautious cost-counting can come close to cowardice, but I think that when it is done wisely it can give good reasons for real, albeit reluctant, toleration.

10. Oberdiek, *Tolerance,* 53, argues against limiting intolerance to coercive interventions. I suspect that Oberdiek means to suggest that words, and not just physical intervention, can be coercive.

11. I admit that power relationships are such that teaching in a context in which the need for a positive evaluation can become intimidating to the point of coercion. (In fact, when I did a survey, many of my students said that college teaching involves coercion, especially when grades are involved, though they added that it was justified coercion.) Also, we cannot draw a sharp moral line between threats and offers, or between coercion and exploitation. Coercion is usually defined as involving the narrowing down of another's options in an unfavorable way; if I threaten to harm you if you do not hand over your billfold, you do have a choice, but it is a coerced one. If you need something from me and I exploit your vulnerability by making you an offer that would be unacceptable apart from your vulnerability, I am increasing rather than decreasing your options; so it is not coercion but it may be as morally unacceptable.

12. Mill, *On Liberty*, 4.

13. "Mutual persuasion is essential to democratic politics. . . . [W] must respect one another's autonomy by being willing to reason with one another about what we ought to do," Richardson, *Democratic Autonomy*, 90. Richardson insists that openness to being persuaded is what distinguishes respectful persuasion from coercive demagoguery. In chapter one, I distinguished using argument to persuade from using it for mutual inquiry. Richardson, in effect, insists that inquiry be part of democratic persuasion. I think there can be issues on which you merely want to persuade, your mind having been made up, and you still respect the autonomy of the other (and avoid coercive intolerance) if you appeal primarily to the other's reason or, insofar as you make an emotional appeal, you avoid mere manipulation. Sharp lines cannot be drawn here.

14. Obviously, there is a sense in which you either tolerate something or do not. But there is just as obviously a sense in which the type and amount of coercion you use are matters of degree. Threatening to badmouth me is less coercive than threatening to shoot me, and threatening to hit me is somewhere in between.

15. "Contempt travels easily under the mask of tolerance. To accept the unacceptable is to tell a child that nothing about him matters." Budziszewski, *True Tolerance*, 272.

16. "Silent toleration" can also be a form of "freeloading," as when one sees that others' intolerance makes one's own as superfluous as it is unpleasant. If you are already successfully taming a loud bully, I may decide not to stick my neck out, which might be as cowardly as allowing him free rein. Might *tolerance*, defined (as I do later) as the *disposition toward toleration*, include the connotation of being a virtue? Paul Weithman claims that "tolerance is a virtue which demands personal integrity. . . . If I refuse to stand up and be counted for the side to which I secretly incline . . . I have engaged in a form of moral draft-dodging" (in a review of T. M. Scanlon's "The Difficulty of Tolerance," *Ethics* 114 [2004]: 838). I believe that tolerance is a moral virtue when it is motivated by moral principle, which is the sort of tolerance and toleration this chapter commends. But toleration can be motivated by prudence and, in a shy person, or one who hates to make a fuss, prudence can come close to timidity. Though I distinguish the latter from toleration, I think clarity is best achieved with a fairly neutral definition of tolerance and toleration, along with the recognition that it can be appropriate or inappropriate, depending on circumstances. But we should remember that sometimes the terms are used in a more morally loaded way. In "What Toleration Is," Cohen argues that toleration requires a "good" reason (68–95), giving as a negative example the parents who are merely "permissive" rather than "tolerant" toward their child's smoking (80). I am inclined to say that overly indulgent parents are inappropriately tolerant.

17. Kant, "What Is Enlightenment?," 5. First published in 1784.

18. Paine, *Rights of Man*, 55. First published in 1791.

19. The element of truth in Kant and Paine's point about the arrogance of toleration is that sometimes we should not be proud when we are tolerant of things we should accept in the first place. For people with racist tendencies to decide to tolerate racial harmony is better than some of the alternatives, but it still says something unattractive about them. See Horton, "Toleration as a Virtue," 34.

20. Admittedly there are limits to how much you can disapprove of my behavior while embracing me as a person, because we cannot draw a sharp line between what we are and what we do. But anybody who has raised children knows the importance of the distinction. The fuzziness of the boundaries is sometimes used by multiculturalists to insist on the sort of recognition and approval of differences that would make toleration itself disagreeable. As I argued earlier, one can celebrate all kinds of cultural differences while merely tolerating—or sometimes not tolerating—others.

21. Cited by Oberdiek, *Tolerance*, 28. Oberdiek here distinguishes among bare toleration (put up with thy neighbor), mere toleration (live and let live—what I will call prudential toleration), and full tolerance (what I will call principled toleration).

22. Williams, "Toleration: An Impossible Virtue?," 18–27.

23. Fotion and Elfstrom, *Toleration*, 124. This "affirmation" sense of tolerance is in the spirit of the 1995 United Nations *Declaration of the Principles on Tolerance*: "Tolerance is respect, acceptance and appreciation of the rich diversity of our world's

cultures, our forms of expression and ways of being human." Anna Elisabetta Galeotti also calls for "a semantic extension from the negative meaning of non-interference to the positive sense of acceptance and recognition." Galeotti, *Tolerance as Recognition*, 10. What she says about "recognition" overlaps what I call "respect" for a view one disagrees with. There is, I concede, a use of "tolerance" that connotes something closer to acceptance than to endurance: "I have a high tolerance for bad puns" probably suggests that I *enjoy* them more than *endure* them. It is in this sense of tolerance that the more tolerance we have, the less toleration we need. The more I accept something, the less reason I have to raise the question whether I should accept the right of others to practice it; that is, the less reason I have to ask whether I should endure it. Obviously, this "acceptance" sense of tolerance is very different from, even the opposite of, tolerance as a trait that disposes one toward toleration. Those with a high tolerance for ambiguity will be disposed simply to admit the former sense and focus on the latter.

24. Gardner, "Propositional Attitudes and Multicultural Education," 72–76. One might try to cope with parental worries about relativism by asserting that "the child's right to an education must be seen as more fundamental than the parents' right to transmit their view of the world" and that "those cultural groups that see children merely as means of perpetuating their culture and not as ends in themselves must be seen as morally flawed," as do Kach and DeFaveri in "What Every Teacher Should Know about Multiculturalism" (quoted by Dwight Boyd in "The Moral Part of Pluralism.") But, whatever one thinks of this hard-line Kantianism, its frank rejection of communitarian values in favor of individualism can hardly serve as an argument for being nonjudgmental.

25. See Laursen, *Religious Toleration,* for essays discussing toleration in various parts of the world from ancient times. It is true that only lately (usually in countries influenced by liberalism) does religious toleration involve full freedom of religion. The Ottoman Empire, for example, allowed Christians and Jews their own "millets" where they could run their own religious affairs, but this toleration involved only certain religions and it came with a number of restrictions and impositions. Paul Seabright's *Company of Strangers* traces liberalism and its toleration back to the agricultural revolution, when humans first had to "get along with" strangers outside the hunting-gathering tribe.

26. See, for example, Rawls, *Political Liberalism*, xxi–xxv; Fotion and Elfstrom, *Toleration*, 75–80; and Mendus, *Toleration and the Limits of Pluralism*, 22–68.

27. Little, Kelsay, and Sachedina, *Human Rights and the Conflict of Cultures*, 85.

28. Locke, *A Letter Concerning Toleration*, first published in 1689. My comments refer to pages 27, 44, and 50–51. The quotation is from page 55. Locke wrote three additional letters on toleration, in which he buttressed his "irrationality" argument with others that support the unjustifiability of intolerance. But an earlier letter to Henry Stubbe (1661) argued *against* religious toleration on the grounds that it is impractical because it would lead to civil unrest. Obviously, Locke allowed experience to change his mind.

29. My comments refer to pages 9, 11, 50, and 54–71.

30. Mill thought that encouraging diversity was *necessary* for progress because only by exposure to diversity could one escape the confines of tradition (54). He thought diversity was *sufficient* for progress because he believed in the perfectibility of humans—that they would, in the long run, choose the better options (60–61, 67).

Edwards, in "Toleration and Mill's Liberty of Thought and Discussion," (94), and Megone, in "Truth, the Autonomous Individual, and Toleration," (140), note that there is a tension in Mill between his celebration of diversity and his belief that, as society is challenged by diversity, it will move toward the truth and thereby toward conformity of belief. I suspect Mill thought that conformity on matters of truth was compatible with diversity in lifestyles and that the latter would always be necessary and sufficient to nurture the best in human nature.

31. Locke, *Letter Concerning Toleration*, 38. The previous quotations are from page 27. When Christians of Locke's time tried to justify coercion of belief, they would appeal to Luke 14:23, "Go out into the roads and lanes, and compel people to come in, so that my house may be filled." Locke could have noted that this is from a passage that gives several "hard sayings" about the cost of discipleship, including the much-debated verse 26: "Whoever comes to me and does not hate father and mother, wife and children, brothers and sisters, yes, and even life itself, cannot be my disciple."

32. Little, Kelsay, and Sachedina, *Human Rights*, 15–20.

33. That Americans are much more influenced by religion than philosophy is obvious to anyone who attends to our political and cultural debates, and is a point made by a philosopher, Rescher, in "American Philosophy Today," 734.

34. Shanks's "Democratizing the Image of God," 2, provides references to biblical scholars who claim that the Hebrews were the first to assert that the "Image of God" applied to all persons, not just to royalty.

35. Stith, "Toward Freedom from Value," 6.

36. Tinder, *The Political Meaning of Christianity*, 35–36. Nicholas Wolterstorff notes that the *free and equal* doctrine of liberalism has its roots in 17th-century Protestantism; in "Why We Should Reject What Liberalism Tells us about Speaking and Acting in Public for Religious Reasons," *Religion and Contemporary Liberalism*, ed. Weithman, 162–81, at 168.

37. Tinder, *Tolerance*, 114. Some theists agree that basing recognition respect on the doctrine of being created in God's image is a firmer foundation than secular appeals to human dignity, but worry about this foundation because the capacities that persons have by virtue of imaging God vary so much in humans. Adults with dementia as well as normal babies, for example, do not have these capacities to any extent higher than do many animals. So Wolterstorff in *Justice: Rights and Wrongs* argues that a firmer grounding for recognizing rights against unjustified coercion is the "bestowed worth" that all humans have by virtue of being loved by God. This difference in theological grounding does not change the theistic insistence on religious toleration.

38. Tinder, *Political Meaning*, 102–16.

39. Mendus, *Toleration and the Limits of Pluralism*, 18. Actually, there are two issues that are often called the paradox of toleration, the other one being the question of tolerating intolerance. Clearly there are limits to the latter, as when we arrest people who physically block abortion clinics (or, at the extreme, try to kill abortion providers), even when we recognize that they have their reasons.

40. Mill famously restricted legal coercion to the harm principle: No one may cause harm to the innocent. There are many questions that emerge about the meaning and degree of harm, and Mill sometimes says things that look like an endorsement of at least the first of these following common justifications for legal coercion: to prevent offense; to prevent harm to self or to benefit self (legal paternalism); to prevent severe immorality (legal moralism); and to benefit others (welfare principle).

Reflection on laws against public nudity, seat-belt laws, laws governing pornography, mandatory social security, and taxation for parks and Medicaid shows that the harm principle probably is not the only criterion for justified legal intolerance. The issue of how a civil society should decide matters of legal intolerance is the subject of the next chapter.

41. When claiming that uncertainty can be a reason for toleration, the qualification "usually" is necessary because we may be uncertain about whether something is harmful but recognize that the risks of great and irreversible harms in tolerating it outweigh the costs (in money or freedom) of preventing it. Consider our earlier example of whether we should take regulatory steps to stop global warming.

42. Graham, "Tolerance, Pluralism, and Relativism," 44–59, argues that tolerance comports *better* with objectivism than with skepticism or relativism. In fact, Lord Patrick Devlin gave an argument for concluding that, in principle, intolerance is appropriate toward whatever society abhors, and he assumed a subjectivist ethics that is skeptical about moral truth. His claim is that when society cannot rely on something other than strong feelings to maintain consensus on morality, it may protect its character by using coercion against sin and immorality. Devlin does say that there are many practical objections to legal intolerance toward sin, objections that often override the argument for intolerance. See Devlin, *The Enforcement of Morals*, 1–25.

43. By empathy I mean either cognitive ("I know what you are feeling") or affective ("I feel what you are feeling") sharing of feelings. By sympathy I mean feeling the compassion to help another.

44. Little and Chidester, "Rethinking Religious Toleration," 3–30, at 10.

45. I agree with the substance of what Oberdiek, *Tolerance*, 132–34, and others say about supporting and sustaining those tolerated, but I think that clarity suggests it be called cooperation rather than toleration.

46. Of course, one can also cooperate with decisions and practices one agrees with, so this definition assumes a context of disagreement. For that matter, one can cooperate with actions one does not tolerate, as when one is resigned to the inevitability of something (so is not *choosing* to endure it) and decides to engage in behavior that helps carry it out. Prisoners condemned to execution generally do not choose to endure their dying, but may for a variety of reasons choose to cooperate with the executioner. "Stance" may connote both the cooperative behavior and the cooperative attitude that disposes one toward it. We noticed earlier in this chapter that tolerance is sometimes defined as a virtue, being identified with what I call principled tolerance. Similarly, cooperation sometimes is identified with principled cooperation. Rawls, *Political Liberalism*, 16, for example, sees in it a commitment to fairness. As with tolerance, I think it is best defined in a neutral way, agreeing that it can be motivated by goodness or by greed.

47. Gilkey, *Shantung Compound*, 122.

48. Quoted in *Law and Politics* (August/September 2004): 15.

49. There can be borderline cases between reaching a new consensus and reaching a true compromise. In *Democratic Autonomy*, Henry Richardson cites the following "gay rights" debate regarding civil unions (in a state legislature) as an example of what he calls "deep compromise": "[S]ome of the legislators initially opposed to gay rights ended up voting for the compromise because their concern or respect for members of the other side led them to take more seriously their opponents'

arguments about the importance of homosexual persons obtaining equal respect. Instead of continuing to regard state recognition of any kind as a position to be opposed for its own sake (as wrong), these swing legislators came to see it as an acceptable means to expressing and promoting respect for homosexuals" (148). In context, Richardson makes it clear that these swing legislators did not come to a new opinion about the acceptability of homosexual behavior; that would not be compromise but a change of mind on the substance of the issue. Rather, they decided that, given gay (disagreeable) views about sex and marriage, and given the discrimination they received because of these views, the compromise was necessary to protect their status as legally and morally equal persons. Presumably, if the latter could be protected without the legal recognition of their unions, the swing legislators would have considered other options. Still, one might claim that the swing legislators did reach a new consensus on the issue of legal recognition of gay civil unions or, at least, that this is a borderline case. A number of important examples of political compromise are perceptively analyzed in Dobel's *Compromise and Political Action*.

50. Implicit here is a debate between utilitarians and others over whether we are as responsible for the consequences we foresee and allow when we intentionally refrain from an action as we are for the consequences that we actively cause. In the literature on ethics, two examples of this dispute have become famous. In the "Jim in the jungle" example, a warlord captures Jim and threatens to kill the twenty natives who are lined up, unless Jim kills one of them himself, in which case the other nineteen will be freed along with Jim. In the "trolley dilemma," you are asked whether, as driver of a trolley that has lost its brakes, you should steer onto a track that has just one workman who will be killed, or allow the trolley to continue on the track that has five workmen who will be killed. Of course, there are variations on these (and other) examples. Without settling the substantive moral issues involved, we might agree that one can allow duty and personal integrity to count in the balance as well as external consequences.

51. When Luther said he could "do no other," we realize that there were several other things he could do, such as recant. But he meant that he could do no other while maintaining his moral integrity and his spiritual identity.

52. See Darwall, "Two Kinds of Respect," 36–49.

53. Charles Larmore distinguishes *appraisal respect* for another's views from *sympathy* for them. The latter involves the belief that, in the other's situation, we would share the beliefs, whereas respect for the other's views connotes only that we think they are justified from the other's perspective without implying that we would share them if we were in the other's situation. See Larmore, *Patterns of Moral Complexity*, 62–63. As I claimed earlier, one can agree that a belief is justified *to* another (as is paranoia to a paranoid) without agreeing that it is justified *for* another. My notion of respect for another's position involves the view both that the position is reasonable from the other's perspective and that the other's perspective is one that can be held reasonably, even if it is thought to be wrong.

54. In the previous chapter I mentioned that our judging a view as reasonable involves commonsense criteria such as consistency, clarity, comprehensiveness, practicability, and plausibility given (at least some of) our other well-established beliefs. As Rawls insisted, the well-established beliefs that we use to decide the plausibility of other beliefs likely include some moral beliefs about reciprocity, rights, and moral

status, though obviously perspective pluralists cannot insist that "reasonable" views be consistent with *all* of the moral beliefs that they think are well established. I doubt that "reasonable" should entail the sort of strong egalitarianism that Rawls seems to include in it; what I see as respectable hierarchical views can assert basic human rights for all while insisting, for example, that the king of Thailand has a higher moral status than ordinary citizens. I claimed that "seems reasonable to me," and by extension, "a position I can respect," apply primarily not to beliefs or believers but believings, which involves less the content of the belief and more the way the believer came to hold it or continues to hold it. I use the terms "a position" and "a view" interchangeably with "a believing."

55. Sometimes people who are otherwise decent seem to have been raised in a way that infects them with moral blindness on a particular issue; for example, certain slave owners in the antebellum South (or, for that matter, Mark Twain's Huck Finn) or Nazi racists. The term "corrupted consciousness" can be applied to them, though not, of course, from their own understanding of their perspective. Obviously, this category must be used carefully or disagreements quickly degenerate into sheer name-calling. Notice that I could *sympathize* (in Larmore's sense described in note 53) with a racist's view (I could imagine myself being raised with the same false consciousness) without *respecting* it.

56. In terms of our earlier distinction, low appraisal respect for persons' views is compatible with recognition respect of their rights as persons. Indeed, low appraisal respect for a few of a person's views is compatible with high appraisal respect for her character as a whole, though it is hard to imagine how one could detest most of what another thinks and still have a high regard for her character (as opposed to respect for her rights, which may remain strong).

57. Assuming that you should follow your conscience when it is reasonable, respect should be interpreted as what has been called "moral nondogmatism." This is the view that if I believe your position is reasonable, then I should agree that you ought to try to do what you think is right, even after I have unsuccessfully tried to convince you that you are wrong. Moral nondogmatism has been rejected by Almond in her *Moral Concerns*, 159, because it seems to contradict what she (correctly, in my view) sees as the central moral doctrine of universalizability. When we make a *moral* judgment, we universalize it in the sense that we agree that anyone who is in a relevantly similar situation is permitted or obliged to do what we think we are permitted or obliged to do. This refusal to make an exception for oneself is thought by many to be what distinguishes morality from prudence, matters of taste, and other types of judgments. But if respect is interpreted as moral nondogmatism, then when I respectfully disagree with your position I seem to say both that if I were in your position I would not do what you think is right and also that you ought to try to do what you think is right. So if I respect your decision and I also universalize my moral judgment about what I should not do, I seem to say both that you should and that you should not try to do what you think is right.

I believe that the above argument is unsound for the same reason that universalizability does not entail specific universal obligations. People are often in relevantly different situations, so universalizability does not entail that they have the same specific obligations. And your having a different but reasonable position from mine will often put us in relevantly different moral situations. Of course, if having any sort of different beliefs would put us in relevantly different moral situations, universalizability would be trivialized. Saddam Hussein would have had different obligations toward the Kurds just because he believed they did not have moral rights. But respect applies only to reasonable believings, so it implies only that different reasonable believings can put us in relevantly different moral situations. Therefore I think that the nondogmatic interpretation of respect is consistent with universalizability and that it can enable us to honor the consciences of those with whom we disagree, even when we feel obliged to oppose them.

58. By "open-minded" some writers mean "undecided" or, in Peter Gardner's words, "that state of mind where, although aware of [a position], in the sense of having entertained it, we neither believe it nor disbelieve it" (Gardner, "Propositional Attitudes and Multicultural Education," 69). This usage at least distinguishes it from broadminded acceptance, but it does mean that we cannot be open-minded about positions with which we disagree. I cannot legislate usage, of course, but I think it is important to recognize that believing someone is wrong is only the first step in deciding how to cope civilly with the disagreement. I think "close-minded" connotes to many people the attitude of "You are wrong; end of discussion." But disagreement should be just the beginning of the discussion, and I think that "open-minded," in distinction from either uncertainty or broadminded approval, connotes the willingness to consider the appropriateness of various combinations of respect, toleration, cooperation, and their opposites. Gardner's narrower notion of open-minded is consistent with skepticism and ambivalence; but I argue that open-mindedness is consistent with commitment and decisiveness. I grant that the term "open-minded" is associated with "broadminded" or even "empty-minded" by some people, so they may want to use a different term to refer to what I call open-mindedness, perhaps a term like "courteous" or "civil."

59. Since six attitudes are discussed (toleration, cooperation, respect, and their oppositions), one might expect eight possible combinations. However, I think that any combination that involves intolerance and cooperation is impossible, although I noted earlier that one can cooperate with an action that one happens not to tolerate. (The case involved lack of toleration due to resignation at the inevitable; whether to endure it was not one's choice.) But when one chooses to be intolerant, one cannot simultaneously choose to cooperate with the same action. Of course, one could combine cooperation and intolerance in a series of actions, as when a former Minneapolis police chief would give his wife a ride to a missile guidance facility and then arrest her and her friends when they illegally blocked the driveway in protest against nuclear arms buildup. As a husband, he cooperated with her getting to the site; as a police chief he was intolerant of her blocking the driveway. That a person fulfills a number of roles can make things complicated, but even in two roles one cannot do something contradictory with respect to the identical action. Related to this point are three more. Within limits, a professional can personally disapprove of a policy while having good reasons to enforce it in his role as a professional, though he may also have the responsibility to try to change the policy. Also, one could tolerate a given *action* without tolerating a *practice* of similar actions. The details of a given situation—the character of the agent, the extremity of consequences—may make an action tolerable or even approvable in that particular case, but it may be too dangerous to allow everyone in that type of situation to do it and too difficult to define explicitly the criteria of acceptable versus unacceptable instances. Thus one might oppose a policy of mercy killing while hoping that a wise

physician might violate it on certain occasions. Of course, if one endorses a legal policy that is intolerant of a type of action, one cannot ignore the consequent moral and prudential considerations against tolerating or cooperating with a particular instance of the illegal practice. Finally, a professional code may allow or require a type of action, but in a given instance a professional may have good reasons to violate or, at least, go beyond the code. What is sometimes labeled "adversary equipose" or "the division of moral labor" is the view of some that the *profession* writes the rules based on the general good, and the *individual professional*, a defense lawyer, say, is thereby mandated to try to acquit a defendant known to be guilty. But there are limits, as Applbaum says in *Ethics for Adversaries*, a book that explores such professional dilemmas: "So what justifies making a rule that in general leads to good social outcomes or in general neutralizes bad outcomes does not by itself justify complying with the rule" (99). Professional practices in a complex and pluralistic society provide complications regarding tolerance and cooperation that we cannot explore here.

60. Given what I said about "moral nondogmatism" in note 57 of this chapter, combining respect and intolerance amounts to saying, "I think you should try to do what you think is right, even though I think I should try directly or indirectly to prevent you from doing it, using coercion when necessary." This strikes some as an incoherent attitude, but notice that it is not unlike the attitude that two friendly competitors have during a game. Of course, in real life the stakes can be much higher. But they are much higher for *both* sides, which is why we need a carefully nuanced understanding of intolerance and respect. Rawls is sometimes interpreted as requiring toleration for actions based on reasonable comprehensive doctrines, which are outlooks that incorporate egalitarianism (Rawls, *Political Liberalism*, 50, 61), but the attitude of respect uses a broader notion of reasonable, and can apply to positions one respectfully refuses to tolerate.

61. Whether they could be justified in being directly intolerant, blocking abortion clinics, for example, is a legitimate question that we cannot pursue here. Of course, even if they could be justified in doing that, others might be justified in being intolerant of that instance of intolerance. Whether there are any moral restrictions on the types of arguments they use for indirect intolerance (trying to make abortions illegal) is discussed in the next chapter. If you think that the combination of intolerance and respect is perhaps theoretically possible but psychologically impossible on life-and-death issues such as abortion, consider these words from Robert George, one of the most forceful opponents of prochoice advocates: "I am not maintaining (nor do I wish to be thought to maintain) that liberal political theorists who abet the culture of death are moral monsters. They are not Nazis or hatemongers. They are our colleagues and very often our friends. Many of them are doing their level best to think through the moral issues at the heart of our cultural struggle and arrive at conclusions that are right and just" (George, *The Clash of Orthodoxies*, 40). These words are quoted approvingly by the late Neuhaus, another vigorous opponent of legalized abortion, in "One Little Word."

CHAPTER FOUR

Laws and Dissenters

Much of what has been discussed so far applies primarily to disagreements and conflicts between individuals in their personal interactions. I have offered a conceptual framework that I hope helps us think through appropriate ways to respond when we have differences on issues that are important to us. For example, we can recognize positions that we can respect, even if we disagree, and then we can raise the question of toleration or cooperation as separate issues. We can distinguish toleration from any number of related and sometimes contradictory concepts. In discussing intolerance, I have noted that we should distinguish direct intolerance, as when a parent personally prevents a child from smoking, and indirect intolerance, as when a citizen supports laws against smoking. In the latter case, the coercion is not directly applied by citizens; rather, they endorse the use of coercion by those who enforce the laws. For example, the issue of which euthanasia practices are tolerable or intolerable often involves political decisions about which laws an individual should favor, and so they are decisions about indirect intolerance. The toleration practiced by persons in their daily interactions is sometimes called *social* toleration, and that practiced by institutions such as governments is sometimes called *political* toleration.[1] In a democracy, political intolerance involves decisions by a majority of citizens to be indirectly intolerant of particular actions and practices. This chapter focuses on the issues involved in such decisions.

One of the most difficult problems a pluralistic society faces is that of legislating on value-laden issues; these often are hotly controversial issues about which the differences are wide and deep and the passions run high. This is the first of two main issues we will discuss in this chapter. The second one derives from the fact that in a pluralistic society we will inevitably find groups whose sense of identity leads them to reject consensus values, including the value or interpretations that most of us give to individual freedom and equality, and who ask to be left alone to live and raise their children in ways that force us to think hard about toleration of differences. Can our discussion of civil disagreement provide guidelines for thinking through these tough issues?

Civil Disagreement about Legislating Laws

At least four factors converge to heighten both the difficulty and the importance of disagreement within a pluralistic nation-state such as the United States. First, the legal power of a state is generally immense, highly coercive (traditionally and evocatively called "the sword power of the state"), and, within its sphere, the final court of appeal. Second, rarely is citizenship a completely voluntary agreement, since relatively few people have the opportunity to change citizenship and, even when they do, the choices are usually quite limited; citizens are typically born into a state and generally they avoid its legal authority only at death. Third, a pluralistic state will include many conflicting decisions about what the laws should be and how to enforce them, decisions that can greatly affect the quality of citizens' lives. Fourth, included within the diversity are conflicting religious and moral convictions that are central to persons' identities and to the commitments that give their lives meaning, structure, and fulfillment. These four factors have motivated much of the debate over what is meant by liberalism and by democracy, as well as the debate over how they are related to each other and to pluralism. A brief summary of these debates will set the stage for examining the disagreements about legislating on controversial issues.

Liberalisms: Classical, Comprehensive, and Political

What is often called *classical* liberalism is the insistence on individuals' rights, usually in opposition to the hierarchies that presided over most of human history—the monarchies, dictatorships, theocracies, and aristocracies that used entrenched power structures or selected traditional authorities to justify the rule of one or a few over the many. The heavy thinkers of classical liberalism include the 17th-century English philosopher John Locke, who emphasized individual property rights; the 18th-century German philosopher Immanuel Kant, who emphasized respect for individuals' autonomy; and the 19th-century English philosopher John Stuart Mill, who emphasized individual freedoms. In today's political debates, important elements of classical liberalism are embraced both by "conservatives" (often called "liberals" in Canada, Europe, and Australia and sometimes called "libertarians" in the United States), as well as by the "L word" liberals, those associated with leftist policies. We find this overlap in political outlooks because classical liberalism asserts individual rights while allowing a wide range of intramural debates over precisely which rights to include as well as over which economic and political policies can best implement them. Classical liberalism emerged from at least two important historical movements: the religious battles of the Reformation and the Enlightenment optimism about using human reason to make social progress. Its resulting hallmarks include favorable dispositions toward toleration, liberty, and individual rights, and the confidence that these can be grounded in self-evident reasons. Typically, it tried to resolve the tension between legitimate authority and individual freedom by using some version of social contract thinking, thereby replacing the top-down theory of the divine right of kings with the bottom-up theory of the consent of the governed. As we will see, this resolution provides one of the links between liberalism and democracy.

The political debates between liberal theorists who emphasize individual liberty rights (conservatives) and those who emphasize equal opportunity rights (L word liberals) usually involve different empirical claims about history, psychology, and other social sciences, including claims about which economic systems are most likely to foster the prosperity necessary for a healthy society. In addition, these debates involve appeals to different rankings of the values associated with liberalism, rankings that can be justified only with rather substantial moral beliefs. For example, consider debates about whether taxes generated to support social welfare programs are violations of individual property rights or are simply the user fees that nurture a wealthy society stabilized by equal opportunity. Arguments here may appeal to facts about history and predictions about the future, but are also likely to reveal a ranking between the value of freedom and the value of equality or, at least, a difference over the extent to which (or the way in which) we are obliged to share one another's burdens. Such debates, therefore, can involve deep and important moral and religious differences, ones that derive from what Rawls calls different and conflicting but reasonable comprehensive doctrines.[2] From these debates *comprehensive* or *philosophical* liberalism has emerged as a way to underscore the point that the debates among different versions of liberalism are not neutral with respect to controversial moral and religious values, to conflicting visions of the good life, or to metaphysical disputes about human nature and the human condition. Indeed, those who affirm *perfectionist* liberalism explicitly insist that their type of liberalism is value-laden with a thick description of the virtues and ideals that are appropriate for liberals.[3] With his recognition of reasonable pluralism, discussed in chapter two, Rawls decided that his effort to argue for his particular version of comprehensive liberalism was not likely to convince those committed to other versions[4] and that, in any case, agreement on a particular comprehensive doctrine of liberalism was not necessary or even desirable in order for liberalism to accomplish its main political task.

So Rawls introduced *political* liberalism: "the problem of political liberalism is: How is it possible that there may exist over time a stable and just society of free and equal citizens profoundly divided by reasonable though incompatible religious, philosophical, and moral doctrines?"[5] Notice that it is the combining of multiple factors that creates this problem; free and equal people can likely have a stable society if the society is homogeneous, and a profoundly divided society can be stable if it is ruled by a powerful elite rather than free and equal citizens; it is the combining of stability, freedom, justice, and pluralism that is problematic. Rawls's proposal is that all varieties of liberalism and, indeed, all religious and philosophical outlooks can get along peacefully and respectfully as long as they are committed to reasonable political restraints.

They can argue vigorously and disagree with each other about the true foundations of human rights and political obligations, but when they come to debate about the essentials of political policy they can and should avoid narrow appeals to a sectarian vision of goodness and truth and restrict themselves to what is publicly reasonable. We will discuss the details and criticisms of this proposed restriction in a later section.

Democracy

What is democracy and how is it related to the varieties of pluralism and liberalism? Democracy should be defined in a neutral way so that we can separately consider the debate over whether it is a good idea or not. Everyone agrees that it has to do with decision making for and by a given group. This need not be a political group; it can apply—for better or worse—to business entities, organizations of all sorts, and even to families. However, we will focus on political democracy, forms of which go back to classical Athens but which, as noted above, is historically associated in Western civilization with such social contract thinkers as Locke and Rousseau. When *consent of the governed* replaced traditional hierarchies—the monarchies justified by divine appointment or others enforced by sheer power—political thinking required clarity about what is meant by "consent."

One obvious answer is that when everyone in a group votes for or at least agrees with a given policy, we have the consent of the governed. The participation of the individuals could be shallow, such as simply voting on referenda or candidates brought up by others, or deep, such as careful mutual deliberations at every step of the process. Of course, the chances of unanimity in a pluralistic society on any interesting political issue are next to zero, so the big question for democracy is how consent of the governed applies to minorities, including those who persistently find themselves in the minority. Majority rule is a simple solution, one that has been justified by claiming that those who participate in the voting process have implicitly agreed to abide by the majority vote.[6] But for liberal democracy, whatever plausibility this answer has depends on ensuring that some basic minority interests and rights are protected. Otherwise democracy becomes a system whereby the winners tyrannize the losers, a sadly too-familiar feature of so many nations today, and one that contradicts all versions of liberalism, with its concern for individual freedoms. Constitutional and procedural features, such as requiring super majorities on certain types of issues, can do much to protect minority rights, but by its very nature a democracy and its constitutional features can be shaped and changed by a determined majority.[7] This fact about democracy underscores the question whether it is desirable, if only, Winston Churchill once quipped, as the least bad form of government.

In the sixth book of his *Republic*, Plato ranks democracies near the bottom of types of government because he feared that they would be ruled by those who were good at winning elections rather than those who were good at governing once elected. Given the ignorance of the average citizens as well as their apathy about the common good combined with their fierce protection of their own interests, Plato expected that special interest groups and demagogues would prevail in the elections, and they would have neither the capacity nor the desire to promote the common good. Observers of political debates and elections in many democracies today cannot merely dismiss Plato's worries as elitist and overblown, though several types of replies can be made.

One reply to Plato is to assert the moral value of the liberty of individuals that democracy accommodates; maybe there are more efficient ways to accomplish legitimate political goals, such as leaving political decisions up to experts, but at least democracy recognizes the autonomy and moral right of each citizen to participate in the decisions that affect their lives. This moral value outweighs the mistakes that inevitably will be made when ordinary people vote on vastly complicated issues or vote for those who will decide on their behalf.

Another reply is to point out that nondemocratic governments have even worse problems—Churchill's "least bad" retort. The horrors of 20th-century dictatorships and totalitarian regimes are evidence, of course, but even decent hierarchical societies, ones that attend to some basic human rights and whose leaders pursue a vision of the common good (often their vision of God's will for the common good), tend to find themselves beset by at least as many political and economic problems as are democracies, and they seem at least as prone to various forms of corruption and self-serving efforts to maintain power. What favors democracy, this reply asserts, is the capacity for nonviolent self-correction, however long and difficult that may be.

A more positive reply to Plato is that democracies can have features that mitigate his worries. First, even those that reduce citizenship to voting for one's own interests can build in various checks and balances that play special interest groups against one another, so that no person or group can hold power indefinitely. A free press by itself can play a crucial role in checking powerful interests; although it is possible for these interests to control some (or even much) of the media, it would be very difficult in a democracy for them to control all (or even most) of the media. Second, the virtues of a citizenship that seeks the common good can be nurtured. Sometimes a narrow "liberal" model of citizenship is contrasted with a broader "republican" or Aristotelian model, the former viewing citizens as simply those who enjoy the legal protections of the government and the latter viewing citizenship as an office that involves active participation in political affairs. There is much debate over the extent to which citizens can or should participate deeply in public deliberation and in the development of political policies. On this issue, some see our political institutions as a *market* in which votes are simply registered and decisions thereby made, whereas others see political institutions as a *forum* in which issues are discussed in a deliberative way—information and ideas are shared and minds are made up and perhaps changed—and decisions thereby evolve into a consensus.[8] Casual familiarity with how American politics actually works suggests that in fact we exemplify a variety of models. There is no consensus on whether our politics should involve a widely deliberative effort to reach agreement (even if the agreement is for a reasoned compromise) or whether we should simply encourage people to vote for their interests. This book is addressed to those who are interested in civil disagreement, and thereby to those who are interested in giving and receiving reasons for their views and differences. I will assume only as much of the deliberative democracy model as requires that citizens be willing to give reasons to their compatriots when proposing or supporting political policies that could affect each other's liberties. When such discussions arise, an important question focuses on what sort of reasons are appropriate in a pluralistic society. This question can be raised either as a *moral* one: "What does moral respect for the rights of others require?" or as a *prudential* one: "How can we best maintain the stability deriving from consent of the governed when we are so politically divided?" The current debate about political debates in the public square raises the question in both ways.

Public Square Debates

Because the controversy over what types of reasons are appropriate is hottest when religious reasons are involved, this debate has become popularly known as the "Religion in the Public Square" debate. We will see that the controversy can involve more than just theology, but we will begin there.

The debate about religion in the public square is similar to but not the same as the debate about the separation of church and state. The latter has become a legal dispute about interpreting the Constitution. If my deeply held religious convictions are not merely private preferences but are integrated with definite implications for my political choices, then to forbid my appealing to them in my political advocacy and voting seems to rub against my First Amendment right to free exercise of religion. But if I and my cobelievers leverage a majority to vote our distinctive religious convictions into coercive law, that seems to invite something like the establishment of religion, forbidden by the First Amendment. Of course, if the establishment clause is interpreted narrowly as forbidding only the establishment of a national ecclesiastical institution, then religiously inspired legislation might not create any constitutional problem. But the Supreme Court has interpreted it more broadly; the *Lemon v. Kurtzman* decision in 1971 forbids legislation that does not have a legitimate secular purpose, or that has the primary effect of advancing or inhibiting religion, or that results in an excessive entanglement of government and religion. This interpretation has been attacked by several current Supreme Court justices, but as long as it stands it may well forbid coercive legislation that is based solely on distinctively religious visions of the good life.[9] The legal debate over the tension between the "free exercise" and the "nonestablishment" clauses has become a perennial American constitutional discussion, and it has influenced the moral debate about what the Constitution should require. Since the Constitution itself can be amended, we must confront the issue of the extent to which it is appropriate for citizens to use their distinctive convictions in the public square, whether for amending the Constitution or for any other issue that affects citizens' freedoms.

"The public square" refers to those locations and forums where one votes or advocates for political candidates, for legislation, or for any public policy that would result in the right of government to use coercion to control the behavior of its citizens. It is this resultant right to use coercion that underscores the importance of controversies in the public square. The public square is often contrasted with the "background culture" of a society—the religious, educational, and cultural institutions, including the media, the journals, the magazines, the sermons, the entertainment industry, and all those venues in society where, among other things, we try to *explain* our views and also try to *influence* opinions and behavior through persuasion, advertising, and so on. Obviously, the contrast here is not between public and private *realms*, but between *aims*, in particular, the extent to which one's aim is to promote particular candidates or legislation. A sermon or letter to the editor, for example, can be in either category, depending on how directly it addresses issues and candidates up for a political vote, and there are likely to be many borderline cases. It is a matter not of when and where but of "conversational pragmatics," including intentions, unspoken conventions, and uncodified practices.[10] Although there are issues of how to disagree civilly in the background culture, we will concentrate on civil disagreement in the public square, where important matters of legislation and legislators are proposed for discussion and voting.

The debate about debate in the public square focuses on whether we have prudential or moral reasons for imposing on ourselves some sort of restraint on the types of arguments we use in the public square or whether, in a pluralistic democracy, we should engage each other with arguments that are frankly and unabashedly based on our religious, moral, and other distinctive particularities. John Rawls insisted that a defining feature of political liberalism is what he called the *restraint principle*. A general version of the restraint principle is that conscientious citizens ought to restrain themselves from using nonpublic reasons to advocate or vote for coercive legislation unless they also are willing and able to provide public reasons for it. This principle comes in many variations; for example, some apply it mainly or only to advocacy, and less or not at all to voting[11]; some apply it to all citizens while others apply it only or mainly to public officials,[12] and others draw the line between executives and judges, on the one hand, and legislators and ordinary citizens, on the other[13]; some restrict it to constitutional essentials and matters of basic justice,[14] while others apply it to all coercive legislation[15]; some propose restraint on theological (nonsecular) reasons but not on controversial secular reasons,[16] while others propose restraint on all controversial reasons.[17] A final variation is that some restrict acceptable reasons to those that actually are sufficient to motivate the advocates,[18] while most others allow advocates to use any public reasons that they think could convince the intended audience, even if the advocates are actually motivated by other reasons. At stake in this latter issue is whether an advocate should appeal to a *consensus* on some public reasons or whether public square civility allows one to appeal to different reasons for different audiences and thereby try to generate a *convergence* in which different people agree on a policy but do so for different reasons.[19]

One thing that all proponents of a restraint principle agree on is that the proposed restriction is a moral and internal restraint, not a legal and external constraint. This is important to remember because sometimes opponents of the restraint principle characterize it as excluding or barring or prohibiting or preventing or banishing distinctly religious appeals from the public square,[20] and such phrasing could lead people to think that political liberals are proposing laws or penalties. Of course, proponents of the restraint principle hope that there will be moral and social pressure to abide by it, and that could cause resentment, a point we will consider later.

The version of the restraint principle cited above is not a call to privatize distinctive doctrines. Instead, it is what Rawls calls the "wide" and what others call the "inclusive" version: One is welcome to appeal to distinctive religious and moral doctrines in the public square, as Martin Luther King did in quoting the Hebrew prophets, as long as one meets the "proviso" that one is willing and able to provide public reasons for the legislation or legislator that one favors. This does not mean that advocates must "translate" their distinctive doctrine into public reason; they simply should feel morally obligated to be willing and able to give independent public reasons for the same conclusion they advocated when using their distinctive doctrines.

Public reasons, according to Rawls, are those that advocates in the public square can reasonably expect their compatriots could reasonably accept. They need not be reasons that compatriots *actually* accept, since the latter may make mistakes about the implications of their own views. And since the range of reasons one could reasonably accept is wider than the range of reasons one cannot reasonably reject, it is important to phrase the restraint principle in the wider sense.[21] Of course, if I think that I am reasonable, there is a sense in which I think that anyone could reasonably accept almost any of my own beliefs, which is why the restraint principle must be understood as applying to my compatriots *given their* reasonable but distinctive and conflicting moral and religious views (what Rawls calls their "comprehensive doctrines" and what is often called their "evidential set"). As Rawls puts it, we must be able in a sincere and nonmanipulative way to conjecture that our compatriots' reasonable comprehensive doctrines allow them to endorse the public reasons we offer, even if, in fact, they reject them.[22]

The actual content of public reason includes not only the well-established claims of the empirical sciences and mathematics and logic, but also normative beliefs that have become part of the public culture: "We collect such settled convictions as the belief in religious toleration and the rejection of slavery and try to organize the basic ideas and principles implicit in the convictions into a co-herent political conception of justice" that becomes a "reasonable overlapping consensus." This overlapping consensus might be regarded as true by one or more comprehensive doctrines, but it can also be formulated as "a freestanding political conception having its own intrinsic (moral) political ideal expressed by the criterion of reciprocity."[23] In his final publication on public reason, Rawls says its content includes a rather fluid *family* of political conceptions of justice that might include "Catholic views of the common good and solidarity."[24] Some liberals propose that Rawls is too loose—even populist—in his view of public justification, so they call for more stringent restrictions for what is sometimes called "justificatory liberalism."[25] However, many critics find even Rawls's view too restricting, so we will focus on it.

Later we will ask whether "public reason" can be defined precisely enough to be used in some version of the restraint principle, but first we need to ask why political liberals propose the restraint. One *prudential* consideration might be the avoidance of conflict, analogous to an argument for religious toleration based on avoiding religious wars. Rawls and other political liberals do some-times sound as if their main concern is that of stability, expressing worries that, if a majority of citizens leverage their controversial views into a majority that encodes sectarian practices into law, we risk at least political divisiveness and perhaps even a high enough degree of alienation that it results in violence and religious wars. Many critics think that this fear is overblown. They admit that there may have been times in history when religious appeals should have been toned down. They even admit that there are geographical locations today (this worry is sometimes called "argument from Bosnia") in which the risk of violence or divisiveness calls for restraint or even the privatization of religious appeals, but they think that there are no such monsters under the bed in demo-cratic societies that are liberal and pluralistic.[26] Indeed, those who insist that they live *inside* their traditions, not *alongside* them, who insist that their reli-gious commitments are overriding and totalizing obligations with definite and important implications for their political deliberations (hereafter "integrated believers"), claim that asking them to restrain this central feature of their iden-tities in the public square—while welcoming secular arguments—is not a way to reduce conflict but is itself a recipe for significant alienation, resentment, and divisiveness.[27]

When evaluating the claim that the restraint principle might cause more resentment and division than it prevents, we must recognize that a democracy will always have voters who find themselves in the minority and that this out-come is not in itself a cause of instability. This point goes beyond the earlier observation that we do not need *consensus* on reasons in order to *converge* on a conclusion that different people accept for different reasons. Apart from con-sensus and convergence, people can *acquiesce* to policies they vote against and, as we noted in the last chapter, sometimes even cheerfully cooperate with them. Consensus-seeking and convergence-seeking societies "aim to maximize the number of people who approve of what is being done; acquiescence-seeking societies seek to minimize the number of people who disapprove very strongly of what is being done."[28] A pluralistic democracy probably has to resort frequently to mere acquiescence, and then maintain stability by relying on constitutional checks and civil regard for minority rights. This point underscores the question whether the restraint principle, which some integrated believers feel discounts in the public square their most important and deepest beliefs, is likely to cause the sort of resentment and alienation that undermines even sullen acquiescence, or makes it more likely that being coerced by the objectionable nonpublic beliefs of others will cause it. This is an empirical question on which there seems to be more anecdote and testimony than research.[29]

We need not settle this debate because lately the main type of argument that political liberals use for the restraint principle is the *moral* one that appeals to civil respect toward one's compatriots. Thus Rawls insists that the sort of stability society needs is not simply a *modus vivendi* in which minorities begrudgingly but reliably acquiesce to offensive coercive legislation; rather, we need stability for the right reasons. And stability for the right reasons requires the moral and political ideal of reciprocity, which in turn associates with civil respect and even civic friendship.[30] Thus, given reasonable pluralism, reciprocity calls for the civic virtue of a liberalism of reasoned respect. For Rawls, what it means to respect our compatriots as free and equal is to refuse to coerce them unless one can give them reasons that one reasonably believes they cannot only *understand* (as Servetus could understand why Calvin decided to burn him at the stake) but which one reasonably believes they reasonably could *accept* whatever their reasonable comprehensive doctrine might be. Lest this view seems overly indebted to Kantian "recognition respect" toward the autonomy of others, it is worth noting that theists have appealed to a reasoned respect that is derived from the Christian ideal of agape or from the doctrine of persons' being created in God's image.[31] The ongoing debate is whether basing the restraint principle on civil respect begs the question about the sort of respect we owe to compatriots. Rawls, for example, seems to build the restraint principle right into the notion of "terms all can accept," which he in turn associates with reasonable persons regarding each other as free and equal, which he sees as an essential part of civil respect. Critics claim that with these moves Rawls implies that anyone who has important reasons for rejecting his notion of civil respect is by definition unreasonable.[32] Meanwhile, integrated believers argue that true reasonableness requires that we respect each other in our particularity, and we do this only if we give each other our true reasons for our political decisions, including our distinctive moral and religious ones.[33] Sometimes called the "consocial" view or—at its radically inclusive extreme—the "agonistic" view (from the Greek *agon*, meaning both "assembly" and "contest"), it advocates frank and full public square discussions of all our differences. After vigorous debate, rather than appeal to a nonexistent consensus or convergence, we should simply vote and expect the minority respectfully to acquiesce without undue resentment, given that their distinctive views were not automatically discounted as illegitimate and that constitutional safeguards protect their basic rights against ill-considered majority decisions. For these critics, respect in the public square involves exchanging *substantive* ideas on religion, and not merely *methodological* ideas about religion's role in the debate. They think it is in vain that liberals hope that a consensus about the latter can emerge from the lack of consensus about the former. Rather than hope for a community consensus—be it substantive or methodological—we need to live with a politics of multiple communities.

Moreover, some critics of the restraint principle argue that encouraging all sincere integrated believers to include their theological commitments in public square debates allows public criticism of what otherwise would likely be hidden, but powerful, motivators. Theological claims can be intelligible and understandable and thereby criticizable even if they are not accessible in the sense of being shared. This approach would also have the healthy effect of preventing the fundamentalists and fanatics—who rush in where others fear to tread—from being the only sectarian voices heard in the square. These critics admit that there will be costs involved in this radically inclusive approach: Sometimes a majority may legislate religious views about marriage, for example, that seem to minorities to impinge on their freedom. But, especially when political liberals base their arguments for restraint on the moral value of civil respect rather than on the prudential value of avoiding violence and instability, liberals must be willing to weigh the costs and benefits of an inclusive public square against a restricted one; just how valuable is the liberal ideal of civil respect compared to the cost of asking integrated believers to keep quiet about values central to their moral, religious, and (thereby) political identity?[34]

In addition to discounting worries about violence and instability, and disagreeing about what respect requires for political advocacy, and weighing differently the costs and benefits of a religiously inclusive public square, critics of the restraint principle are also skeptical of the resources of public reason to settle controversial political issues, either because there are too few public reasons or they are too vague and ambiguous to give guidance on controversial issues.[35] To this latter important point, political liberals can reply that, given Rawls's expanded concept of public reason mentioned above, while there can be reasonable debate over the extent of public reason, it provides a guideline that works better in practice than in theory, and that a look at the debates over hot-button issues such as abortion, euthanasia, and gay marriage shows that fair-minded believers can and do engage in public reason arguments about them. Consider, for example, the argument from biology and genetics that the fetus is a unique, individual, live human being and that there is no nonarbitrary line to draw for its moral standing other than at conception; this argument can be defended and criticized using only public reason. That the argument continues is confirmation that reasonable persons can disagree, not that we cannot take a stand based on public reasons. A similar point can be made about arguments that physician-assisted suicide will put undue pressure on patients to ask for it, or that marriage between a man and a woman is the foundation of the family ethos that is central to civilization. Even if some public reasons can be found for use in hotly contested issues, we will not settle soon the dispute over whether there are enough of them. Meanwhile, there may be room for compromise over the restraint principle.

First Proposal for Compromise

Why not grant political liberalism the content of its restraint principle, but make it an obligation of *pursuit* rather than *restriction*? This proposal from Christopher Eberle addresses both sides in the argument. To avoid intransigent sectarianism, it tries to persuade the "anything goes" audience that they are morally obliged "to exit their parochial worldviews, to do what is within their power to inhabit the respective points of view of their compatriots, and to attempt to articulate reasons . . . that are convincing to their compatriots."[36] And it tries to persuade the political liberal that, if citizens have sincerely pursued public justification but have failed to find public reasons, then they are not morally bound by the restraint principle, and they may in good conscience vote and advocate for coercive legislation based only on their distinctive religious beliefs. Too often people collapse the pursuit principle into the restraint principle, thinking too hastily that any obligation to pursue public reasons implies the obligation to restraint if one cannot find them. But we should distinguish them, because if integrated religious believers were disposed to satisfy the pursuit principle, resentment toward religiously based coercion would be reduced, and acquiescence toward it would be more palatable. Political liberals seem most deeply offended when an integrated believer simply announces, "My God tells me so, and I don't need to have or to use any other arguments." If the integrated believer would conscientiously pursue public reasons, many political liberals might be more sympathetic to the avoidance of the restraint principle when public reasons for coercive legislation cannot be found. Notice that if political liberals are right in thinking that public reasons can usually be found for political decisions, then the practical results of the pursuit principle by itself would largely overlap those of the restraint principle. And, if public reasons cannot usually be found, that would underscore the cost the restraint principle imposes on integrated believers. Of course, political liberals may worry that without the restraint principle, integrated believers may too quickly give up on the pursuit of public reasons, and too quickly feel justified in appealing to their sectarian beliefs in voting and advocacy. Countering this worry is the fact that finding public reason arguments for their favored candidate or legislation would be very prudent for those integrated believers who are motivated to have their favored candidate or legislation win. Of course, there may be some integrated believers who are less interested in winning than in testifying, Still, combined with the ones who work harder to find public reasons, they may be able to leverage a legislative victory. So it is uncertain how often this proposal for compromise by itself would morally sanction the effective use of distinctive religious beliefs in the public square. The next proposal makes explicit some additional important considerations relevant to respecting the restraint principle.

Second Proposal for Compromise

A second—perhaps additional—route to compromise, one that I propose, is to admit that at least sometimes the pursuit of public reasons will fail but, rather than reject the obligation of restraint, claim that it remains an important *prima facie* obligation, one that can be morally overridden only in certain carefully considered circumstances. This approach simply develops what a number of political liberals and integrated believers themselves say. Some prominent political liberals, for example, concede that integrated believers have a moral *right* to vote and advocate solely on religious grounds, and that what the restraint principle proposes is an *ideal* that yields a prima facie obligation, the overriding of which can sometimes be acceptable.[37] Meanwhile, some critics of the restraint principle agree that political liberalism proposes an appropriate ideal or excellence of citizenship. Some of these raise questions of how one moves from ideals to obligations, even prima facie obligations,[38] while others see no problem in moving from seeing the restraint principle as an ideal to claiming that violating it is morally criticizable. Some of the latter add that any religious or moral duty for religious citizens to reject the restraint principle is itself a prima facie one, one that can be overridden by morally appropriate reluctance to impose coercive laws on their compatriots.[39]

This "prima facie obligation" approach could be implemented by conscientious citizens with the following types of considerations. These are not ranked in importance, as there can be reasonable disagreement about the ranking; but within each consideration the answers can be put on sliding scales indicating how much weight they should have when making an overall judgment:[40]

1. What is the degree and type of coercion (or vulnerability)[41] that would be imposed on others? Even taxation is enforced with the sword power of the state, as Henry Thoreau's prison experience reminds us, but being forced to pay a small percentage of one's income is clearly not as coercive as, say, forbidding abortion when a woman's health is at stake.[42]

2. How basic and far-reaching is the legislation? When we consider all coercive legislation, and not just Rawls's constitutional essentials and matters of basic justice, some proposals, such as amendments to the Constitution, have a broader scope for good or ill than others do.[43]

3. What is the type and degree of harm the legislation is proposed to prevent? Sabbath observance is very important to ultra-Orthodox Jews in Jerusalem, but for most of us it does not involve the type and degree of harms forbidden by the Commandments against stealing and murder.

In the abortion case, however, disagreement over the moral status of the fetus entails disagreement over whether abortion involves the harm of murder. Hence even those who deny that abortion is murder can appreciate why it is higher on the agenda of some integrated religious believers than is Sabbath desecration or divorce, both of which some believers have had reasons to see as coercive legislation issues.

4. How distinctive or controversial is the norm appealed to? It may range from being a borderline public reason one to being one of the more idiosyncratic features of a religious or moral outlook, one that, if legislated, would seem to be an especially sectarian imposition.[44] Even those who deny that the restraint principle is a moral duty might agree that, when the reasons used are narrowly sectarian, there must be some other compelling considerations to justify not conforming to it.

5. How central to one's identity and integrity is the belief to which one appeals? Most political liberals can agree that no one is obliged to violate his deepest convictions or to annihilate essential aspects of his very self. And by the same token, integrated believers can distinguish between, on the one hand, convictions central to one's integrity, the compromising of which would do psychological or spiritual damage, and, on the other, those that might involve strong feelings—as matters of sex, for example, often do—but which are possible subjects for principled compromise or toleration.

6. How volatile is the social and political situation? Even some integrated believers agree that in some areas of the world or periods in history religious differences should be politically restrained or even privatized. As we noticed earlier, given that these areas and periods are volatile precisely because integrated believers are in conflict, it means that what they call the "overriding and totalizing duty to obey God"[45] implies specifically a *prima facie* duty to integrate one's religion with one's political advocacy, since God is also interested in peaceful conflict resolution.

7. Can the favored coercion be enforced, and at what costs? The costs can be financial or impingements on important values. Coercion is always an impingement on liberty, of course, but if enforcement requires extensive surveillance, which in turn requires significant impingement on privacy, then the fallout for both pocketbook and quality of life must be weighed.

8. Is the proposed legislation susceptible to slippery slope objections? Sometimes one's justification for proposed legislation implicitly justifies something unacceptable; or, apart from justification, a proposed practice might involve the risk of sliding into an unacceptable practice.[46] Both types of slippery slope arguments have been used when debating physician-assisted suicide, for example.

9. How certain is one of the truth of the relevant belief, and how readily do others who are in a similar cognitive position agree that one is entitled to affirm it confidently? Even those who believe that the Bible is inerrant can be fallibilists about their apprehension of it. And the more exegetical debate there is among those who share one's basic beliefs, the less certain one should be about the wisdom of legislating one's interpretation of the disputed religious demands.

10. Is one deciding and advocating as a citizen, a public opinion leader, a member or leader of a religious or secular organization, a legislator, or a government official? One need not draw bright lines here to agree that roles are relevant to how strong a prima facie duty one has to exercise restraint. Many religious believers who reject the restraint principle for ordinary citizens would get nervous about having their legislators exegete scripture on the floor, or having judges rely on it in court decisions.

Let us consider a few applications of the above considerations. Suppose I advocate in the public square for unilateral disarmament, basing my view on various well-known New Testament texts such as "Love your enemies" and "When someone strikes you on one cheek, turn to him the other cheek," as well as what I see as the demands of agape, or self-sacrificing love. I know there are prudential and other public reason arguments for pacifism, but they do not convince me; instead, I have devoted my life to passionate advocacy for agape-based nonviolence, and it has become a defining feature of my moral identity. I am convinced that vengeance is the Lord's and that using violence in self-defense is a kind of practical apostasy that thinks it has to help Almighty God make history turn out right. Notice that my policy, if legislated, could make others highly vulnerable to coercion and violence by well-armed and possibly brutal enemies. The harm I want to protect people from is the interminable violence that wars engender, though, of course, others fear that my policy would engender even more violence against the innocent. Although my interpretation of the sacred texts is distinctive, it is one shared by many of my cognitive peers, and I am confident that our minority view is right. My advocating my view in the public square will not risk riots or even public discord, though largely because the public sees my view as a quaint and touchingly naïve one that has no chance of becoming public policy. When others have pointed out that my view is susceptible to a slippery slope argument—it seems to require the disarming of police and the repudiation of the Second Amendment—I cheerfully agree to ski down that slope and accept the implications. How should political liberals respond? It seems that as long as I am not a high official—certainly not the chair of the Joint Chiefs of Staff—political liberals, after mulling over the above considerations, reasonably could arrive at an all-things-considered judgment that admits my moral right to override the restraint principle. That others could reasonably arrive at the opposite judgment simply illustrates reasonable pluralism.

Now suppose I argue for an amendment to the Mississippi State Constitution stipulating that personhood begins at fertilization, my reasons consisting primarily of biblical texts such as this from Psalm 139:13–16: "[Y]ou knit me together in my mother's womb. . . . Your eyes beheld my unformed substance." Even if I am and have been completely devoted to antiabortion causes, so consideration five would weigh heavily in favor of my restrained pushing for this amendment, most of the other considerations would raise red flags. The amendment would likely prohibit in vitro fertilization, the use of IUDs, the use of "morning after" pills, and all or almost all abortions. It would be a constitutional matter, so quite basic and hard to change. Enforcement would be difficult if not impossible, and would involve significant impingement on privacy. If it passed, a sizable majority would regard it as an especially egregious and sectarian violation of their rights, and likely there would be demonstrations and counterdemonstrations that could become violent. The biblical interpretation involved in my argument is a highly distinctive doctrine, though one that might well be shared by a majority in Mississippi. Its justification does seem open to a slippery slope objection: If a zygote has full moral status because God knows it, what about Jeremiah 1:5: "Before I formed you in the womb I knew you," or Judges 13 where God announces to Samson's mother that she will conceive a son who will be called Samson and he will save Israel from the Philistines? Does God's knowing which sperm and egg will eventually produce Samson grant them full moral status? Although the latter argument smells like suspicious logic chopping to me, I decline to rebut it. Here it seems that political liberals could reasonably tell me that they do not think I have the moral right to override the restraint principle. They could say that the above considerations should make me wonder about how certain I am of my interpretation of the texts, especially seeing that other Bible-believing people have different interpretations. Also, they would say, the above considerations should prompt me to call into question the type of harm I thought I was trying to prevent: Is preventing implantation the moral equivalent of murdering persons? At any rate, perhaps enough voters in Mississippi explicitly or implicitly let some of the above considerations move a healthy majority of them in 2012 to vote down the proposed amendment, even though a significant majority of that state's citizens consider themselves to be firmly prolife.[47]

Maybe the above cases are too easy. In my home state of Minnesota, we also had controversial proposed amendments to the state's constitution in the 2012 election, including one that would limit marriage to male and female pairs. Although most of the motivation seemed heavily influenced by biblical interpretations, a fair number of the arguments seemed to be public reason arguments having to do, for example, with the welfare of children and how traditional marriage is the foundation of our civilization.[48] However, many proponents of the amendment simply argued that a vote against it would violate God's will and perhaps bring God's wrath down upon us. Some, though not all, were willing to compromise, allowing "civil unions" for those who would otherwise be deprived of the legal advantages of marriage. This proposed compromise would change the type of harm that would have been imposed on the minority, though it certainly would not eliminate their sense of being discriminated against. An important consideration regarding the relevance of the restraint principle was the extent to which enforcing traditional marriage was a central feature of the proponents' moral and spiritual identities. Passionate intensity on sexual and marital matters does not automatically mean that one's very integrity is at stake, though this is hard for oneself, to say nothing of others, to judge. In short, enough of the above ten considerations seemed to yield ambiguous enough results, that for conscientious Minnesotans who were inclined to base their vote on biblical texts, the considerations probably did not provide very clear guidance regarding the restraint principle, especially if they saw its passage as a way to introduce civil unions. Even open-minded political liberals might have seen this as a borderline case, though most of the opponents of the amendment urged voters not to impose their distinctive religious beliefs on others. In any case, some of the ten considerations or others like them may have made a difference; there were lots of "Another Catholic voting No" yard signs and, to the surprise of many, the amendment failed.[49]

The upshot is that these ten considerations are hardly exhaustive, and no one can claim that using them provides an algorithm or clear-cut procedure for citizens deciding when to exercise or advise restraint in the politics of a pluralistic society.[50] That the vague and sometimes conflicting considerations provide less an algorithm than a way to zigzag toward a useful degree of discernment would be a devastating problem if we were talking about legal rules. Instead we are talking about civic virtue and responsibilities that suggest prima facie moral obligations, the strength of which can be a matter of thoughtful disagreement among those genuinely interested in the implications of civil respect in a pluralistic democracy. Hence I believe that this second proposal for compromise provides a conceptual framework that can help conscientious citizens take stands that support both their own integrity and political civility.

Accommodating Dissenters

A pluralistic and democratic society that is influenced by the various strands of liberalism discussed above will inevitably be asked to accommodate groups that reject or reinterpret some of its core values, values such as individual autonomy, open-mindedness, equality, and the examined life. Even if we agree that any accommodation must stop short of tolerating serious physical or mental harm,[51] we are faced with difficult questions about where to draw the line. For example, the Old Order Amish in Wisconsin believe that requiring formal education for their children beyond the eighth grade is worse than useless—it is unnecessary for the work God provides and it introduces modern ideas that could tempt their children away from the sound doctrine, the righteous customs, and the simple life that constitute their distinctive identity. Meanwhile,

Wisconsin requires mandatory schooling until age sixteen for very good reasons: Children should be educated until at least age sixteen so that they can get a job that contributes to a modern economy and to their own welfare and so that they can develop their autonomy and ability to participate responsibly in civic life. However, the Amish are not interested in the modern economy or civic life and they think that obedience to God's demands trumps autonomy. This conflict led to the famous *Wisconsin v. Yoder* Supreme Court decision in 1972; it accommodated the Amish but it also elicited this oft-quoted dissent from Justice William Douglas:

> It is the future of the students, not the future of the parents, that is imperiled by today's decision. If a parent keeps his child out of school beyond the grade school, then the child will be forever barred from entry into the new and amazing world of diversity that we have today. The child may decide that that is the preferred course, or he may rebel. It is the student's judgment, not his parents', that is essential if we are to give full meaning to what we have said about the Bill of Rights and of the right of students to be masters of their own destiny. If he is harnessed to the Amish way of life by those in authority over him and if his education is truncated, his entire life may be stunted and deformed. The child, therefore, should be given an opportunity to be heard before the State gives the exemption which we honor today.[52]

Surely Douglas is right in denying that the only two sets of interests at stake are those of the parents and those of the state. It is that presumption that elicited the controversial decision about the state's having no compelling interest that overrides the parents' interest in nurturing their children into the parents' distinctive outlook. But Douglas's point is that the children's interests—the quality of their future lives and choice—are a third powerful set of interests.

However, it is not at all clear that hearing from the children is the way to protect their interests, since there is strong evidence that children can be socialized into simply accepting their parents' views.[53] Young Christian Scientist children usually agree with their parents in rejecting scientific medicine, but the state does not allow that to override their interests if their life or physical health is at stake. This insistence on limits to how controlling parents can be over their children is motivated by more than concern for the child's interest; the health of the economy and of the civic life of the wider society are also motivations.

Here is where a division emerges within the liberal tradition, one that may be linked to the two different historical sources of classical liberalism that were mentioned earlier in this chapter: One was the Enlightenment emphasis on trusting reason to enhance individual autonomy and social progress, and the other was the post-Reformation emphasis on tolerating and accommodating diversity. Often these emphases harmonize, since respect for autonomy and desire for social progress go hand in glove with tolerance of and even appreciation for diversity. But an issue such as the education of children reveals a tension. On one side of the spectrum are those who insist that a liberal democracy should take an active role in shaping the curriculum to promote the critical thinking that is conducive to autonomy, and also to promote the skills and attitudes conducive for a healthy technological economy and a vibrant civic life. This side argues that a liberal democracy is not a suicide pact, so the state should insist on strict guidelines for the amount and type of education that molds our children.[54] On the other side are those who promote maximal feasible accommodation to diversity, insisting that liberal pluralism involves the expressive liberty to believe and practice any variety of visions of the good life, and that only compelling societal interests should override the right to act on one's beliefs and to inculcate them into one's children. There is a compelling societal interest against human sacrifice, for example, so that limits expressive freedom for the Aztecs, but probably there is no compelling societal interest that requires the Amish to go to high school.[55]

As long as Americans believed that everyone wanted to be assimilated into a melting pot, we avoided such issues, and that belief was widespread through much of our history. When Eleanor Roosevelt headed the United Nations Human Rights Commission that drew up the *Universal Declaration of Human Rights* in 1948, she replied to several European countries, including Yugoslavia, who wanted to write in protections of minority groups:

> All of the Americas' delegates declared that this problem did not exist with them because people who come to our shores do so because they want to become citizens of our countries. They leave behind certain economic, religious and social conditions that they wish to shed and prefer to be assimilated into the new country they are adopting as their own. They are accepted by us with that understanding, and from our point of view we would like to see the committee recognize the fact that the European problem should be handled differently.[56]

Quite apart from the fact that this statement ignores indigenous minority groups, it is worth noting that one of the most intelligent, sensitive, and informed people of the mid-20th century had this view of the cultural dynamics of our democracy. The assumption view might be favored today by many Americans, but even they would reject it as a description of the desires of all minority groups.

Dissent against consensus comes not just from well-defined groups wanting to have their distinctive identities recognized, such as the Amish or Native American tribes, it also comes from individuals or small subgroups uniting for a cause. For example, in 1983, a group of parents in Church Hill, Tennessee, all of whom were Christian fundamentalists albeit from different denominations, protested that the books used as readers in the public school violated their religious convictions, in particular their belief that they must protect their children from exposure to such evils as mental telepathy, situation ethics, human evolution, and the idea that one religion is as good as another.[57] They asked that their children be excused from classroom reading sessions and be allowed to read from alternative readers in sessions that the parents were willing to tutor. The district court ruled that the school system should accommodate these parents, perhaps by excusing the students from reading class, having the parents

tutor them in reading at home, and having the county administer standardized
tests. It concluded that the refusal to so accommodate them violated the parents' constitutional rights, including the free exercise of religion. But the Sixth
Circuit Court of Appeals overruled the lower court, and the Supreme Court
refused to accept an appeal, with the result that most of the students left the
public schools for home schooling or private Christian schools.

The three circuit judges concurred in their conclusion but gave different
reasons for it. Chief Justice Lively argued that the plaintiffs' rights were not
violated because, unlike in cases of Seventh-Day Adventists being required
to work on their Sabbath, the children were not asked to say or do anything
against their religious beliefs. Moreover, mere exposure to repugnant ideas did
not constitute teaching these ideas. And he said that analogies with the *Yoder*
case were flawed because, unlike the Amish who wanted to avoid participation
in modern American culture and politics, these parents wanted their children
to acquire all the skills necessary to participate in modern life. This point was
enlarged upon by Judge Kennedy, who argued that even if reading the assigned
books imposed a burden on the children, this burden was overridden by the
compelling interest of the state to expose students to controversial issues as
part of their preparation for citizenship and civil life in a pluralistic society.
Judge Boggs disagreed with Lively's claim that students were not asked to violate their beliefs; referring to the pre-Vatican II Catholic list of forbidden books,
he argued that requiring Catholics to read them would require them to violate
their beliefs even if it were merely a matter of simply exposing them to the
ideas in these books. Indeed, some parents believed that their allowing their
children to read such material would consign both the parents and the children to eternal punishment.[58] Moreover, Boggs thought that the school system
could and should have accommodated these students without causing any bad
educational effects. But he argued that the requirement that all students read
the same books, while unfortunate and unnecessary, did not violate anyone's
constitutional rights since the parents could withdraw their children from the
public school; the burden—financial and otherwise—that the latter option imposed on the parents and students, while significant, did not violate their constitutional rights.

It is not difficult to predict that liberals devoted to shaping children with
liberal values, especially the critical thinking necessary for autonomy, reacted to
this decision in a way very different from that of the liberal pluralists devoted to
maximal feasible accommodation. The latter noted that, while the capacity for
critical deliberation is one element of good citizenship, there are other important ones such as "law-abidingness, personal responsibility, and the willingness
to do one's share"[59] that the fundamentalists may do a good job of nurturing.
And even if critical thinking is important for democratic citizenship, liberal
pluralism should accommodate "diverse legitimate ways of life, limited only
by the minimum requirements of civic unity."[60] So there is no compelling state

interest in insisting on the same reading curriculum for all public school students; the court's decision is wrong. Meanwhile, those liberals who think that society's need for informed citizens and the child's right to a modern education override the parents' desire to transmit their parochial views, they agreed with the decision, arguing as follows:

> The basic question of principle is, Do families have a moral right to opt out of reasonable measures designed to educate children with very basic liberal virtues because those measures make it harder for parents to pass along their particular religious beliefs? Surely not. To acknowledge the legitimacy of the fundamentalist complaint as a matter of basic principle would overthrow reasonable efforts to inculcate core liberal values. It would provide religious fundamentalists with a right to shield their children from the fact of reasonable pluralism. Liberal civic education is bound to have the effect of favoring some ways of life or religious convictions over others. So be it.[61]

Notice that this defense of mandatory civic education implies that children should be exposed not only to the fact of sheer diversity but also to the "fact of reasonable pluralism." The *Mozert* parents said that exposure to ideas that contradicted the Bible was acceptable, as long as those ideas were presented as wrong. This concession highlights the point that, while pluralism in the sense of sheer diversity is an empirical fact, "reasonable pluralism" is an interpretation of the diversity, saying that contradictory views may both be reasonable. This interpretation may be a fact to most liberals, but it is a slant on diversity that includes normative elements. It was the *sympathetic* exposure to diversity that grated on these parents.

Some commentators on this case have pointed out that, although their pedagogical theory was extreme, the actual demands of the parents were more moderate; they wanted their children to remain in school while opting out of the reading class (and their home-schooled reading skills could be gauged by outside proficiency tests).[62] Given that parents can withdraw their children from public schools and either home-school them or send them to private schools teaching their distinctive worldview, it might be better to accept the compromise. Keeping the children in public school for all but the reading class would at least expose them to the fact of diversity, and their interaction with friends of diverse views would likely nurture something like reasonable pluralism. This pragmatic suggestion raises the question of the extent to which public school boards and teachers should cooperate with (and not merely tolerate) a practice that is based on an outlook they regard as wrong and perhaps one that they cannot even respect as reasonable. As we saw in the previous chapter, the decision whether to respect a view is largely based on intellectual criteria, but the decision whether to tolerate and cooperate with a view one regards as wrong and perhaps even unreasonable is based on the morally relevant results of what one decides, including the social, political, and educational results. Given that education is compulsory, and given that home-schooling or private schooling is an option, it is not surprising that the author of a highly regarded book on the *Mozert* case argues for compromise and cooperation, not necessarily based on the maximal accommodation principle that some liberal pluralists push, but largely on prudential grounds:

> If we truly believe that pluralistic public education is an essential foundation of a peaceful multicultural society, then we should do what we can to keep fundamentalists (and other religious dissidents) in the public schools. Even skipping the occasional book or class, they benefit from and contribute to the democratic mission of public education. They acquire information and attitudes that they wouldn't otherwise get. (In a 1993 study, Albert J. Menendez asserts that textbooks used in fundamentalist schools "create a permanent ghetto of the mind.") By their presence, fundamentalists also give other students an object lesson in diversity. We shouldn't panic when differentness manifests itself, as when some students leave the room or read a different book.[63]

Many people might find this an acceptable compromise but, of course, when you play the results card, you are open to rebuttal from alternative scenarios. What if the above cooperation would lead to chaos, as scores of other parents seek accommodation from having their children in biology classes that teach evolution, history classes that undermine American exceptionalism, or religion classes that highlight theological diversity? "Grant this one, a voice whispers to each judge, and you will be confronted with an endless chain or exemption demands from religious deviants of every stripe."[64] The question whether such compromise would put us on a slippery slope to chaos is an empirical one and so far there is not much evidence one way or the other. Some commentators are skeptical about the slippery slope argument, observing that the *Yoder* decision did not lead to others asking for exemptions from compulsory education, but others point out that that result may be due to the Amish combining their dissident views with an isolationist mentality. Dissidence is much more common than isolationism, so the *Yoder* case may not provide evidence about the effects of accommodation in other types of cases. But evidence may be coming. In 2011, the New Hampshire legislature passed a law that allows parents to request alternative course material whenever they find the assigned material objectionable.[65] Since this law applies to any material in any course, it may provide evidence for or against the slippery slope worries, though the fact that parents must pay for any additional costs throws some gravel on the slope.

Legal rights and laws can come and go, of course. The question we have is whether there are moral principles and other considerations that should inform our decisions about what to legislate and which accommodations are appropriate. Here is where those supporting maximal accommodation differ from those who are less flexible about exempting individuals or groups from democratic legislation regarding education and other social norms. Much of the debate involves the sort of considerations we have noted above: prudential appeals to results or philosophical differences over the type of society we should strive to be. One question we have not yet discussed is whether a particular group might have a right as a group to maintain its distinctive identity.

Group Rights?

Group rights are sometimes thought of as part of the third generation of rights.[66] The first generation consists of individuals' negative human rights not to be harmed or even interfered with; they are the sort of civil and political rights listed in our Bill of Rights, such as freedom of speech, religion, and assembly, and the right to a fair trial. The second generation consists of positive human rights to be aided; they are social and economic welfare rights, such as the right to free education, to social security, medical care, and unemployment benefits.[67] Most people see a correlation between rights and duties; if you have a right, then others have the duty to respect that right. It is relatively easy to see how we can respect negative rights; usually, if we just leave others alone and mind our own business, we are simultaneously fulfilling the negative rights of billions of people. But with positive rights to be helped it is sometimes very difficult to specify who has the obligation to fulfill them. This difficulty came to the fore when after World War II the United Nations drew up *The Universal Declaration of Human Rights*.[68] Western nations pushed hard for the first generation of rights, and the Soviet bloc pushed just as hard for the second generation, the latter refusing to put them into a different and less important category of rights. But since the *Declaration* included such second-generation rights as Article 24's right to "periodic holidays with pay" and Article 25's right to "food, clothing, housing, and all medical care and necessary social services," it became clear that these rights were more idealistic and were more relative to resources than the rights not to be tortured or discriminated against. Poor countries might be excused for not meeting the former but never excused for violating the latter. That is why some delegates wanted to put the second generation of rights into a separate listing, one that classified them more as aspirations than the hardcore rights in the first generation. But President Franklin D. Roosevelt, in his annual address to Congress on January 6, 1941, listed his famous "Four Essential Freedoms." Here he combined such first-generation rights as freedom of speech and religion with "freedom from want," which he said "means economic understandings."[69] So many delegates, including Eleanor Roosevelt, were reluctant to make economic rights look less essential than the other freedoms; however, they could not deny that some of the economic rights listed depended on economic resources that some countries simply did not have. Hence Article 22 was added: It specifies that the second generation of rights were to be met "in accordance with the organization and resources of each State."

Specifying the details regarding the second generation of rights has proved to be controversial enough, but the *Declaration* also mentions such rights as Article 27's "right freely to participate in the cultural life of the community." Such rights are classified by many as third-generation rights, the first generation being said to incorporate the French Revolution's appeal to *Liberty*, the second to *Equality*, and the third to *Fraternity*. The subset of third-generation rights that are relevant to our discussion are labeled "group rights," the rights that apply to particular groups rather than the rights that apply to all human persons.

It is not difficult to see how the second-generation rights to equality can rub against first-generation rights to liberty: Even those who support a strong safety net for the poor and disadvantaged can agree that taxing me to support Medicaid interferes with my liberty to spend that money elsewhere, though they claim that the interference is justified. But talk about group rights is even more controversial. Of course, if by group rights we mean rights that an individual has by virtue of being part of a particular group, such as those involved in affirmative action, reverse discrimination, and quota systems, such rights are definitely controversial, but at least they can be reduced to individual human rights, albeit of a special kind. But if by group rights we mean that a particular group has human rights as a group, we make into human rights bearers something other than individuals, and that is controversial in several ways.[70]

One important disagreement is over the sort of entities that can be bearers of rights, with some arguing that only individuals—not groups—have the sort of status that allows for the attribution of rights. There is debate over whether the individual must be a person, since rights have been asserted for human fetuses as well as for animals and even for trees, but those who disagree about, say, animal rights can agree that rights apply only to individuals. One must be careful here, since it is clear that organizations such as corporations can be granted certain rights and, indeed, have been granted by the US Supreme Court the legal status of persons at least with respect to the conferring of certain rights. But such *conferral* is a legal matter, and our question is whether groups have *moral* human rights that call for legal *recognition*. For example, some people claim that groups have moral rights to maintain their distinctive cultural identities, and some nation-states, such as India and Egypt, recognize that by granting to religious groups the right to decide on family laws for their members, notably marriage, inheritance, and divorce laws. Others argue that such laws are justified if and only if *individuals* have a right to cultural identity, and thus any so-called group rights are reducible to the rights of individuals. This may seem to be an abstract conceptual or metaphysical issue, but it is related to what is probably the most controversial issue about group rights, which is that they can easily conflict with individual rights. For example, Egypt grants the Christian Copt community the right to decide which divorces are legitimate. The church authorities have decided that adultery and conversion to another religion are the only justifications for divorce; ongoing and severe spousal abuse is not grounds for divorce. Since Copts must be married within the church, individuals are controlled by whatever marriage rules this religious community decides are necessary for its cultural identity. So, for Copts, an abused spouse must live with the abuser or else convert out of the group to another religious community.[71]

Given that group rights can so impinge on individual rights, it is not surprising that group rights are rarely appealed to in the United States, where individual rights are hallowed.[72] For example, *Wisconsin v. Yoder* can be argued not as a conflict between state laws and the group rights of the Amish, but as a conflict between state laws and the rights of parents to raise their children in a way consistent with parents' religious and cultural beliefs. Could state laws themselves be seen as involving a type of group rights that can conflict with individual rights? Perhaps, but few people argue for extending such rights to dissident subgroups within the state even while they argue for accommodating the interests and defending the rights of dissident individuals who are shaped and socialized by those dissident groups.

Right of Exit?

Whether one appeals to group rights or to individual rights of a parent, and whether one seeks maximal accommodation to dissidents or seeks to avoid exceptions to laws that should apply to all, one thing that almost everyone agrees on is that, whatever accommodation is made for dissident groups, individuals within the groups must retain important civil and political rights, especially the right to leave the group.[73] Dissident groups may socialize and shape their members in identity-defining ways, but groups may not turn their members into prisoners. The question is what this exit right involves. It must mean more than a merely formal right; even if nobody coercively prevents you from leaving a group, you do not have an effective or realistic right to leave unless you are able to leave. If you would lose all possessions (that you shared with the group) and you are not educated enough to make a living outside the group, the right to leave would amount to the right to starve, hardly a real right. Feminists have pointed out that an effective right to exit is especially problematic for girls and women. Girls in illiberal groups often receive little education, are socialized into very restricted roles, and simply do not have the external and internal resources to go against their parents' demands.[74] Since such groups often shun those who leave, the choice is usually "take it all or leave it all"; young people do not have the option of saying "I want to stay but be allowed more freedom and be treated with dignity." So the feminists' point is that the choice to leave is not a very realistic one for most females.

The insistence that the right of exit must be a substantive one and not just a formal one is accepted by most of those who argue for maximal feasible accommodation. For example, William Galston gives a formidable list of necessary conditions for a right of exit:

> A meaningful right would seem to include at least the following elements: *knowledge conditions*—the awareness of alternatives to the life one is in fact living; *capacity conditions*—the ability to assess these alternatives if it comes to seem desirable to do so; *psychological conditions*—in particular, freedom from the kinds of brainwashing that give rise to heartrending deprogramming efforts of parents on behalf of their children, and more broadly, forms of coercion other than the purely physical that may give rise to warranted state interference on behalf of affected individuals; and finally, *fitness conditions*—the ability of exit-desiring individuals to participate effectively in at least some ways of life other than the ones they wish to leave.[75]

One can wonder whether this extensive array of conditions could be met by dissident groups without their losing the very distinctiveness that maximal accommodation tries to respect. Indeed, the acceptance of substantive conditions for the right of exit seems to narrow the difference between the sides in this debate; the fitness condition, for example, overlaps the insistence of liberals that all students should have an education that enables them to participate in the economic and civic life of the wider society. Of course, Galston specifies that they need be fit for only *some* alternative ways of life, so the overlap is hardly total. Also, compatible with the psychological condition is allowing the parents to socialize their children in such a way that it would be very difficult and painful for them to leave. Even the liberals that stress autonomy allow for inculcation of values in young children; few people would say that children should simply be taught a variety of moral, religious, and cultural ideals among which they are invited to choose when they come to the age of discretion. Children are raised to think and feel that the moral and religious views of their parents are right, and not just one option among several, though many parents make sure that, as they get older, children learn about alternatives and acquire the tools of critical and independent thinking.

Dissident groups are generally thought to discourage critical and independent thinking, but it is worth noting that such groups may have a good reason for exposing their members to lifestyles that differ from their own; making the choice to be part of the group a deliberate one may actually increase loyalty to the group, and a deliberate choice requires awareness of alternatives. The Old Order Amish practice of *Rumspringa* (running around) illustrates this point. Before they are baptized the teenagers in this group are allowed to run free in the outside world for as long as it takes for them to decide whether to join or abandon the church and community. All restrictions on driving, drinking, dating, and so on are lifted during this time, and there is evidence that at least some of these youths take full advantage of the materialistic and consumerist side of American culture.[76] In fact, one can wonder whether they get an accurate impression of American life, since they tend to experience the hedonistic side rather than museums, alternative religious outlooks, and educational options.

Having left school after the eighth grade, they cannot explore higher education and most entry-level jobs would not be available to them. Most males have some vocational skills, but the skills taught to the females are related mainly to motherhood. Perhaps this is why 80 to 90 percent reject the outside world and join the Old Order Amish by taking baptismal vows (and many of those who leave simply join the more liberal Mennonite sect where their skills are valued). So it is not clear that even this remarkable feature of Amish life demonstrates a realistic right of exit.

Hence what looks like an agreement that narrows differences among the various sides of the debate—that there must be a substantive right of exit— becomes a debate over whether and how a dissident group can meet the conditions for such a right while maintaining the distinctiveness that liberal pluralists wish to respect. The courts will continue to deal with the legal battles case by case, while the moral and political principles that give guidance to the various sides are in tension with each other. Should a pluralistic liberal democracy emphasize toleration and even cooperation when it confronts groups that reject some of its key values, such as individual autonomy, or should it emphasize the need to nurture the education and dispositions that enhance individual opportunities and civic responsibility even if that undermines the distinctiveness of the group? Clarity about what is at stake is easier to obtain than a coherent and agreed-on policy.

Notes

1. Sistare, *Civility and Its Discontents*, 75. If *social toleration* is between persons as private citizens, and *political toleration* is a matter of what is tolerated within and between governments, it may be useful to notice that intolerance within and between *nongovernmental* institutions, while generally lacking legally coercive powers, can involve other sorts of pressures, some of which can be quite coercive. The threat of getting fired from one's job or excommunicated from one's church can be more coercive than the threat of many legal punishments.
2. In *Political Liberalism*, Rawls notes that just how comprehensive and explicitly articulated our worldviews (or comprehensive doctrines) are is a matter of degree (13); they include our basic moral, religious, and metaphysical convictions, but they are not always explicit or organized and are rarely complete.
3. The title of Raz's *The Morality of Freedom* underscores the value-laden character of his perfectionist liberalism, which focuses on moral autonomy as the central ideal.
4. One wades into controversy when distinguishing the different types of liberalism that are active in today's political debates, but here is what I see as some main differences. *Libertarianism* is a philosophical or comprehensive version of classical liberalism that emphasizes individual freedoms (negative rights not to be interfered with) over other liberal values such as equality of opportunity and community cohesiveness. In the United States, this version of liberalism is associated with right-wing conservatives, but it should be distinguished from the social conservatism deriving from Burke's *Reflections on the Revolution in France* that emphasizes

the value of tradition over fast changes advocated by appeals to abstract rights and radical ideas. Of course, libertarians can and often do link up with social conservatives to gain political leverage against other types of liberals. *Egalitarian liberalism* (sometimes identified with comprehensive liberalism and usually with left-wing liberalism) emphasizes equality of economic opportunity (positive entitlement, or welfare rights) and the value of solidarity—sharing each other's burdens—over individual economic freedom. Of course, all of these claim to support individual freedom as well as economic opportunity; the difference is in the details of defining what these mean and in ranking them. What is called *"the liberalism of fear"* (Judith Shklar) is sometimes contrasted to what is called "the liberalism of rights"; the former seeing the latter as too optimistic about governments' being able to support a full panoply of human rights (without risking totalitarianism) and instead advocates the more modest goal of avoiding cruelty, though the cruelty to be avoided includes economic deprivation and exploitation (see Yack, *Liberalism without Illusions*). *Communitarianism* is sometimes projected as an alternative to liberalism, or least political liberalism, one that insists on allowing political appeals to thick descriptions of moral and religious goods, in contrast to what is seen as liberalism's reducing politics to consensus on thin rights that can settle few if any substantive political debates (see Sandel's *Democracy's Discontent*). But one of the most prolific communitarians is Amitai Etzioni, who advocates a type of liberalism that emphasizes social responsibility and civic engagement as well as individual rights. Of course, there are overlaps among these types of liberalism, and many thinkers should be put on spectrums rather than into sharp categories. At any rate, a main point of this brief survey is that liberalism is a big tent in political philosophy and should not be reduced to leftist politics.

5. Rawls, *Political Liberalism*, xx. Perceptive discussions of the move to political liberalism can be found in Weithman's *Why Political Liberalism* and Nussbaum's "Perfectionist Liberalism and Political Liberalism," 3–45.

6. The justification for accepting the majority outcome sometimes goes beyond moral appeal (to an implicit agreement). Rousseau, in *On the Social Contract* (first published in 1762), famously asserted that the "general will" is authoritative for members of a democracy and that it is determined by majority vote. So voters who find themselves in the minority should realize that they were wrong. This remarkable view is thought by some to have empirical evidence, recently claimed by Surowiecki in *Wisdom of Crowds* and traditionally asserted by the Condorcet Jury Theorem (see Goodin's *Reflective Democracy*, 94–96). The claim is that majority rule is not just a matter of fairness, given the implicit agreement to abide by the voting result, but is also a way of tracking the actual truth of the disputed issue. Majorities are more likely than minorities to decide correctly. If we can believe this, we can have some sympathy for Rousseau's view that the minority should see that what they *really* want is what the majority decided, and maybe even some sympathy for his infamous conclusion that the minority has tacitly agreed to be coerced by the general will, because "[t]his means merely that [it] will be forced to be free" (150). The problem is that even the defenders of crowd wisdom agree it works only if each individual thinks independently and is not influenced by what Rousseau calls "intrigues and partial associations" (156). But even casual familiarity with elections in contemporary democracies shows that this stipulation rarely holds.

7. Even a determined minority could change constitutional safeguards. Although this route has yet to be used in the United States, an amendment to the Constitution could be engineered by majorities in three-fourths of the smaller states, which could be a minority of the population in the combined states, including the one-fourth larger states.

8. See Elster, "The Market and the Forum," 3–34. According to Elster, the market model treats the political process as purely instrumental; citizens privately vote their interests with the goal being the optimal compromise among opposed interests. The forum divides into two views: the classical "republican" view that participatory democracy aims at nurturing good citizenship apart from other outcomes; and the deliberative democracy view, associated with Jurgen Habermas and others, that the aim is rational agreement. Many supporters of democracy accept aspects of all three models, since political civility does require the nurturing of conversational virtues while constraints of time, competence, and knowledge require simply voting at some point, voting that inevitably will involve considerations of both the common good and private interests. In addition to the above anthology, see Macedo's *Deliberative Politics* for a robust debate between critics and defenders of deliberative democracy. The subtitle of the Macedo anthology refers to the seminal work by Gutmann and Thompson, *Democracy and Disagreement*. See also Gutmann and Thompson's follow-up to the debate, *Why Deliberative Democracy?*

9. Perry, *Religion in Politics*, 66–70.

10. Weithman, *Religion and the Obligations of Citizenship*, chapter 5.

11. Weithman, *Religion and the Obligations of Citizenship*; and Greenawalt, *Private Consciences and Public Reasons*.

12. Greenawalt, "Religion and the Public School Teacher," 217–30.

13. Wolterstorff, "The Role of Religion in Political Issues," 117.

14. Rawls, *Political Liberalism*, 227–30.

15. Eberle, *Religious Conviction in Liberal Politics*.

16. Audi, *Religious Commitment and Secular Reason*.

17. Rawls, *Political Liberalism*.

18. Audi, *Religious Commitment and Secular Reason*.

19. Could the different reasons that converge on a given policy include nonpublic reasons? Those who reject the restraint principle would, of course, have no trouble with this sort of diversity and in fact they claim that respectful democratic politics typically appeals to such a diverse set of reasons in trying to leverage a winning convergence on a favored policy. Audi's insistence that advocates actually be sufficiently motivated by the secular reasons they appeal to does allow some variation in appeals, since one could find different secular reasons that are sufficiently motivating but, of course, he insists that the reasons be secular ones. I see no reason why political liberals should avoid leveraging a convergence by appealing to different reasons for different audiences, even reasons that do not sufficiently motivate themselves and even nonpublic reasons, as long as they believe that they could back up their appeal with sufficient public reasons for each audience.

20. All of these terms are used in an otherwise useful book, *Religion in Public Life: Must Faith Be Privatized?* by Trigg.

21. Most of the conclusions I am unsure about are ones that I could reasonably accept or reject. Rawls's phrasing is sometimes ambiguous, and other political liberals

unambiguously use the narrower interpretation (Scanlon, *What We Owe Each Other*, 4), so it is understandable that some interpreters use the narrower interpretation for Rawls (Stout, *Democracy and Tradition*, 65), but I think the wider interpretation is fairer. Also, it follows (*pace* Wolterstorff, "Role of Religion," 106) that if you reasonably believe a compatriot reasonably could accept your reasons, you also reasonably believe that about your conclusion, since the inferences from reasons to conclusion can be debated using only public reasons, even when one realistically expects disagreement to remain. Wolterstorff argues that if we are willing to coerce people with *conclusions* they do not actually accept (as we must, since legislatures are not Quaker meetings and there will never be unanimity on legislation), it seems strange to single out *premises* as something we should reasonably believe they could reasonably accept. However, even if we were talking about actual acceptance, I think unshared premises are in a different boat than unshared conclusions, since presumably the debate about who made the invalid inference (from the shared premises to the unshared conclusion) would be a public reason debate in which we could reasonably expect that, in principle, we could reach agreement. Consider the difference between being convicted because the jury made a different inference than you do from evidence that you agree is relevant, on the one hand, and, on the other, being convicted because the jury accepted evidence (a message from a soothsayer, say) that they know you cannot reasonably agree is relevant. The conviction and coercion are the same, but I believe you would have more grounds for legitimate resentment at injustice in the latter case, resentment that would affect more deeply your loyalty to the system.

22. Rawls, *Political Liberalism*, 156.
23. Ibid., 8, xvii.
24. Rawls, *Law of Peoples*, 142.
25. See Gaus, *Justificatory Liberalism*. Some writers, such as Eberle in *Religious Conviction in Liberal Politics*, assimilate political liberalism and justificatory liberalism, but others see the latter as a more restrictive version of the former.
26. Eberle, *Religious Conviction in Liberal Politics*, chapter 6. This critic of the restraint principle agrees that there are regions today where the argument is (and times in history when it would be) "compelling" and "privatization is essential" (158). Notice that "privatization" (religious arguments are excluded from public political advocacy) is a much stronger version of restraint than the "inclusive" version political liberals call for today, which allows—even encourages—any religious arguments that can be backed up by public arguments. Since the most volatile areas, such as Bosnia and Palestine, are ones that include believers with the "overriding and totalizing obligation to obey God" (149) that Eberle uses to reject the inclusive restraint principle in the United States, it is worth noting that in other circumstances he sees this commitment as compatible with a privatization that is even more restricting than the restraint principle. So the overriding and totalizing duty to God yields only a prima facie duty to integrate one's religion with one's political advocacy. I emphasize what may seem an obvious point because Eberle quotes approvingly (145–46) some powerful passages from Wolterstorff and Perry ("To 'bracket' such convictions is therefore to bracket—to annihilate—essential aspects of one's very self.") that might be interpreted as almost absolutizing a duty to integrate one's religion with one's political advocacy, even in Bosnia, where religious believers are as likely as in the United States to be sensitive to the "anathema" of "knowingly and willingly" disobeying God (183).

27. This argument is made by Eberle in *Religious Conviction in Liberal Politics*, 143–49, where he quotes other authors who make the same argument. The "living inside rather than along side one's religion" distinction is made by Wolterstorff in "The Role of Religion", 89.

28. Rescher, *Pluralism*.

29. When I survey my students they overwhelmingly worry more about the possible coercion from others' nonpublic beliefs than the possible discounting of their own, but they are hardly a representative sample of all citizens.

30. Rawls, *Political Liberalism*, xliii, xlvii–li. The phrase "liberalism of reasoned respect" in the next line is also used by Weithman in *Religion and Contemporary Liberalism*, 5, who disagrees somewhat with Rawls on what it implies.

31. Dombrowski derives reasoned respect from agape in *Rawls and Religion*, 21, and I derive it from respecting imagers of God; see my "Theism and Toleration," 606–13. Although one need not appeal to Kant's version of "recognition respect" (discussed in the previous chapter) to argue for the liberalism of reasoned respect, some theists who reject the restraint principle do appeal to it in developing their own views; see Eberle, *Religious Conviction in Liberal Politics*, chapter 4. And other theists use entirely different theological arguments to *support* the restraint principle. For example, Audi provides a well-reasoned "theo-ethical equilibrium" argument to the effect that God sees to it that people using only secular reason are aware of the basic norms that should shape good legislation, and that therefore theists should be suspicious of any sectarian arguments that they cannot back up with public reasons (Eberle, *Religious Commitment and Secular Reason*, chapter 5). Of course, some integrated believers fear that this argument does not have a robust enough regard for the cognitive effects of sin and other difficulties in our epistemic situations (chapter 9).

32. Stout, *Democracy and Tradition*, 67. If the restraint principle is indeed embedded in Rawls's notion of reasonable, it underscores the need for him to *defend* and not just *define* what he means. In chapter three, note 54, I assert that "reasonable" and "respectable" can apply to outlooks that are mildly unegalitarian, including what Rawls in his *Law of Peoples* calls "decent hierarchical" views.

33. Eberle, *Religious Conviction in Liberal Politics*, chapter 5, and Wolterstorff, "Role of Religion," 110. Wolterstorff calls this a "politics of multiple communities" (109) or the "consocial" view (114).

34. The views summarized in this paragraph come from, among others, Sandel, *Public Philosophy*, 144–46.

35. Wolterstorff, "Role of Religion," 102; Greenawalt, *Private Consciences and Public Reasons*, 65; and Perry, *Religion in Politics*, 57.

36. Eberle, *Religious Conviction in Liberal Politics*, 22. The ideas in this paragraph come from Eberle's chapters 4–5. Of course, prudence suggests that advocates for a policy or candidate should try to appeal to as wide an audience as possible, which is why even those who use sectarian arguments in the public square also use public reason arguments whenever they can. Eberle argues that integrated believers also have a moral obligation to use public reason whenever they can, appealing to the same sort of respect for autonomy as political liberals. Of course, Eberle's own view is not a compromise for himself; it would be a compromise for any political liberals who otherwise would urge silence in the public square when public reason arguments cannot be found.

37. Audi, *Religious Commitment and Secular Reason*, 95, 114, 203. Audi says that at other times the overriding of the restraint principle may not be morally acceptable but still excusable. Insofar as political liberals explicitly treat the restraint principle as a prima facie moral obligation, my proposal is not a compromise for them; as with the first proposal, it would be a compromise for those who otherwise would urge silence in the public square when public reason arguments cannot be found. My proposal overlaps what some call "aspirational public reason liberalism." See Kelly Sorensen's review of Nicholas Wolterstorff's *Understanding Liberal Democracy*.

38. Weithman, *Religion and the Obligations of Citizenship*, 129, 151, 161–63, 211. In an earlier article, "Citizenship and Public Reason," Weithman argues that Rawls sees the restraint principle as a role-specific obligation of citizenship rather than a prima facie obligation of persons (128) or something derived from the morality of ideals (142), but Weithman does say that sometimes citizens' role-specific duties can be overridden by the demands of their other roles (146).

39. Eberle, *Religious Conviction in Liberal Politics*, 56, 105, 188. Regarding the debate about associating ideals with prima facie obligations, Mellema's *Beyond the Call of Duty* argues for a spectrum of levels of responsibility, including "quasi-supererogatory" responsibilities, whose nonperformance is blameworthy in a way that the nonperformance of supererogatory ones is not but in some lesser way than is the nonperformance of obligatory ones. Mellema suggests some level of responsibility for living up to even high ideals, at least in the sense that we are morally criticizable if we develop a disposition to never go the second mile (119). I suspect that if Audi, Eberle, and Weithman (and the spirit of Rawls) could discuss a suitably nuanced approach to levels of moral responsibility, they would find a fair amount of common ground.

40. These considerations are phrased in terms of voting for legislation, but they can be used for voting for political candidates as long as voters are informed about where the candidates stand on the relevant issues.

41. "Vulnerability" is added because some integrated believers argue solely on theological grounds for pacifism based on the biblical virtue of agape, self-sacrificing love. If this pacifism became national policy one could interpret it as coercing non-pacifists from forming a defensive army; in any case it would make them highly vulnerable to aggressors.

42. Audi, *Religious Commitment and Secular Reason*, 88–89, provides a set of distinctions that can help us think through this consideration; for example, taxation may be less coercive than forcing one to be inoculated, but unlike hunting fees, it is unconditional, so it may raise more resentment when it funds abortions or other things that are abhorrent to a taxpayer. Eberle agrees that the degree of rational justification required for coercive legislation rises with how averse those affected are to the proposed coercion (93).

43. Thus, even Weithman—not one to generate obligations out of mere responsibilities—agrees in *Religion and the Obligations of Citizenship* that "when the consequences of political outcomes are important enough . . . responsible commitment to political outcomes becomes obligatory" (100). So those who reject the restraint principle as a general rule may be willing to give it some weight when deciding on basic constitutional issues.

44. Noting that some distinctive doctrines, or parts of them, are more widely shared than others are, Eberle, *Religious Conviction in Liberal Politics,* suggests that we can appeal to the less controversial parts to make it as easy as possible for others to acquiesce to disagreeable legislation (127).
45. Ibid., 149.
46. See chapter two, note 8, for an explanation of slippery slope arguments.
47. See www.huffingtonpost.com/2011/11/08/mississippi-personhood-amend ment_ n_1082546.html (February 26, 2013).
48. Public reason arguments are often used by integrated believers whose main motivation may come from their distinctive doctrines. In the Mississippi case, for example, a common public reason argument was that if we do not draw the line at fertilization, there is no other nonarbitrary place to draw it. I do not think that this use of public reason arguments makes my ten considerations irrelevant, even for the integrated believer, since if their main result is to motivate people to find public reason arguments, the audience can debate the adequacy of those reasons in a way they could not always do with distinctive doctrine reasons. Plus, a conscientious integrated believer could use the ten considerations privately when deciding how to vote.
49. See www.startribune.com/politics/statelocal/177544631.html?refer=y (February 26, 2013). That careful considerations may have influenced the outcome is quite compatible with my admitting in the first chapter that hugs change more minds than arguments. Heterosexuals voting against the marriage restriction often had friends or family who have alternative sexual orientations.
50. In discussing Audi's example of a religiously inspired law that protects dandelions as sacred, Eberle, *Religious Conviction in Liberal Politics,* agrees that he would be resentful about such a law, but mainly because of the content of the law, rather than the distinctly religious rationale (138–39). He says he would feel as much frustration if environmentalists got the law passed on the grounds that dandelions are an endangered species. I do not share his view, since I think I could argue with environmentalists in a way that I could not with the Dandelionists. In both cases, I could challenge the validity of inferences, but with the environmentalists I could also argue about the premises with a much higher probability of using reasons both sides could reasonably believe the other side could accept. But in any case, I think the ten considerations could help us decide the extent to which we should encourage the Dandelionists to use the restraint principle.
51. Of course there is plenty of room for disagreement about what constitutes serious physical or mental harm; liberal societies tend not to tolerate, much less accommodate, the practice of forced marriages, the insistence of parents on infibulation for their young daughters, and the refusal of Jehovah's Witnesses to permit blood transfusions for their infants. But liberals are divided on whether to tolerate, for example, significant corporal punishment for young children.
52. *Wisconsin v. Yoder*, 406 U.S. 245–46 (1972), Justice Douglas dissenting.
53. Okin, in "'Mistresses of Their Own Destiny," 205–30, notes that cultural factors result in girls being especially susceptible to becoming products of their environment. The depth of their inculcation is controlled by their relative lack of education, their enculturation into defined gender roles, early arranged marriages, and so on (216–22). In an earlier work, *Justice, Gender, and the Family*, Okin argued

that the nurturing of children is a matter of public justice, not something that can simply be left to the private intimacy of family life.

54. Macedo, in *Diversity and Distrust* and other works, has been a vocal and articulate proponent of the side of the spectrum that emphasizes the need for the state to shape students so that they practice liberal virtues.

55. Galston has vigorously and perceptively defended the side of the spectrum that emphasizes maximal feasible accommodation to diversity, and some of the ideas and examples in my exposition come from his *Liberal Pluralism*. Accepting the sort of value pluralism we discussed in chapter two, Galston, *The Practice of Liberal Pluralism*, insists that liberals can be committed to their vision of the good life while recognizing that there are incommensurable and even incomparable visions of the good life that are reasonable to and for others, including ones shaped by strange religious dogma. "It is one thing to say that X is true, another to say that truth is good, yet another to insist that truth is the highest good. . . . Many forms of what value pluralists must regard as illusions will embody other kinds of goodness" (190).

56. Quoted in Glendon's *A World Made New*, 161.

57. A comprehensive and fair-minded account of the Mozert v. Hawkins case is Bates's *Battleground*. My summary is indebted to this book, though my paraphrases of the judges come directly from the ruling. The final ruling can be accessed at www.soc.umn.edu/~samaha/cases/mozert_v_hawkins_schools.html (January 11, 2012).

58. This point is emphasized in Stolsenberg's "'He Drew a Circle That Shut Me Out,'" 600–610, at 631. This author notes that of the judges, only Boggs perceived that requiring even silent reading of the forbidden material violated what these parents saw as a religious commandment.

59. Galston, *Practice of Liberal Pluralism*, 118.

60. Ibid., 119.

61. Macedo, "Liberal Civic Education and Religious Fundamentalism," 485.

62. Appiah, *The Ethics of Identity*, 209–10.

63. Bates, *Battleground*, 316. The Menendez book is *Visions of Reality*. The view that, given the right to privatize education, we should compromise in order to keep children in the public schools turns on its head the claim of Gutmann and Thompson, *Democracy and Disagreement*, that with the compromise the children "would fail to receive the education that is necessary for developing their capacities as democratic citizens. The parents would deny the school board the authority to teach future citizens the skills and knowledge that are necessary for protecting the liberties and opportunities of all citizens" (65).

64. Law Professor Lupu paraphrases this common objection, which he criticizes as "the spectral march" in "Where Rights Begin," 947. Quoted in Bates, *Battleground*, 272.

65. The ruckus in New Hampshire got started when a parent objected to assigning Barbara Ehrenreich's *Nickel and Dimed: On (Not) Getting By in America*, which among other things made the point that Jesus would have been sympathetic to low-wage workers by describing him as a "wine-guzzling vagrant and precocious socialist." See the *New York Times* blog by J. Dell'Antonia, http://parenting.blogs.nytimes.com/2012/01/17/when-parents-can-opt-out-of-school-curriculum. The law itself can be seen at www.gencourt.state.nh.us/legislation/2011/HB0542.html. Governor John Lynch vetoed the bill right after it passed, listing several slippery slope worries: "[P]arents could object to a teacher's plan to: teach the history of France or the history of the civil or women's rights movements. Under this bill,

a parent could find 'objectionable' how a teacher instructs on the basics of algebra. In each of those cases, the school district would have to develop an alternative educational plan for the student. Even though the law requires the parents to pay the cost of [the] alternative, the school district will still have to bear the burden of helping develop and approve the alternative. Classrooms will be disrupted by students coming and going, and lacking shared knowledge." See www .governor.nh.gov/media/news/2011/071311-hb542.htm. In early January 2012, the House voted 255–112 and the Senate 17–5 to override the veto. See www .huffingtonpost.com/2012/01/04/new-hampshire-legislature-curriculum-objec tion-law_n_1184476.html. The size of the override vote suggests that the law may stay around long enough to provide some empirical evidence about whether this maximal accommodation is feasible. All of the above websites were accessed February 20, 2012.

66. For a summary of the "three generations of rights" vocabulary and history, see Griffin's *On Human Rights*, 256.

67. The distinction between the negative right not to be harmed and the positive right to be helped is complicated by the fact that sometimes not helping the helpless violates their negative rights. In other words, not helping the helpless can be a way of harming them, especially when they are related to others through special roles created by past events or promises: If parents refuse to nurture their children, lifeguards refuse to save the drowning, or doctors refuse to continue treating their patients, their refusals to help can be inflictions of harm, since omitting to fulfill a legitimate expectation can inflict as much harm as committing an action. This point can be pushed further than some people want to go, as when one argues that not providing basic medical care is to commit harm, just as not providing police or fire protection or basic education would be.

68. The story is well told in Glendon's *World Made New*. She points out that when various countries from around the globe listed what they regarded as basic human rights, there was surprising overlap in the lists, but not in theories about the foundation of human rights. There was widespread acceptance of human *dignity* as central to human rights, but sharp disagreement about the grounding of dignity, with the atheists disagreeing with theistic natural law theories and Confucian communitarians disagreeing with individualistic social contract theorists. These disagreements sometimes implied disagreements over substantive issues such as whether responsibilities were prior to rights or the other way around. Finally, Eleanor Roosevelt, the chair of the UN's Human Rights Commission, convinced the participants that if they could agree on a universal *declaration* of what are the human rights, they could agree to disagree about the foundation of human dignity or the grounding that makes the rights universal. Glendon's Appendix Seven consists of the version of the Declaration that passed without a negative vote (though some countries abstained because of the inclusion of such rights as Article 13's right to leave and return to one's country and Article 18's right to change one's religion).

69. Roosevelt, "Four Freedoms."

70. Appiah, *Ethics of Identity*, gives the label "membership rights" to rights an individual has by virtue of membership in a group, and "collective rights" to rights that groups are asserted to have, noting that such groups would require well-defined membership criteria and an accepted way of making decisions for the group (72).

71. The conservative Copt rules on divorce became politicized in 2011 when 130 Copts threatened to leave the church if the grounds for divorce and remarriage were not changed. See Alex Murashko's article, "Coptic Christians Threaten to Leave Denomination over Divorce, Remarriage Laws," *The Christian Post*, September 17, 2011, at www.christianpost.com/news/coptic-christians-threaten-to-leave-denomination-over-divorce-remarriage-laws-55819 (April 2, 2012). Copts can convert to certain Protestant denominations, a move that given current Egyptian law would put them under Islamic family rules. With the overthrow of the Mubarak regime in 2011 and the death of Coptic Pope Shenouda in 2012, to say nothing of recent conflicts, the situation may change, of course.

72. Donnelly, in *Universal Human Rights in Theory and Practice,* probably speaks for most Americans when he says, "[G]roup human rights are fraught with theoretical and practical difficulties. Liberal human rights approaches usually are capable of accommodating the legitimate interests of even oppressed groups—and where they are not, group human rights rarely are more likely to provide an effective remedy" (205). It may be that the strongest case for group rights is for indigenous peoples, such as Native American tribes, but that is because such groups, who see themselves as resisting colonization if not oppression by invading immigrants, are more like autonomous nations than dissenting groups among ordinary citizens.

73. I specify that *almost* everyone agrees to a right of exit because some defenders of group rights have argued that a true pluralist realizes that a right of exit would undermine those dissident groups that cannot exist if members are free to leave. An excellent discussion of this and most other issues related to group rights and the right of exit can be found in the third chapter of Appiah's *Ethics of Identity*. The millet system of the Ottoman Empire looked much like the system of religious group rights in Egypt that is discussed above, but it did not involve a right of exit. For a good discussion of the millet system, see Walzer, *On Toleration*, 18 and throughout.

74. See Okin's "Mistresses of Their Own Destiny," 216–28.

75. Galston, *Practice of Liberal Pluralism*, 123.

76. See Mazie's "Consenting Adults?," 748–51, for a description of a number of Amish youth on *Rumspringa*. He mentions the bad publicity connected with the 1998 arrest of two Amish men in their early 20s for running a cocaine ring (with a motorcycle gang) and selling drugs to unbaptized Amish youth and the public puzzlement when the Amish elders said that these young people weren't really Amish because they had not yet joined the church. He quotes a 90 percent "return" rate but also mentions an 80 to 90 percent rate (752). Kraybill, *The Riddle of Amish Culture*, 184–87, questions whether the Amish have a realistic right of exit.

CHAPTER FIVE

Civil Disagreement: Conclusion

The preceding chapters have raised at least as many questions as they have provided answers. Indeed, the viewpoint underlying this book is that, in a society with interesting diversities, questions and disagreements are more likely than agreement on answers. The issue is whether we can share our disagreements in a civil way, one that recognizes the importance of personal integrity while also insisting on respecting our differences. The latter means not only being courteous toward and respecting the rights of the people we disagree with, but also being open-minded enough to consider whether and when we can respect their viewpoints and tolerate and perhaps cooperate with the actions and practices that flow from them.

In the first chapter we took seriously Aristotle's claim that what makes the human species distinctive is our ability to converse with one another, especially about values. We distinguished various types of arguments, noticing that they can be used for mutual inquiry and not just for persuasion or for scoring political points. We observed that, contrary to Mill's worry about open-minded inquiry eventually exposing all errors and leading to a lazy consensus, it more often clarifies and underscores our differences. So conversations and arguments, while sometimes revealing common ground, often reveal how broad and deep and important our disagreements are. No person of integrity can paper over all these differences with broad-minded acceptance of all sides of the arguments or even polite silence about them.

In the second chapter we observed that although sometimes the concept of pluralism simply refers to the empirical fact of diversity and disagreement, including moral conflict, it more often refers to coping with diversity and disagreement in a civil way. One helpful insight is that the burdens of judgment often result in conflicts of reasonable opinions; all the positions that contradict each other are reasonable to and for those who hold them. To be able to say, "I disagree with you but your position is one that I respect as reasonable," is the essence of what is called reasonable pluralism. This does not imply that all differences involve conflicting but reasonable viewpoints; apart from the all-too-human tendency toward confirmation bias—underscoring evidence we like and ignoring the rest—there is sheer ignorance, stupidity, and greed that can influence our thinking. Of course, a wise policy is to not presume corruption when confusion will do, and not confusion when reasonable pluralism will do. Although sometimes people combine reasonable pluralism with relativism about truth, we noticed how people can believe that they are right and that others are wrong insofar as they disagree, and still respect the others' views as reasonable. This "perspective pluralism" embraces relativism of justification without relativism of truth, and it helps us think more clearly about such issues as religious pluralism, intellectual humility, and skepticism. It enables us to have sincere dialogue with others, and a willingness to learn from them, while maintaining in an authentic way our own commitments.

Perspective pluralism does not in itself settle the issue of when we should tolerate or even cooperate with actions or practices that flow from views we regard as wrong (whether or not we respect these views as reasonable). The third chapter addresses this issue, and it concludes by considering how various combinations of toleration, cooperation, and respect (and their opposites) can be used in civil disagreement. It thereby helps us understand how we can be open-minded toward differing viewpoints without embracing a broad-minded approval of them.

In particular, we saw that "cooperation and compromise" is distinct from finding common ground or reaching a consensus. In fact, it is precisely when we cannot agree that we have to rank our own convictions and commitments in order to ask what we are willing to give up if the other side gives up something comparable. When it is conflicting interests at stake, it may be less hard to split the difference than when principle is at stake. For example, during the Constitutional Convention at Philadelphia in 1787, there was a fierce fight over proportional representation, the small states fearing that proportional representation in both houses of Congress could amount to a dictatorship of the big states over the small ones, and the big states fearing that equal representation could yield control to a small minority of voters. The Connecticut Compromise called for splitting the difference: the House would have proportional representation and the Senate equal representation. A similar effort at compromise failed earlier, with the large states threatening to leave, so the Connecticut effort sweetened the deal for the large states by stipulating that the House would have more control over the budget. Both sides were very dissatisfied, but both knew that the alternative was failure, so they reluctantly and even angrily voted to give up some of their important interests as long as the other side did too.[1] Tough prudence.

Another compromise at that same convention has become notorious: The northern states wanted proportional representation to be based on the number of franchised citizens in each state while the southern states wanted it to be based on the number of human beings; the difference, of course, was that the South wanted to count slaves while, somewhat ironically, the North did not. The compromise was that slaves would count as three-fifths of a person. It seems that most delegates saw this as simply another splitting the difference of interests[2] (after all, it was the slave owners who wanted the slaves to count as a full person, simply to ensure southern political strength), but today one can get into trouble defending this as an example of what compromise is all about. That is because today many of us think that the compromise lent at least symbolic support to the wicked prejudice that slaves were unequal to full persons, and that therefore moral and religious principles should have been invoked.[3] If they had been invoked, that would not have made a compromise impossible, just more difficult; in chapter three I give some examples of principled moral compromise in which people are forced to rank their morally relevant considerations. Underscoring the difference between finding common ground and reaching compromise is important because our politics today too often conflates them. Moreover, countering the quip that I quoted in the third chapter—that unlike the French, Americans make matters of principle into matters of interests—it seems that too often matters that primarily have to do with interests, such as whom and how much to tax, are being treated primarily as matters of principle. This in itself would not prevent compromise, but too often people seem to think that compromise on matters of principle shows lack of integrity. Instead, people of integrity should not accept stalemate when there are alterations with much better moral consequences.[4] Hence I highlight in this summary the sections on moral pluralism and on cooperation with disagreeable viewpoints.

The final chapter applies the book's conceptual framework to political issues that arise in a pluralistic and liberal democracy. Since laws can be extremely coercive and since we cannot expect consensus on what the laws should be, political liberalism has focused on the types of arguments that we should encourage in the public square about those laws and about the legislators that shape them. Proposing moral restraints on public square arguments makes lots of people in a pluralistic democracy nervous, especially those who worry that their distinctive convictions and commitments, which form their identities and purposes and which provide them with political direction, will be discounted as inappropriate in comparison to the public reasons that ignore faith and God's will. But political liberals worry that encouraging sectarian arguments could lead to legislation based on religious demands that others find especially offensive. Both sides have legitimate concerns, and we looked at some proposals for compromise.

A pluralistic democracy will inevitably be asked to accommodate groups that reject the liberal values that the majority see as central to the sort of society where liberty, justice, and economic opportunity flourish. A major problem is the conflict between conditions that are conducive to a group's flourishing and the rights of individuals within that group to lead their own lives and perhaps leave the group. We saw that the trade-offs involved are easier to clarify than to solve in a general way.

Of course, in today's world we need to consider not just the interactions of citizens and groups within a given pluralistic society or state, which is the subject of this book; we also face the complicated issue of how states and governments should interact with each other. What are the limits to toleration when rogue governments or tyrants blatantly violate the rights of their citizens? Or when civil war includes terrorism against innocent people? Or when failed states cannot protect the rights of citizens? These questions raise the issue of humanitarian intervention, where difficulties and dangers abound no matter what is decided.[5] And what about cooperation with nonliberal states that treat their citizens decently but have little or no commitment to what we see as equal rights or individual freedoms?[6] The ideas in this book are not sufficient to settle arguments about such questions, but I hope they do illuminate important details about how we should and should not debate them.

Notes

1. See Robertson's *The Original Compromise*, 97–105.
2. Ibid., 85.
3. See this *New York Times* site for a lively debate about the morality of this compromise: www.nytimes.com/roomfordebate/2013/02/26/the-constitutions-immoral-compromise/three-fifths-compromise-was-an-understandable-deal-on-slavery (February 27, 2013). It is clear that both sides thought the other would leave the convention without the compromise, and that the failure to pass a constitution risked a number of political as well as moral consequences. Not only might there be up to thirteen nations in place of the United States, the number of slaves that would continue to be imported may have been multiplied many times beyond what the compromise projected.
4. As chapter three insists, the weighing of morally relevant consequences need not be simply a utilitarian calculus; categorical moral imperatives can carry heavy moral weight. This point underscores the importance of not confusing important and highly favored economic and political interests with unconditional commitments.
5. Humanitarian intervention, especially when it uses military force as a last resort, goes beyond the traditional "just war" criteria since the latter typically include the requirement that a just war must be a defensive war against an invader. In 2005, after massacres in Rwanda, the United Nations endorsed a document on "The Responsibility to Protect." It asserts that governments have the responsibility to protect its citizens and, when they fail to do so, the international community has that responsibility, at least in cases of mass atrocity crimes such as genocide, war crimes, crimes against humanity, and ethnic cleansing. The following website, maintained by the International Coalition for the Responsibility to Protect (ICRtoP), provides the relevant documents and information: www.responsibilitytoprotect.org (June 8, 2012).
6. Rawls's *Law of Peoples* argues that liberal societies should cooperate with what he calls decent hierarchical societies such as some of the Muslim countries and that, out of respect for them, we should not attach strings that would force or even nudge them toward our ideals of equality and individual liberty. This view is opposed by the "cosmopolitan" view that liberal societies should use pressure to support individual rights in countries where women, for example, do not have equal opportunities. A good anthology of different opinions on this debate is Rawls's *Law of Peoples: A Realistic Utopia*, edited by Rex Martin and David Reidy.

WORKS CITED

Adams, Robert. "Vocation." *Faith and Philosophy* 4, no. 4 (October 1987): 448–62.

Adeney, Bernard. *Strange Virtues: Ethics in a Multicultural World*. Downers Grove: InterVarsity Press, 1995.

Almond, Brenda. *Moral Concerns*. Atlantic Highlands: Humanities Press International, 1987.

Appiah, Kwame Anthony. *The Ethics of Identity*. Princeton: Princeton University Press, 2005.

Applbaum, Arthur. *Ethics for Adversaries: The Morality of Roles in Public and Professional Life*. Princeton: Princeton University Press, 1999.

Aristotle. "Politics." Translated by T. A. Sinclair and T. J. Saunders. In *A New Aristotle Reader*, edited by J. L. Ackrill. Princeton: Princeton University Press, 1987.

Asch, Solomon. *Social Psychology*. Englewood Cliffs: Prentice Hall, 1953.

Audi, Robert. *The Good in the Right*. Princeton: Princeton University Press, 2004.

———. *Religious Commitment and Secular Reason*. Cambridge: Cambridge University Press, 2000.

Austen, Jane. *Pride and Prejudice*. 1813.

Barker, Evelyn. "Socratic Intolerance and Aristotelian Toleration." In *Philosophy, Religion, and the Question of Intolerance*, edited by Mehdi Amin Razavi and David Ambuel. Albany: State University of New York Press, 1997.

Bates, Stephen. *Battleground: One Mother's Crusade, the Religious Right, and the Struggle for the Control of Our Classrooms*. New York: Poseidon Press, 1993.

Beauchamp, Thomas, and James Childress. *Principles of Biomedical Ethics*, 6th ed. Oxford: Oxford University Press, 2008.

Benjamin, Martin. *Splitting the Difference: Compromise and Integrity in Ethics and Politics*. Lawrence: University of Kansas Press, 1990.

Berdal, Mats, and David Malone, eds. *Greed and Grievance: Economic Agendas in Civil War*. London: Lynne Rienner Publishers, 2000.

Berger, Peter. *A Far Glory*. New York: The Free Press, 1992.

———. *The Heretical Imperative*. Garden City: Doubleday, 1979.

Berlin, Isaiah. *The Crooked Timber of Humanity*. New York: Knopf, 1991.

Bloom, Allan. *The Closing of the American Mind*. New York: Simon and Schuster, 1987.

Bok, Sissela. *Common Values*. Columbia: University of Missouri Press, 1995.

Boyd, Dwight. "The Moral Part of Pluralism as the Plural Part of Moral Education." In *The Challenge of Pluralism*, edited by F. Clark Power and Daniel Lapsley, 155–56. Notre Dame: University of Notre Dame Press, 1992.

Brody, Baruch. *Taking Issue: Pluralism and Casuistry in Bioethics*. Washington, DC: Georgeown University Press, 2003.

Buber, Martin. *Autobiographical Fragments*. New York: Routledge, 2002.

Budziszewski, J. *True Tolerance: Liberalism and the Necessity of Judgment*. London: Transaction Publishers, 1992.

Burke, Edmund, and J. C. D. Clark. *Reflections on the Revolution in France*. Stanford, CA: Stanford University Press, 2001.

Buss, Sarah. "Appearing Respectful: The Moral Significance of Manners." *Ethics* 109, no. 4 (July 1999): 795–826.

Calhoun, Cheshire. "The Virtue of Civility." *Philosophy and Public Affairs* 29 (2000): 251–75.

Carter, Stephen. *Civility: Manners, Morals, and the Etiquette of Democracy*. New York: Basic Books, 1998.

Chang, Ruth, ed. *Incommensurability, Incomparability, and Practical Reason*. Cambridge, MA: Harvard University Press, 1997.

Clottes, Jean. "Chauvet Cave." *National Geographic Magazine* 200, no. 2 (2001): 104–21.

Cohen, Andrew Jason. "What Toleration Is." *Ethics* 115 (2004): 68–95.

Colby, Anne, and William Damon. *Some Do Care: Contemporary Lives of Moral Commitment*. New York: The Free Press, 1992.

Cuddihy, John Murray. *The Ordeal of Civility*. Boston: Beacon Press, 1987.

Darwall, Stephen. "Two Kinds of Respect." *Ethics* 88 (1977): 36–49.

Dees, Richard. *Trust and Toleration*. New York: Routledge Publishers, 2004.

Devlin, Baron Patrick. *The Enforcement of Morals*. London: Oxford University Press, 1965.

Dobel, J. Patrick. *Compromise and Political Action: Political Morality in Liberal and Democratic Life*. Savage: Rowman and Littlefield Publishers, 1990.

Dombrowski, Daniel. *Rawls and Religion: The Case for Political Liberalism*. Albany: SUNY Press, 2001.

Donagan, Alan. *The Theory of Morality*. Chicago: University of Chicago Press, 1977.

Donnelly, Jack. *Universal Human Rights in Theory and Practice*, 2nd ed. Ithaca: Cornell University Press, 2003.

Dreyfus, Hubert and Stuart E. Dreyfus. "What Is Morality? A Phenomenological Account of the Development of Ethical Expertise." In *Universalism vs. Communitarianism*, edited by David Rasmussen, 237–64. Cambridge: MIT Press, 1990.

Eberle, Christopher. *Religious Conviction in Liberal Politics*. Cambridge: Cambridge University Press, 2002.

Eck, Diana. *Encountering God: A Spiritual Journey from Bozeman to Banaras*, 2nd ed. Boston: Beacon Press, 2003.

Edwards, David. "Toleration and Mill's Liberty of Thought and Discussion." In *Justifying Toleration*, edited by Susan Mendus. Cambridge: Cambridge University Press, 1988.

Ehrenreich, Barbara. *Nickel and Dimed: On (Not) Getting By in America*. London: Picador Press, 2001.

Elgin, Catherine. *Between the Absolute and the Arbitrary*. Ithaca: Cornell University Press, 1977.

Elster, Jon. "The Market and the Forum: Three Varieties of Political Theory." In *Deliberative Democracy: Essays on Reason and Politics*, edited by James Bohman and William Rehg. Cambridge: MIT Press, 1997.

Erlewine, Robert. *Monotheism and Tolerance: Recovering a Religion of Reason*. Bloomington: Indiana University Press, 2010.

Feldman, Richard. "Plantinga on Exclusivism." *Faith and Philosophy* 20 (2003): 85–90.

Fish, Stanley. "Postmodern Warfare." *Harper's Magazine* (July 2002): 33–40.

Fogelin, Robert. *Walking the Tightrope of Reason: The Precarious Life of a Rational Animal*. Oxford: Oxford University Press, 2003.

Forni, P. M. *Choosing Civility: The Twenty-Five Rules of Considerate Conduct*. New York: St. Martins Griffin, 2002.

Fotion, Nick, and Gerhard Elfstrom. *Toleration*. Tuscaloosa: University of Alabama Press, 1992.

Frankfurt, Harry G. "The Faintest Passion." *Proceedings and Addresses of the APA* 66, no. 3 (November 1992): 5–16.

———. "On the Necessity of Ideals." In *Necessity, Volition, and Love*, 108–16. Cambridge: Cambridge University Press, 1999.

———. *The Reasons of Love*. Princeton: Princeton University Press, 2004.

Galeotti, Anna Elisabetta. *Tolerance as Recognition*. Cambridge: Cambridge University Press, 2002.

Galston, William. *Liberal Pluralism: The Implications of Value Pluralism for Political Theory and Practice*. Cambridge: Cambridge University Press, 2000.

———. *The Practice of Liberal Pluralism*. Cambridge: Cambridge University Press, 2005.

Gardner, Peter. "Propositional Attitudes and Multicultural Education, or Believing Others Are Mistaken." In *Toleration: Philosophy and Practice*, edited by John Horton and Peter Nicholson, 69. Aldershot, UK: Avebury, 1992.

Gaus, Gerald. *Justificatory Liberalism: An Essay on Epistemology and Political Theory*. Oxford: Oxford University Press, 1996.

George, Robert. *The Clash of Orthodoxies: Law, Religion and Morality in Crisis*. Wilmington: ISI Books, 2001.

Gilkey, Langdon. *Shantung Compound*. New York: Harper and Row, 1966.

Gilligan, Carol. *In a Different Voice*. Cambridge: Cambridge University Press, 1982.

Glendon, Mary Ann. *A World Made New: Eleanor Roosevelt and the Universal Declaration of Human Rights*. New York: Random House, 2001.

Goodin, Robert. *Reflective Democracy*. Oxford: Oxford University Press, 2003.

Gowan, Christopher. *Innocence Lost: An Examination of Inescapable Wrongdoing*. Oxford: Oxford University Press, 1994.

Graham, Gordon. "Tolerance, Pluralism, and Relativism." In *Toleration: An Elusive Virtue*. Princeton: Princeton University Press, 1998.

Gray, John. *Two Faces of Liberalism*. New York: The New Press, 2000.

Greenawalt, Kent. *Private Consciences and Public Reasons*. Oxford: Oxford University Press, 1995.

———. "Religion and the Public School Teacher." In *Religion in the Liberal Polity*, edited by Terence Cuneo. Notre Dame: University of Notre Dame Press, 2005.

———. *Religious Convictions and Political Choice*. Oxford: Oxford University Press, 1988.

Griffin, James. *On Human Rights*. Oxford: Oxford University Press, 2008.

Griffiths, Paul. *Problems of Religious Diversity*. Oxford: Blackwell Publishers, 2001.

Gutmann, Amy, and Dennis Thompson. *Democracy and Disagreement*. Cambridge: Harvard University Press, 1996.

Gutmann, Amy, and Dennis Thompson. *Why Deliberative Democracy?* Princeton: Princeton University Press, 2004.

Habermas, Jurgen. *Moral Consciousness and Communicative Action*. Translated by Christian Lenhardt and Shierry Weber Nicholsen. Cambridge: MIT Press, 1990.

Haidt, Jonathan. *The Righteous Mind: Why Good People Are Divided by Politics and Religion*. New York: Pantheon Books, 2012.

Hampshire, Stewart. *Justice Is Conflict*. Princeton: Princeton University Press, 2000.

Hanvey, Robert. *An Attainable Global Perspective*. Center for War/Peace Studies, 1975. The University of Michigan.

Headland, Thomas, ed. "The Tasaday Controversy." *American Anthropological Association Special Publication* 28 (1992).

Heim, S. Mark. "Orientational Pluralism in Religion." *Faith and Philosophy* 13, no. 2 (April 1996): 201–15.

———. *Salvations: Truth and Difference in Religion*. New York: Orbis Books, 1995.

Hemley, Robin. *Invented Eden: The Elusive, Disputed History of the Tasaday*. New York: Farrar, Straus and Giroux, 2003.

Hick, John. *God Has Many Names*. Philadelphia: Westminster Press, 1980.

———. *An Interpretation of Religion: Human Responses to the Transcendent*. New Haven: Yale University Press, 1989.

———. *Philosophy of Religion*, 4th ed. Upper Saddle River: Prentice Hall, 1990.

———. "Religious Pluralism and Salvation." *Faith and Philosophy* 5 (1988): 365–77.

Hinman, Lawrence. *Ethics: A Pluralistic Approach to Moral Theory*, 2nd ed. New York: Harcourt Brace Publishers, 1998.

Hobbes, Thomas. *Leviathan*. 1651.

Horton, John. "Toleration as a Virtue." In *Toleration: An Elusive Virtue*, edited by David Heyd. Princeton: Princeton University Press, 1996.

Hsieh, Nien-he. "Incommensurable Values." *Stanford Encyclopedia of Philosophy*, http://plato.stanford.edu/contents.html#value-incommensurable-Hsieh (17 January 2012).

Ignatieff, Michael. "Nationalism and Toleration." In *The Politics of Toleration in Modern Life*, edited by Susan Mendus. Durham: Duke University Press, 2000.

Kach, N., and I. DeFaveri. "What Every Teacher Should Know about Multiculturalism."

Kant, Immanuel. *Critique of Pure Reason*. 1781.

———. "What Is Enlightenment?" Translated by Leo Rauch. In *Kant's Foundations of Ethics*. Millis: Agora Publications, 1995.

Kekes, John. *The Morality of Pluralism*. Princeton: Princeton University Press, 1993.

Kingwell, Mark. *A Civil Tongue: Justice, Dialogue, and the Politics of Pluralism*. University Park: Pennsylvania University Press, 1995.

Knitter, Paul F. *Introducing Theologies of Religions*. Maryknoll: Orbis Books, 2002.

Kolodiejcuk, Brian, and Mother Teresa. *Mother Teresa: Come Be My Light*. New York: Doubleday, 2007.

Kraybill, Donald. *The Riddle of Amish Culture*, 2nd ed. Baltimore: The Johns Hopkins University Press, 2001.

Langerak, Edward. "Theism and Toleration." In *A Companion to Philosophy of Religion*, edited by Paul Draper Charles Taliaferro and Philip Quinn, 606–13. Oxford: Blackwell Publishers, 2010.

Larmore, Charles E. *Patterns of Moral Complexity*. Cambridge: Cambridge University Press, 1987.

———. "Pluralism and Reasonable Disagreement." In *Cultural Pluralism and Moral Knowledge*, edited by Ellen Frankel Paul et al. Cambridge: Cambridge University Press, 1994.

Laursen, John Christian, ed. *Religious Toleration: "The Variety of Rites" from Cyrus to Defoe*. New York: St. Martin's Press, 1999.

Lindemann, Hilde, ed. *Stories and Their Limits*. New York: Routledge, 1997.

Little, David, and David Chidester. "Rethinking Religious Toleration: A Human Rights Approach." In *Religion and Human Rights: Toward an Understanding of Tolerance and Reconciliation*. Atlanta: Emory Humanities Lectures, the Academic Exchange, 2001.

Little, David, John Kelsay, and Abdulaziz Sachedina. *Human Rights and the Conflict of Cultures: Western and Islamic Perspectives on Religious Liberty*. Columbia: University of South Carolina Press, 1988.

Locke, John. *Discourse on the Origins of Inequality*. 1755.

———. *A Letter Concerning Toleration*. Indianapolis: Hackett Press, 1983. First published in 1689.

———. *Second Treatise of Government*. 1690.

Lockhart, Ted. *Moral Uncertainty and Its Consequences*. Oxford: Oxford University Press, 2000.

Lupu, Ira C. "Where Rights Begin: The Problem of Burdens on the Free Exercise of Religion." *Harvard Law Review* 102 (1989): 933–90.

Macedo, Stephen. *Diversity and Distrust: Civic Education in a Multicultural Democracy*. Cambridge: Harvard University Press, 2000.

———. "Liberal Civic Education and Religious Fundamentalism: The Case of God v. John Rawls?" *Ethics* 105 (1995): 458–96.

Macedo, Stephen, ed. *Deliberative Politics: Essays on Democracy and Disagreement*. Oxford: Oxford University Press, 1999.

MacIntyre, Alasdair. *After Virtue*, 2nd ed. Notre Dame: University of Notre Dame Press, 1984.

Martin, Rex, and David Reidy, eds. *Rawls's Law of Peoples: A Realistic Utopia?* Oxford: Blackwell Publishing, 2006.

Marty, Martin. *Education, Religion, and the Common Good*. San Francisco: Jossey-Bass, 2000.

May, Larry. *The Socially Responsive Self: Social Theory and Professional Ethics*. Chicago: University of Chicago, 1996.

Mazie, Steven. "Consenting Adults? Amish *Rumspringa* and the Quandary of Exit in Liberalism." *Perspectives on Politics* 3 (2005): 745–59.

McFall, Lynn. "Integrity." In *Ethics and Personality: Essays in Moral Psychology*, edited by John Deigh. Chicago: University of Chicago Press, 1992.

McKim, Robert. *Religious Ambiguity and Religious Diversity*. New York: Oxford University Press, 2001.

McLennon, Gregor. *Pluralism*. Minneapolis: University of Minnesota Press, 1995.

Megone, Christopher. "Truth, the Autonomous Individual, and Toleration." In *Toleration: Philosophy and Practice*, edited by John Horton and Peter Nicholson. London: Ashgate, 1992.

Melchert, Norman. *Who's to Say: A Dialogue on Relativism*. Indianapolis: Hackett Publishing, 1994.

Mellema, Gregory. *Beyond the Call of Duty*. Albany: SUNY Press, 1991.

Mendus, Susan. *Toleration and the Limits of Pluralism*. Atlantic Highlands: Humanities Press, 1989.

Menendez, Albert J. *Visions of Reality: What Fundamentalist Schools Teach*. Buffalo: Prometheus, 1993.

Mercier, Hugo, and Dan Sperber. "Why Do Humans Reason? Arguments for an Argumentative Theory." *Behavioral and Brain Sciences* 34 (2011): 57–111.

Midgley, Mary. *Can't We Make Moral Judgments?* New York: St. Martin's Press, 1991.

Mill, John Stewart. *On Liberty*. Indianapolis: Hackett Publishing, 1978. First published in 1859.

Miller, Barbara. *Cultural Anthropology*, 2nd ed. Boston: Allyn and Bacon, 2002.

Moody-Adams, Mitchell. *Fieldwork in Familiar Places: Morality, Culture, and Philosophy*. Cambridge: Harvard University Press, 1997.

More, Thomas. *Utopia*. 1516.

Moser, Paul, and Thomas Carson, eds. *Moral Relativism: A Reader*. Oxford: Oxford University Press, 2001.

Mouw, Richard, and Sander Griffoen. *Pluralisms and Horizons*. Grand Rapids: Eerdmans Publishing, 1993.

Nagel, Thomas. "The Absurd."

———. "Concealment and Exposure." *Philosophy and Public Affairs* 27 (1998): 3–30.

———. "Fragmentation of Value." In *Mortal Questions*.

———. *Mortal Questions*. Cambridge: Cambridge University Press, 1979.

Nance, John. *The Gentle Tasaday*. New York: Harcourt Brace Jovanovich, 1975.

Nasr, Seyyed Hossein. "Metaphysical Roots of Tolerance and Intolerance: An Islamic Interpretation." In *Philosophy, Religion, and the Question of Intolerance*, edited by Mehdi Amin Razavi and David Ambuel. Albany: SUNY Press, 1997.

Netland, Harold. *Encountering Religious Pluralism*. Downers Grove: InterVarsity Press, 2001.

Neuhaus, Richard John. "One Little Word." *First Things: A Monthly Journal of Religion & Public Life* 149 (2005): 60–61.

Nussbaum, Martha. "Perfectionist Liberalism and Political Liberalism." *Philosophy and Public Affairs* 39 (2011): 3–45.

Oberdiek, Hans. *Tolerance: Between Forbearance and Acceptance*. Lanham: Rowman and Littlefield Publishers, 2001.

Okin, Susan Moller. *Justice, Gender, and the Family*. New York: Basic Books, 1989.

———. "'Mistresses of Their Own Destiny': Group Rights, Gender, and Realistic Rights of Exit." *Ethics* 112 (2002): 205–30.

Oliner, Samuel, and Pearl Oliner. *The Altruistic Personality: Rescuers of Jews in Nazi Germany*. New York: The Free Press, 1988.

Paine, Thomas. *Rights of Man*. Indianapolis: Hackett Publishing, 1992. First published in 1791.

Palmquist, Stephen. *The Tree of Philosophy: A Course of Introductory Lectures for Beginning Students of Philosophy*. Hong Kong: Philopsychy Press, 2000.

Perry, Michael. *Religion in Politics*. Oxford: Oxford University Press, 1997.

Perry, William. *Forms of Intellectual and Ethical Development in the College Years*. San Francisco: Jossey-Bass Publishers, 1998.

Pippen, Robert. "The Ethical Status of Civility." In *Civility*, edited by Leroy Rouner. Notre Dame: University of Notre Dame Press, 2000.

Plantinga, Alvin. "Pluralism: A Defense of Religious Exclusivism." In *The Philosophical Challenge of Religious Diversity*, edited by Philip Quinn and Kevin Meeker. Oxford: Oxford University Press, 2000.

Plato. *The Republic*. 380 BCE.

Pojman, Louis. *Ethics: Discovering Right and Wrong*, 4th ed. Belmont: Wadsworth, 2002.

Quine, Williard Van Orman, and J. S. Ullian. *The Web of Belief*, 2nd ed. New York: McGraw Hill, 1978.

Quinn, Daniel. *Ishmael*. New York: Bantam Books, 1995.

Rahner, Christian Karl. "Theological Investigations." In *The Christian Theology Reader*, edited by Alister McGrath. Oxford: Blackwell Publishers, 1995.

Raphael, D.D. "The Intolerable." In *Justifying Toleration*, edited by Susan Mendus. Cambridge: Cambridge University Press, 1988.

Rawls, John. *The Law of Peoples with "The Idea of Public Reason Revisited."* Cambridge, MA: Harvard University Press, 1999.

———. *Political Liberalism*. New York: Columbia University Press, 1996. First edition published in 1993.

Raz, Joseph. "Incommensurability and Agency." In *Incommensurability, Incomparability, and Practical Reason*, edited by Ruth Chang. Cambridge: Harvard University Press, 1997.

———. *The Morality of Freedom*. Oxford: The Clarendon Press, 1986.

Rescher, Nicholas. "American Philosophy Today." *The Review of Metaphysics* 46 (1993): 717–45.

———. *Pluralism: Against the Demand for Consensus*. Oxford: The Clarendon Press, 1993.

———. *The Strife of Systems: An Essay on the Grounds and Implications of Philosophical Diversity*. Pittsburgh: The University of Pittsburgh Press, 1985.

Rest, James. *The Defining Issues Test*. www.ethicaldevelopment.ua.edu (June 9, 2012).

Richardson, Henry. *Democratic Autonomy: Public Reasoning about the Ends of Policy*. Oxford: Oxford University Press, 2002.

Robertson, David Brian. *The Original Compromise: What the Constitution's Framers Were Really Thinking*. Oxford: Oxford University Press, 2013.

Rokeach, Milton. *The Nature of Human Values*. New York: The Free Press, 1973.

Roosevelt, Franklin D. "Four Freedoms." Franklin D. Roosevelt Presidential Library, www.fdrlibrary.marist.edu/fourfreedoms (January 17, 2012).

Rorty, Richard. *Contingency, Irony, and Solidarity*. Cambridge: Cambridge University Press, 1989.

Ross, W. D. *The Right and the Good*. Oxford: The Clarendon Press, 1930.

Rousseau, Jean-Jacques. *On the Social Contract*. In *The Basic Political Writings*, trans. Donald Cress. Indianapolis: Hackett Publishing, 1987.

Ruse, Michael. *Can a Darwinian Be a Christian?* Cambridge: Cambridge University Press, 2001.

Sachs, David. "How to Distinguish Self-Respect from Self-Esteem." *Philosophy and Public Affairs* 10, no. 4 (1981): 346–60.

Sandel, Michael. *Democracy's Discontent: America in Search of a Public Philosophy*. Cambridge: Harvard University Press, 1996.

———. *Public Philosophy: Essays on Morality in Politics*. Cambridge: Harvard University Press, 2005.

Santurri, Edmund. "Nihilism Revisited." *The Journal of Religion* 71, no. 1 (1991): 67–78.

———. *Perplexity in the Moral Life: Philosophical and Theological Considerations*. Charlottesville: University of Virginia Press, 1987.

Sartre, John Paul. *Being and Nothingness*, trans. Hazel Barnes. New York: Washington Square Press, 1966.

Scanlon, T. M. *What We Owe Each Other*. Cambridge, MA: Harvard University Press, 1998.

Schmidt, James. "Is Civility a Virtue?" In *Civility*, edited by Leroy S. Rouner. Notre Dame: University of Notre Dame Press, 2000.

Schuurman, Douglas. *Vocation: Discerning Our Callings in Life*. Grand Rapids: Eerdmans Publishing, 2004.

Schweder, Richard A. *Why Do Men Barbecue Other Men?: Recipes for Cultural Anthropology*. Cambridge, MA: Harvard University Press, 2003.

Seabright, Paul. *The Company of Strangers*. Princeton: Princeton University Press, 2004.

Shanks, Hershel. "Democratizing the Image of God." *Bible Review* 15, no. 1 (February 1999): 2.

Shaw, R. Paul, and Wong, Yuwa. *Genetic Seeds of Warfare: Evolution, Nationalism, and Patriotism*. Boston: Unwin Hyman, 1989.

Shermer, Michael. *The Science of Good and Evil*. New York: Times Books, 2004.

Sire, James W. *Naming the Elephant: Worldview as a Concept*. Downers Grove: Inter Varsity Press, 2004.

Sistare, Christine T. *Civility and Its Discontents: Civic Virtue, Toleration, and Cultural Fragmentation*. Lawrence: University of Kansas Press, 2004.

Skitka, Linda, and Elizabeth Mullen. "The Dark Side of Moral Conviction." *Analyses of Social Issues and Public Policies* 2, no. 1 (2000): 35–41.

Smith, Christian. *Moral, Believing Animals: Human Personhood and Culture*. Oxford: Oxford University Press, 2003.

Sorensen, Kelly. "Review of Nicholas Wolterstorff's *Understanding Liberal Democracy: Essays in Political Philosophy*." *Notre Dame Philosophical Reviews* (Sept. 2013). http://ndpr.nd.edu/news/42380/ (September 19, 2013).

Staub, Ervin. *The Roots of Evil: The Origins of Genocide and Other Group Violence*. Cambridge: Cambridge University Press, 1989.

Stith, Richard. "Toward Freedom from Value." *Bioethics Digest* 3, no. 1 (1978): 1–10.

Stolsenberg, Nomi Maya. "'He Drew a Circle That Shut Me Out': Assimilation, Indoctrination, and the Paradox of a Liberal Education." *Harvard Law Review* 106 (1993): 581–667.

Stout, Jeffrey. *Democracy and Tradition*. Princeton: Princeton University Publishing, 2004.

———. *Ethics after Babel: The Languages of Morals and Their Discontents*. Boston: Beacon Press, 1988.

Surowiecki, James. *Wisdom of Crowds*. New York: Bantum Dell, 2004.

Tannen, Deborah. *The Argument Culture: Moving from Debate to Dialogue*. New York: Random House, 1998.

Taylor, Charles. "Leading a Life." In *Incommensurability, Incomparability, and Practical Reason*, edited by Ruth Chang. Cambridge, MA: Harvard University Press, 1997.

———. *Sources of the Self*. Cambridge, MA: Harvard University Press, 1989.

Taylor, Paul. *Normative Discourse*. Englewood Cliffs: Prentice Hall, 1961.

Thurman, Judith. "Letter from Southern France: First Impressions." *The New Yorker* (June 23, 2008).

Tinder, Glen. *The Political Meaning of Christianity*. Columbia: University of Missouri Press, 1989.

———. *Tolerance: Toward a New Civility*. Amherst: University of Massachusetts Press, 1976.

Tolstoy, Leo. *A Confession and Other Religious Writings*. Translated by Jane Kentish. New York: Penguin Books, 1987.

Trigg, Roger. *Religion in Public Life: Must Faith Be Privatized?* Oxford: Oxford University Publishing, 2007.

Twiss, Sumner. "The Philosophy of Religious Pluralism." In *The Philosophical Challenge of Religious Diversity*, edited by Philip L. Quinn and Kevin Meeker. Oxford University Press, 2000.

Van Fraassen, Bas. *The Empirical Stance*. New Haven: Yale University Press, 2002.

Walzer, Michael. *On Toleration*. New Haven: Yale University Press, 1997.

———. "Political Action: The Problem of Dirty Hands." *Philosophy and Public Affairs* 2 (1973): 160–80.

Warnock, Mary. "The Limits of Toleration." In *On Toleration*, edited by Susan Mendus and David Edwards. Oxford: Oxford University Press, 1987.

Weithman, Paul. "Citizenship and Public Reason." In *Natural Law and Public Reason*, edited by Robert P. George and Christopher Wolfe. Washington, DC: Georgetown University Press, 2000.

Weithman, Paul. "The Difficulty of Tolerance." *Ethics* 114 (2004): 836–42.

———. *Religion and the Obligations of Citizenship*. Cambridge: Cambridge University Press, 2002.

———. *Why Political Liberalism: On John Rawls's Political Turn*. Oxford: Oxford University Press, 2011.

Weithman, Paul, ed. *Religion and Contemporary Liberalism*. Notre Dame: University of Notre Dame Press, 1997.

Williams, Bernard. "Toleration: An Impossible Virtue?" In *Toleration: An Elusive Virtue*, edited by David Heyd. Princeton: Princeton University Press, 1998.

Wolff, Robert Paul. *A Critique of Pure Tolerance*. Boston: Beacon Press, 1969.

Wollheim, Richard. *The Thread of Life*. Cambridge, MA: Harvard University Press, 1984.

Wolterstorff, Nicholas. "Can Belief in God Be Rational If It Has No Foundations?" In *Faith and Rationality*, edited by Alvin Plantinga and Nicholas Wolterstorff. Notre Dame: University of Notre Dame Press, 1983.

———. *Divine Discourse: Philosophical Reflections on the Claim That God Speaks*. Cambridge: Cambridge University Press, 1995.

———. *Justice: Rights and Wrongs*. Princeton: Princeton University Press, 2008.

———. "The Role of Religion in Political Issues." In *Religion in the Public Square: The Place of Religious Convictions in Political Debate*, edited by Robert Audi and Nicholas Wolterstorff. Lanham: Rowman & Littlefield Publishers, 1997.

———. "Thomas Reid on Rationality." In *Rationality in the Calvinian Tradition*. Lanham and London: University Press of America, 1983.

———. "Why We Should Reject What Liberalism Tells Us About Speaking and Acting in Public for Religious Reasons." In *Religion and Contemporary Liberalism*, edited by Paul J. Weithman. Notre Dame: University of Notre Dame Press, 1997.

Yack, Bernard, ed. *Liberalism without Illusions: Essays on Liberal Theory and the Political Vision of Judith N. Shklar*. Chicago: University of Chicago Press, 1996.

INDEX